THE HISTORICAL ATLAS OF
NEW YORK CITY

A VISUAL CELEBRATION OF NEARLY 400 YEARS
OF NEW YORK CITY'S HISTORY

THE HISTORICAL ATLAS OF
NEW YORK CITY

A VISUAL CELEBRATION OF NEARLY 400 YEARS
OF NEW YORK CITY'S HISTORY

ERIC HOMBERGER

Alice Hudson, Cartographic Consultant

A HENRY HOLT REFERENCE BOOK

HENRY HOLT AND COMPANY
NEW YORK

A Henry Holt Reference Book
Henry Holt and Company, Inc.
Publishers since 1866
115 West 18th Street
New York, New York 10011

Henry Holt ® is a registered
trademark of Henry Holt and Company, Inc.

Library of Congress Cataloging-in-Publication Data
Homberger, Eric.
    The historical atlas of New York City : a visual celebration of
    nearly 400 years of New York City's history / Eric Homberger. —
    1st ed.
            p.   cm.
    "A Henry Holt Reference Book"
    Includes bibliographic references and index.
    1. New York (N.Y.) — History.   2. New York (N.Y.) — History — Maps.
    3. New York (N.Y.) — History — Pictorial works.   I. Title.
    F128.3.H65   1994   94–18992
    974.7'1 — dc20   CIP
ISBN 0-8050-2649-5

First Edition — 1994
Second edition — 1996

Printed in Great Britain

10   9   8   7   6   5   4   3   2

EDITOR: Elizabeth Wyse

INDEX AND PICTURE RESEARCH: Catherine Jones

DESIGN AND ILLUSTRATION: Ralph Orme
MAPS DESIGNED BY: Malcolm Swanston
MAPS PRODUCED BY: David McCutcheon
Andrea Fairbrass, Isobelle Lewis, Simon and Sunita Yeomans
PRODUCTION: Norman Fahy, Barry Haslam, Jeanne Radford, and Charlotte Taylor

Foreword

In late July 1994 I re-checked details of the careers of Billie Holiday and George Gershwin in the Second Air Division, Eighth Air Force, U.S.A.F. Memorial Room at the Norwich Central Library. Veterans of the Second World War who had flown out of U.S. Air Force bases in Norfolk and Suffolk had presented the room, and its useful collection of Air Force memorabilia and books about the United States, to the people of East Anglia in memory of the American fliers who had died in the war. The whole library was lost ten days later in an electrical fire. Perhaps as many as 400,000 books, including a unique local studies collection, were destroyed. It will be a long time before people in this provincial English city, so well-served by its public library, can find out just where *Rhapsody in Blue* was written, and the name of the speakeasy where Lady Day had her first job as a singer.

The gloomy experience of seeing a library in charred ruins made me think about the places where I had done research for this atlas. The Norwich fire was also a reminder of the terrifying vulnerability of our knowledge of the past. The consequences of a fire in the New York Public Library or at Widener Library (with its extraordinary collection of material about New York donated by Evert Jansen Wendell, brother of a Harvard Professor of English, Barrett Wendell), are unthinkable.

The best part of several years was spent working on the *Historical Atlas of New York City* in libraries in Durham, New Hampshire, and in Newton, Boston, and Cambridge, Massachusetts – not forgetting Cambridge, England (where there are two books about baseball, tucked away behind the endless shelves of books about cricket in the University Library). And, of course, at the NYPL, with an occasional excursion to the New-York Historical Society, when it was open. The Map Division of the NYPL, and its chief Alice C. Hudson, was the place where cartographical questions could almost *always* be answered.

Research for this book was also done in bookstores in central New York State and at Broadway and 12th Street, in Hay-on-Wye, Herefordshire, on Route 1 in Maine, at the New England Mobile Book Fair, the Hay Cinema Bookshop, G. David, New York Bound, and the much-missed Goodspeed's on Milk Street, Boston. Elliot Willensky and Norval White's *AIA Guide to New York City* (Third edition, 1988) has been my unfailing guide to the city and its structures. Even at nearly a thousand pages long, one still wishes for more detail, more opinions, and better maps.

The biographical notes were written by students at the University of East Anglia.

Eric Homberger
Norwich, England, 1994

A reprint has allowed me to make appropriate revisions and corrections. Grateful thanks to Mr. Richard Pollard of California, Mr. Jim Maguire of New Jersey, and Mr. Kenneth Kowald, Mr. Andrew M. Manshel, Mr. August Matzdorf, and Mr. Stephen T. Whelan, all of New York City, for their sharp eyes, and knowledge of the city.

DEDICATION
For my aunt Harriett Friedner,
and in memory of my uncle
Martyn J. Friedner of Cherry Hill, N.J.

Contents

Frederic Auguste Bartholdi created New York's best known icon, "Liberty Enlightening the World." It was engineered by Gustave Eiffel, transported from France, and assembled on Bedloes Island (renamed Liberty Island in 1956). The statue was dedicated on October 28, 1886.

A plaque fixed to the base of the statue in 1903 bears a poem written in 1883 by Emma Lazarus. The final and most famous lines read:

"Give me your tired, your poor,
Your huddled masses yearning to breathe free,
The wretched refuse of your teeming shore.
Send these, the homeless, tempest-tost to me,
I lift my lamp beside the golden door!"

PART 1

NIEUW AMSTERDAM OFTE NUE NIEUW IORX

‘t TEYLANT MAN

"On this river there is great traffick in the skins of beavers, otters, foxes, bears, minks, wild cats, and the like. The land is excellent and agreeable, full of noble forest trees and grape vines, and nothing is wanting but the labor and industry of man to render it one of the finest and most fruitful lands in that part of the world ..."
Johan de Laet, *Nieuwe Werldt ofte Beschrijvinghe van West-Indien (New World, or Description of West-India)* Leyden, 1625.

The southern tip of Manhattan, with the settlements along the Hudson (left) and the East River, as seen from a ship in the harbor. The large buildings on the left were the Dutch West India Company's storehouse. The Stadt Huys (City Hall) was at the outer edge of the community when this drawing was made in the 1650s.

Chapter 1 Hilly Island

The geography of New York City was the city's supreme advantage. It surpassed Philadelphia as the nation's principal port not because of the superiority of its people, but due to the superiority of its harbor, and its unimpeded access up the Hudson River to the rich agricultural lands to the west. The city's natural setting was a blessing occasionally mentioned in a sermon or patriotic address but there was little knowledge of geology or of the processes which had led to the formation of the seemingly solid and immovable material upon which the city's streets and buildings were built. Nor was there much inclination to explain how or why the coastal plain upon which New York was located had emerged from the sea. Until the work of Louis Agassiz in the 1840s, there was no notion that most of the city had been covered by the great Laurentide glacier only some 20,000 years ago. Traces of the past in New York are buried, hidden, and need deciphering.

Why did the Dutch come in the first place? In the 15th century, the European trading and mercantile powers extended their

Before the native tribes acquired European weapons, bows and arrows, and axes and knives were the staples of war materièl. Tactics - as represented by European writers and engravers - bore an uncanny resemblance to the conduct of sieges by European armies. More commonly, struggles between tribes were a tale of lightning raids, ambushes and high mobility. Europeans attributed these tactics to an innate disposition for deception and deceit among the natives.

economic interests over much of the globe. The hope of finding gold, the great commercial value of the sugar produced on the Cape Verde islands, and the slave trade (which provided the labor force for the sugar plantations) were powerful motives for maritime activities, particularly after the *conquistador* Hernando Cortes encountered the Aztec empire in Mexico in 1519. The Spanish, with skills honed on the reconquest of Spain from the Moors (Granada, the last great Moorish territory in Spain, surrendered in 1492) led the way in plunder and conquest. Merchants in northern Europe were determined to muscle their way into this lucrative trade.

After the accession of Philip II of Spain as ruler of the 17 provinces of the Netherlands in 1555, the bitter and violent revolt against Spanish rule was extended outwards into direct attacks upon Spanish economic interests throughout the world. The Union of Utrecht in 1579 formed a Dutch Republic of seven provinces. When the Spanish reconquered Antwerp six years later, Protestant refugees, Flemish and Walloon, flooded north into the province of Holland, making it the leading commercial center of resistance. Although the combined fleets of Spain and Portugal were the largest in the world, Sir Francis Drake's raid on the Spanish settlement at St. Augustine in 1586 showed that hungry, daring men might prosper at the expense of the Spaniards.

The defeat of the Spanish Armada in 1588, and the successful military campaigns of Maurice, *stadtholder* of Holland and Zeeland, in 1590–94, sharpened the enthusiasm of the Protestant powers for the task of supplanting the Spanish in the New World and the Portuguese in the East. For this purpose the Dutch East India Company was formed in 1602 with a monopoly of the valuable spice trade. Four years later the English Crown gave to the Virginia Company a charter which included virtually the whole territory of North America.

Hudson

At first it was only a handful of maritime districts on the west coast of England and in the Iberian peninsula which possessed the seafaring navigational skills, shipbuilding expertise, and capital resources needed to launch extended voyages of exploration and trade. But skilled mariners like Columbus, a Genoese by birth, who provided invaluable technical skills necessary for the extension of national power and commercial interest, could be hired by trading cartels or crowned heads. By the end of the 16th century, there was a flourishing army of explorers for hire. Henry Hudson was one such. An experienced navigator and trader, he was hired in 1607 by the Muscovy Company, an English trading cartel, to discover a northern route to the spice

"Our master and his mate determined to try some of the chief men of the country, whether they had any treachery in them. So they took them down into the cabin and gave them so much wine and aqua vita that they were all merry. In the end one of them was drunk... for they could not tell how to take it."
Robert Juet, a member of Hudson's crew

islands and to China, a voyage which was both dangerous and slow by the traditional route around the Cape of Good Hope. Hudson sailed north from Holland and reached the island of Spitzbergen, 80° north, in 1607. A year later he tried again, but found the route blocked by frozen seas. Still fervently believing in a route to the east beyond 83° north, he was hired in 1609 by the Dutch East India Company to try the northern route again. He reached as far north as Novaya Zembla in the Barents Sea, but failed once again to discover the Northeast Passage. Rather than abandon the voyage altogether, Hudson followed the advice of another English explorer-promoter, Captain John Smith, and turned the *Halve Maen* (Half Moon), a vessel of 80 tons, west to Newfoundland, and then followed the southerly route along the coast. At each estuary he paused, looking for an entrance to the fabled great northern route to the east. On September 2, 1609 Hudson entered the bay formed by the "Great River of the Mountains," "as fine a river as can be found, wide and deep, with good anchoring on both sides."

He was not the first European to visit the waters of New York. Giovanni da Verrazano, in the employment of the King of France, sailed from Dieppe in 1524 and briefly entered the Lower and Upper Bay of the Hudson. With their voyages, the European history of New York begins.

The seal of New Netherlands.

"Friendly and polite people"

Unlike the rather more benign images commonly made in the 19th century of Hudson's meeting with the natives, he found the native inhabitants of the lower part of the river to be warlike and threatening (two large canoes filled with armed natives greeted his ship, and in the ensuing confusion one member of his crew was killed by an arrow), but upriver there were "friendly and polite people" who were happy to trade valuable skins and pelts for what the Europeans regarded as trinkets. In truth, relations with the natives were from the first uneasy. An officer on the *Halve Maen* published a diary of Hudson's third voyage recording the tense, violent passage of the ship:

"This after-noone [October 1, 1609], one Canoe kept hanging under our sterne with one man in it, which we could not keepe from thence, who got up by our Rudder to the Cabin window, and stole out my Pillow, and two shirts, and two Bandeleeres. Our Masters Mate shot at him, and strooke him on the breast, and killed him. Whereupon all the rest fled away, some in their Canoes, and so leapt out of them into the

New Netherland was, in the eyes of Dutch merchants, a source of furs. From the first voyages, an active trade with the natives brought beaver pelts on to the Dutch market for resale throughout Europe. In the 16th century there was an immense demand for otter and beaver pelts. They were used to trim clothes, and make hats and cloaks. It was believed that beaver fur had medicinal properties.

The first settlement on Manhattan, 1626.

water. We manned our Boat, thinking to get our things againe. Then one of them that swamme got hold of our Boat, thinking to overthrow it. But our Cooke tooke a Sword, and cut off one of his hands, and he was drowned. By this time the ebbe was come, and we weighed and got down two leagues..."

Detailed knowledge of an exceptionally good port on the North American coast, and the existence of a broad river enabling navigation far into the unknown interior, excited much interest in northern Europe. Hudson's reports to the East India Company formed the basis of the Dutch claim to their colony on the Hudson. The Dutch East India Company took no immediate action on the news of Hudson's voyage. In their eyes, the voyage was a failure. Hudson had not discovered a northern route to the east. But other commercial interests in the United Provinces, particularly the fur traders, were interested in news that the Hudson River promised to be a rich fur-trading region, and agitated for the creation of a West India Company. The Dutch came to New York, like so many after them, to make a buck.

Stone, Water, Ice

The stone upon which New York City sits is hard metamorphic rock, Manhattan schist, and Inwood dolomite, formed during the Archeozoic Era. That is, the dark stone which nudges above the surface of Central Park, and which was so forcefully striated during the Ice Age, dates virtually from the formation of the earth's crust. The erosion of the late Mesozoic period (between 70 and 220 million years ago) produced most of the geological features which have remained until the present, especially the Hudson River and the drainage system which cut a deep and narrow gorge through the Hudson Highlands which lie south of the Catskills. (The Hudson is a tidal inlet which opened the land as far as Troy to the Atlantic tide.)

An era of subtropical temperatures began about 65 million years ago, and persisted until about one million years ago. This was the period of the emergence of modern mammals. New York disappeared below the sea approximately 25 million years ago, before the coastal plain rose in time for the Hipparion, the three-toed horse, and the mastodons which followed.

The climate then perceptibly cooled, and an era of glaciation followed. The earliest records of Palaeo-Indians in North America date from about 25,000 years ago, some 5,000 years before the period of maximum glaciation. The settlement of New York by *homo sapiens* was disrupted by the vast ice sheet of the Laurentide glacier as it slowly flowed south and west from Canada. The maximum territory covered by the Laurentide ice sheet some 20,000 years ago reached a line dipping south to the Missouri and Ohio Rivers, and running east to New York. It is this period of glaciation which accounts for the erratic boulders strewn across New York's landscape, with its gravel ridges, striated rock, and deposits of surface drift.

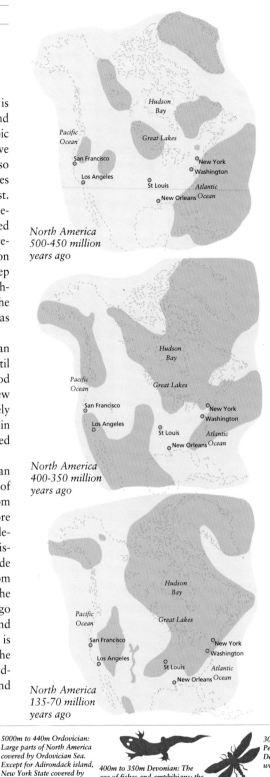

North America 500-450 million years ago

North America 400-350 million years ago

North America 135-70 million years ago

NORTH AMERICA 500-70 million years ago
- land
- water
- present-day coastline

For a billion years after the formation of the Earth's crust, New York City lay beneath the shallow seas which covered most of the gradually subsiding land mass of North America. By 350 million years ago, the climate had warmed, and the land around New York was swampy. It was with the rise of the Appalachian range, which began 220 million years ago, that the state of New York – like most of the American continent – emerged significantly above sea level (maps left).

The map (above right) shows the maximum territory covered by the Laurentide glacier. The farthest terminal moraines, deposited when the glacier began to retreat about 17,000 years ago, are found from Cape Cod to Long Island, and on a line across Brooklyn and Staten Island (map right).

GEOLOGY OF NEW YORK

5,000m to 1,500m Archaeozoic; formation of earth's crust

1,500m to 600m Proterozoic: Earliest known lifeforms: bacteria, algae; primitive multicellular organisms

600m to 500m Cambrian: Upper Cambric Sea covers whole of New York, except part of Adirondacks which stand out as great islands. Emergence of marine invertebrates

5000m to 440m Ordovician: Large parts of North America covered by Ordovician Sea. Except for Adirondack island, New York State covered by vast shallow sea

440m to 400m Silurian: Due to gradual sinking of the land, all of New York south of Ontario, the Mohawk valley, and land west of the Hudson River, was covered by sea water. Emergence of air breathing animals

400m to 350m Devonian: The age of fishes and amphibians: the sea still covers much of the state

350m to 300m Mississippian: A period of warm climates and swampy land; winged insects; development of large reptiles and insects. The sea still covers much of the state

300m to 270m Pennsylvanian: Development of winged insects

270m to 220m Permian: The age of reptiles. Rocks of the permian era are not present in New York State

Paleozoic era ends with great volcanic activity and the rise of the Appalachian range raising the whole state well above sea level

220m to 180m Triassic: The age of amphibians. Continued growth of Appalachians. Sheets of igneous rock forced upward between sedimentary strata, forming Hudson River Palisades

PALEOZOIC						
ARCHAEOZOIC	PROTEROZOIC	CAMBRIAN	ORDOVICIAN	SILURIAN	DEVONIAN	MISSISSIPPIAN	PENNSYLVANIAN	PERMIAN	TRIASSIC

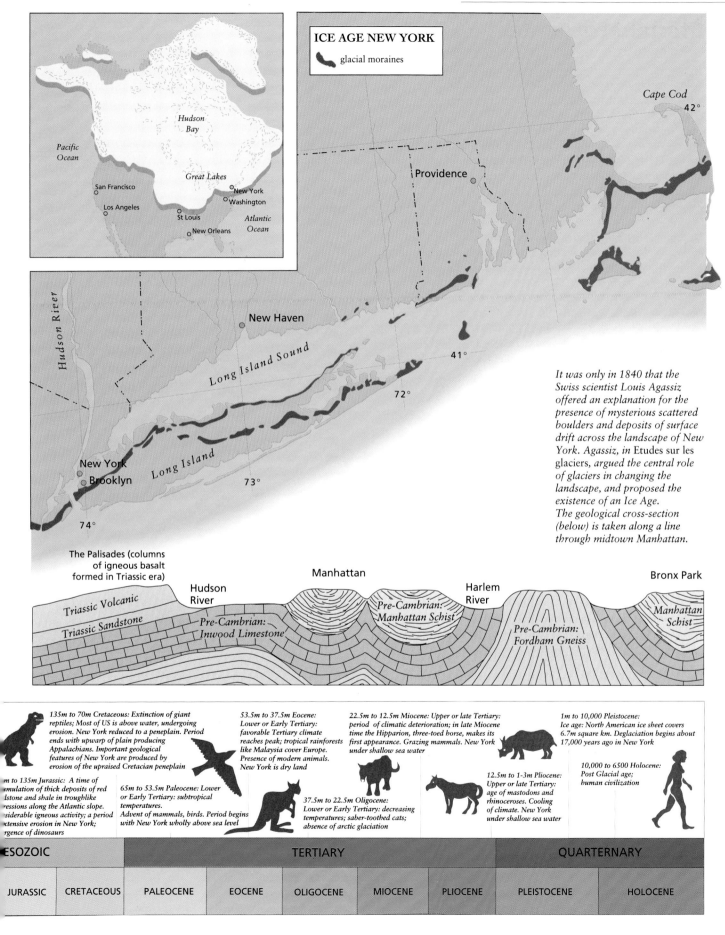

ICE AGE NEW YORK

glacial moraines

Cape Cod
42°

Hudson
Bay

Pacific
Ocean

Great Lakes

San Francisco

Los Angeles

St Louis

New York
Washington

Atlantic
Ocean

New Orleans

Providence

Hudson River

New Haven

Long Island Sound

41°

72°

New York
Brooklyn

Long Island

73°

74°

It was only in 1840 that the
Swiss scientist Louis Agassiz
offered an explanation for the
presence of mysterious scattered
boulders and deposits of surface
drift across the landscape of New
York. Agassiz, in Etudes sur les
glaciers, argued the central role
of glaciers in changing the
landscape, and proposed the
existence of an Ice Age.
The geological cross-section
(below) is taken along a line
through midtown Manhattan.

The Palisades (columns
of igneous basalt
formed in Triassic era)

Manhattan

Bronx Park

Hudson
River

Harlem
River

Triassic Volcanic

Triassic Sandstone

Pre-Cambrian:
Inwood Limestone

Pre-Cambrian:
Manhattan Schist

Pre-Cambrian:
Fordham Gneiss

Manhattan
Schist

135m to 70m Cretaceous: Extinction of giant
reptiles; Most of US is above water, undergoing
erosion. New York reduced to a peneplain. Period
ends with upwarp of plain producing
Appalachians. Important geological
features of New York are produced by
erosion of the upraised Cretacian peneplain

53.5m to 37.5m Eocene:
Lower or Early Tertiary:
favorable Tertiary climate
reaches peak; tropical rainforests
like Malaysia cover Europe.
Presence of modern animals.
New York is dry land

22.5m to 12.5m Miocene: Upper or late Tertiary:
period of climatic deterioration; in late Miocene
time the Hipparion, three-toed horse, makes its
first appearance. Grazing mammals. New York
under shallow sea water

1m to 10,000 Pleistocene:
Ice age: North American ice sheet covers
6.7m square km. Deglaciation begins about
17,000 years ago in New York

10,000 to 6500 Holocene:
Post Glacial age;
human civilization

m to 135m Jurassic: A time of
mulation of thick deposits of red
dstone and shale in troughlike
ressions along the Atlantic slope.
siderable igneous activity; a period
xtensive erosion in New York;
rgence of dinosaurs

65m to 53.5m Paleocene: Lower
or Early Tertiary: subtropical
temperatures.
Advent of mammals, birds. Period begins
with New York wholly above sea level

37.5m to 22.5m Oligocene:
Lower or Early Tertiary: decreasing
temperatures; saber-toothed cats;
absence of arctic glaciation

12.5m to 1-3m Pliocene:
Upper or late Tertiary:
age of mastodons and
rhinoceroses. Cooling
of climate. New York
under shallow sea water

ESOZOIC

TERTIARY

QUARTERNARY

JURASSIC | CRETACEOUS | PALEOCENE | EOCENE | OLIGOCENE | MIOCENE | PLIOCENE | PLEISTOCENE | HOLOCENE

Manahatta

When the Dutch came to New Netherland, they intruded upon a native culture of the "eastern division" of the Algonquian family, a linguistic stock of tribes occupying the Atlantic coast from Maine to the Chesapeake. The many tribes and sub-groups making up the Upper Delawaran or Munsee formed a confederacy which occupied the entire Delaware basin, including eastern Pennsylvania and southeastern New York.

The Delawares encountered on the lower Hudson called themselves Lenape, or "real men". The inhabitants of Manhattan were the Manates, a Munsee tribe, who were regarded by the Dutch as troublesome and aggressive. After selling Manahatta (variously translated as "hilly island" or "the small island"), for trinkets in 1626, the tribe moved west of the Bronx River. The Canarsies in Brooklyn, Matinecooks in Flushing, Rockaways (who settled near Rockaway Beach in Queens) and the Wecquaesgeeks (a Mahican tribe in the vicinity of Yonkers) made their own accommodation with the settlers.

The Lenape were hunters and fishermen, with substantial woodland clearings where they cultivated Indian corn (to make maize or meal for bread cakes), beans, pumpkins, and tobacco. The long, narrow native canoe was carved out of a hollowed tree trunk, and was used for fishing, whether with hooks made of bone, spears with sharpened stone or bone heads, or nets woven of "Indian hemp", a milkweed which grew in the swamps. Meat and fish were dried for consumption in the winter.

They introduced the Dutch to maple sugar, hominy and succotash, as well as tobacco. Natives on Manhattan ate oysters in great quantity, leaving piles of discarded shells near their settlments. The Dutch named Pearl Street after the piles of shells which lined the shore. Beans, meat, fish and roots were all cooked as a mash in large, clay pots.

They used wooden plates, made water buckets out of bark, and had mats and baskets made of rush, husks, grasses and bark. Every item of domestic use was decorated with woven designs or painted figures of animals.

Tanned animal skins were used for clothing, and feathers and embroidery for decoration. In summer, a simple leather breech-cloth sufficed for the men; in the winter, robes of bear, beaver or deerskin were worn. For ceremonial and warlike occasions the men decorated their faces with paint. The women wore decorated headbands, and a cloth around their bodies which was fastened by an ornamented girdle which extended to the knee.

The French explorer, Samuel Champlain, encountered Iroquois on the border between Canada and New York state (below) in 1609, the year Henry Hudson reached New York. He used his musket to shoot two chiefs – the Iroquois had never seen firearms before and this alienated the powerful Iroquois confederacy. The French made common cause with the Huron. The Dutch made alliances with local tribes and were occasionally drawn into traditional tribal conflicts. The wisest diplomacy could seldom prevent violent conflict between natives and Dutch settlers.

The Iroquois and Huron longhouses were customarily arranged around an open space in the center of the settlement. They could be as much as 50 yards long, and 12 or 15 yards wide, and were made of flexible saplings covered with sheets of bark. Smoke holes in the roof and several entrances made the longhouse suitable for a number of families.

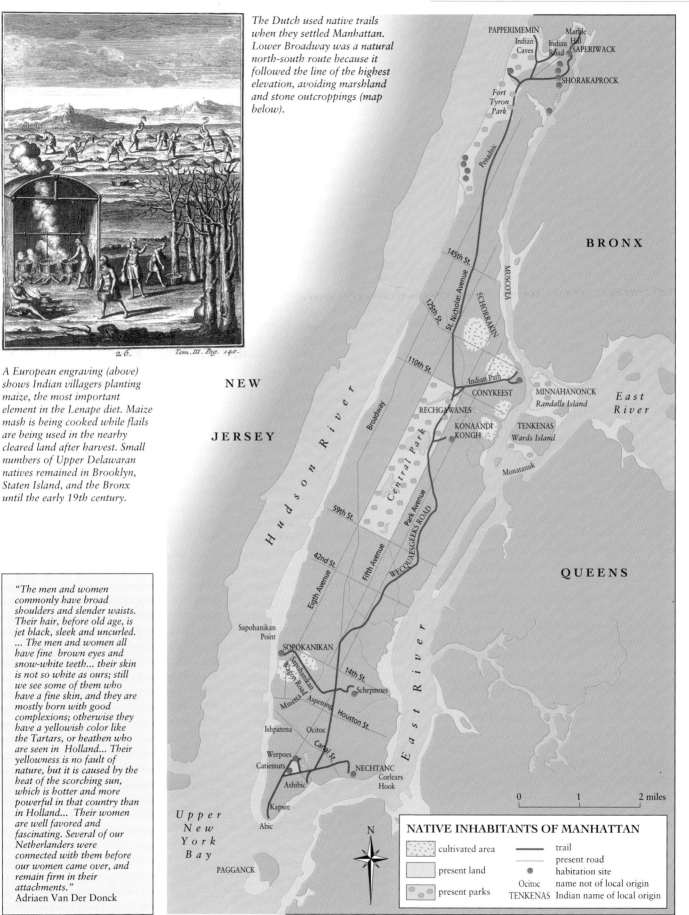

The Dutch used native trails when they settled Manhattan. Lower Broadway was a natural north-south route because it followed the line of the highest elevation, avoiding marshland and stone outcroppings (map below).

A European engraving (above) shows Indian villagers planting maize, the most important element in the Lenape diet. Maize mash is being cooked while flails are being used in the nearby cleared land after harvest. Small numbers of Upper Delawaran natives remained in Brooklyn, Staten Island, and the Bronx until the early 19th century.

"The men and women commonly have broad shoulders and slender waists. Their hair, before old age, is jet black, sleek and uncurled. ... The men and women all have fine brown eyes and snow-white teeth... their skin is not so white as ours; still we see some of them who have a fine skin, and they are mostly born with good complexions; otherwise they have a yellowish color like the Tartars, or heathen who are seen in Holland... Their yellowness is no fault of nature, but it is caused by the heat of the scorching sun, which is hotter and more powerful in that country than in Holland... Their women are well favored and fascinating. Several of our Netherlanders were connected with them before our women came over, and remain firm in their attachments."
Adriaen Van Der Donck

NATIVE INHABITANTS OF MANHATTAN

cultivated area — trail
present land — present road
present parks ● habitation site
Ocitoc name not of local origin
TENKENAS Indian name of local origin

0   1   2 miles

Explorers Arrive

The first explorers to reach New York were the descendants of the bands of hunters who first crossed the Bering Land Bridge from Siberia into Alaska about 25,000 years ago. In time they settled in every region of this vast continent, shaping its landscape with the usc of fire and agriculture. Explorers from the Old World encountered a landscape which was used, occupied, known, and named.

Between the 8th and 11th centuries, the native inhabitants along the Newfoundland coast encountered Swedes, Norwegians, and Danes who had created a first, distant settlement on Iceland in the 9th century. From Iceland the Norse made two settlements on Greenland, and from Greenland initial contact was made with the New World. These first, brief encounters left little beyond legend to document them.

When, in 1492, Columbus reached America, he was unaware of the existence of the large continent to the west, and failed to grasp that he had not landed on a remote Asian island, but on a new continent. In 1493, when Columbus sailed on his second voyage, there were six priests accompanying the crew. For the Spanish Crown, conversion of the natives was an important motive. The other declared motive was the creation of a trading colony. The mixture of motives – commerce, national aggrandizement, and hunger for riches – gave the early voyages of exploration their unique flavor of evangelism and greed.

In 1523, Francis I of France was persuaded by Verrazano to support a voyage to find a sea passage to Cathay. From a reconaissance of the eastern seabord, he brought back a description of the land and its aboriginal inhabitants which greatly stirred interest. In 1534, Jacques Cartier was commissioned to find a route to Asia. Contact with Indians after his 27-day journey to Newfoundland inaugurated the French fur trade. On a return voyage in 1535, Cartier sailed up the St. Lawrence to explore, leaving a winter camp near the present site of Quebec. He traveled as far as Montreal, where he found a large native settlement.

In 1539, Hernando De Soto recruited 700 men, all treasure-seekers, and sailed in ten ships to the southwest coast of Florida. De Soto led his men on a vast journey into the interior of the continent, from North Carolina to Texas. Although he died during the journey and was buried in the Mississippi River, 300 Spaniards survived the ordeal, reaching Mexico in 1543. Sir Walter Raleigh made his first expedition to Roanoke Island in 1584. His first plantation of

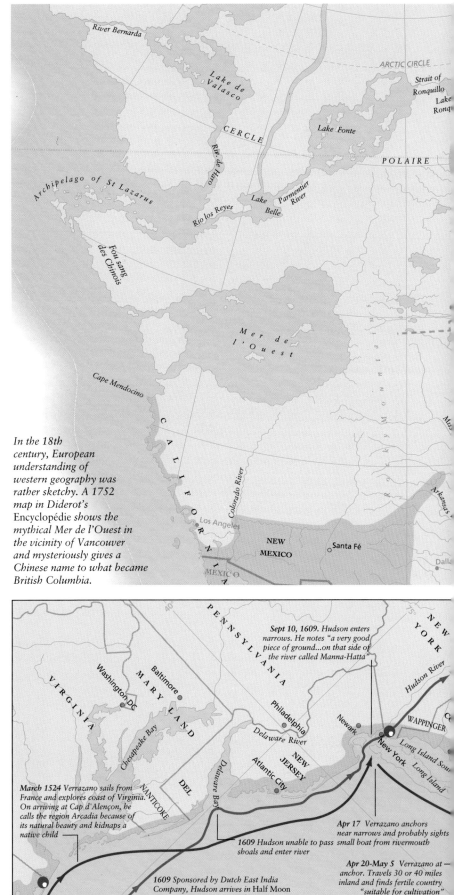

In the 18th century, European understanding of western geography was rather sketchy. A 1752 map in Diderot's Encyclopédie *shows the mythical Mer de l'Ouest in the vicinity of Vancouver and mysteriously gives a Chinese name to what became British Columbia.*

Sept 10, 1609. Hudson enters narrows. He notes "a very good piece of ground...on that side of the river called Manna-Hatta"

March 1524 Verrazano sails from France and explores coast of Virginia. On arriving at Cap d'Alençon, he calls the region Arcadia because of its natural beauty and kidnaps a native child

1609 Hudson unable to pass shoals and enter river

Apr 17 Verrazano anchors near narrows and probably sights small boat from rivermouth

Apr 20-May 5 Verrazano at anchor. Travels 30 or 40 miles inland and finds fertile country "suitable for cultivation"

1609 Sponsored by Dutch East India Company, Hudson arrives in Half Moon to negotiate passage to Cathay

MAPPING A NEW CONTINENT

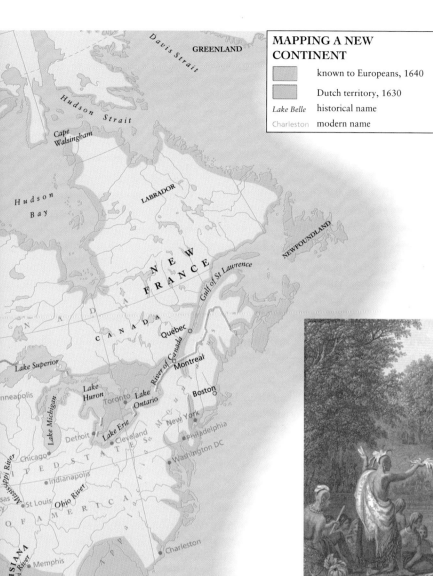

known to Europeans, 1640

Dutch territory, 1630

Lake Belle historical name

Charleston modern name

110 settlers was made in 1587, but by the time a relief expedition could return in 1590 there was no trace of the settlers.

When the first Dutch traders arrived in the Hudson Bay, the disappearance of Cabot in 1498, the killing of Verrazano in Central America in 1527, the brutal hardships experienced by the party Cartier left at Quebec in the winter of 1535-6, and the mysterious disappearance of the Roanoke settlers in 1587-90, had made it abundantly clear that the exploration and settlement of this new land was extremely dangerous. Harsh weather, threats from rival European powers, disease, dangers of mutiny, and the likelihood of attack by natives, made the New World a nightmare of violence and danger, leavened by the hope of gold.

The landing of Henry Hudson in 1609 (above) from an original by R.W. Weir. Hudson, still searching for a northwest passage, made a final voyage to Hudson Bay where he spent the winter of 1610-11. The hardships of the winter enraged the crew, who set Hudson, his son and seven crew members adrift in a small boat with no supplies. They were never heard from again.

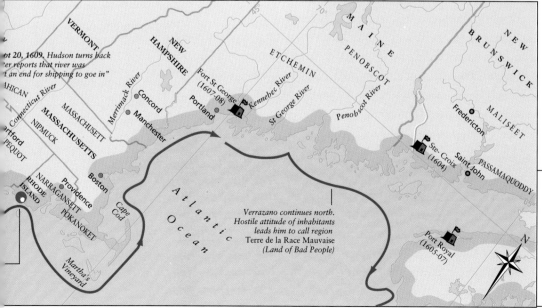

Verrazano continues north. Hostile attitude of inhabitants leads him to call region Terre de la Race Mauvaise (Land of Bad People)

EARLY EXPLORATION OF NEW YORK

known to Europeans, 1524

→ route of Verrazano, 1524

→ route of Hudson, 1609

◗ encounter with native people

Chapter 2 Dutch New Amsterdam 1610–1664

In May 1623, the *Nieuw Nederlandt*, a vessel of 260 tons captained by Cornelis Jacobsz May, brought 30 Protestant families, mostly Walloons (French-speaking refugees who had fled from the Spanish Netherlands) to New Netherland. Their party consisted of 110 men, women, and children, who agreed to settle in the wild colony for six years. They brought with them livestock, seeds, and farm implements. A group of eight men were left on Governor's Island, where a fort was to be built. Other traders were sent to the Connecticut River and to the Dutch settlement on the Delaware. The rest were planted at Fort Orange, near Albany. To survive the first winter, the Fort Orange settlers built bark huts, and planted a crop of grain. Conditions were harsh and their lives were unenviable.

Further settlers arrived on the first ships of the sailing season early in 1625, and among their number was the Amsterdam engineer, Crijn Fredericxsz, who brought with him plans for a new fort to be erected on a site chosen by the Director-designate, Willem Verhulst. It was to be located near the sharp tip of the island, thus commanding naval access to both the Hudson River and the East River. Within the fort there was space for a marketplace, houses, a hospital, school, and a church.

From the efforts of Fredericxsz and Verhulst, the first permanent settlement on Manhattan was established. The existing huts, built at random by the first settlers, followed no recognizable street pattern until the engineer laid out a pattern of streets and lots for houses, and larger sites along the main north–south path for Dutch farms or *bouweries*. Slaves were imported to build the fort and the many dwellings needed. However, Dutch attitudes towards slaves did not vary greatly from the prejudiced views common among all Europeans in the 17th century. When the Rev. Jonas Michaëlius, the first Reformed Church *dominie* to arrive at New Amsterdam, complained in 1629 that "the Angola slave women are thievish, lazy, and useless trash" contemporaries merely took his comments as reconfirming the commonplace stereotypes and prejudices.

Encountering the natives

The first natives encountered by the colonists at Jamestown and Plymouth were Algonquian tribes who lived along the Atlantic seaboard, from Virginia to the St. Lawrence. The Algonquin were the first native tribes to occupy central New York, New England, and lower Canada, but had been displaced by a migration from the west of Huron-Iroquois in the 13th century. The surviving remnants of the Algonquins in New York state were

The seal of the city of New Amsterdam, with a beaver prominently placed at the center of the shield.

"... of his own free will he released and liberated from servitude ... Manuel the Spaniard ...provided that the above named Manuel promises to pay ... for said freedom the sum of three hundred Carolus guilders within the term of three consecutive years ... in seawan (wampum), grain or such pay as is current here ..." Manumission declaration, February 1649. Two years later a debt of 250 guilders was repaid in New Amsterdam by "25 good, merchantable winter beavers."

"[There is little] authority known among these nations. They live almost all equally free... all are well fashioned people, strong and sound of body, well fed, without blemish." Nicholael Van Wassenaer, *Historisch Verhael* ("Historical Account") 1624–30.

Mahicans, who were the first to be devastated by the diseases, such as smallpox, which accompanied the Europeans. The Dutch successfully traded with the Mahicans who lived along the Hudson, and formed a pact of friendship with other tribes (the Delawares and Mohawks) living within the theoretical borders of New Netherland. These commercial relationships were only seriously strained when the Dutch were inveigled by the Mahicans to join in an attack on the Mohawks. The intervention ended disastrously for the garrison at Fort Orange (one of their soldiers was cooked and eaten by the Mohawks), but amicable trade was resumed and Dutch contacts extended through the Mohawk River valley to the territory which was settled by the Oneida and Onondaga tribes.

In Central and Western New York the powerful Five Nations of Iroquois tribes (Mohawks, Oneidas, Onondagas, Cayugas and Senecas, who together had formed a great Confederacy in the 15th century) lived in settled villages, often protected by palisades. They farmed and stored corn, grains, nuts, and wild fruits for trade. The pelts they trapped and treated were avidly sought by the French traders on the St. Lawrence, and by the Dutch at Fort Orange. The Dutch had no imperial design to extend their influence northwards into the territory of the Iroquois, and sent no missionaries, like the French Jesuit "Black Robes," to convert the Indians. Thus, Dutch trade with the Five Nations was built on mutual self-interest. From the 1640s, Dutch traders began to sell muskets and powder to the Iroquois which were turned with devastating effect upon the Iroquois' old foes, the Algonquins and the Hurons, and upon the French.

A view of the city of New Amsterdam made in 1650. The ramshackle wooden buildings which line the shore, as well as the fort and windmill are all clearly visible.

"... *Petrus Stuyvesant, director general of New Netherland and Curaçao,... acknowledges that he purchased the Company's farm in New Netherland ... with the appurtenances thereof, consisting of a dwelling house, barn, hayrick, land, six cows, two horses and two young Negroes ...*"
Deed of Sale, March 1651.

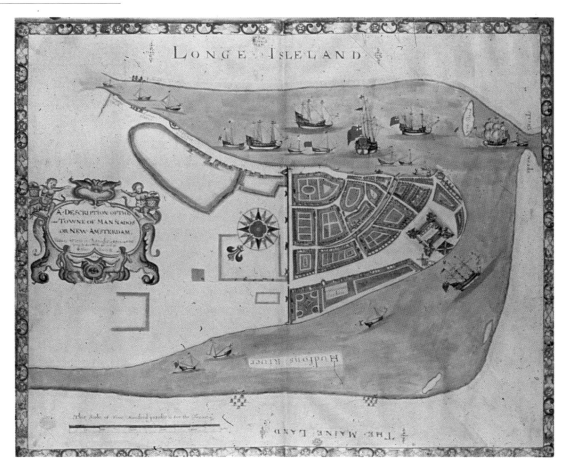

The "Duke" map of New Amsterdam, 1664. By the time the English seized the colony, development was confined to the area below Wall Street.

Trade and conflict

For their protection from attack, the families at Fort Orange were moved down to Manhattan to form a larger, more compact settlement which might be better defended. To encourage the self-sufficiency of the colony, over 100 head of cattle were sent from the Netherlands. There were good reasons to fear the natives, but New Amsterdam depended upon trade for its very existence. Indian cereals (maize and corn) soon became a staple of the colony's food, as did tobacco. Native wampum or seawan (pierced seashells) was for many years the only currency used in the Dutch colony. But the Dutch, no more than the English in Virginia or Massachusetts, had little sense of the complexity of native life and values, its diverse languages and customs. Their encounter with the natives was less bloody than the English colonists', but in the end living harmoniously together proved impossible. Instructed to deal fairly with the natives, Dutch laws punished those who committed offenses against them. Petty irritations led to outbreaks of violence and relations deteriorated. Work proceeded on the fort, and reprisals were made (on both sides) for slights, theft, and violence. In March 1633, 104 well-armed soldiers accompanied the new Director General Krol when he arrived in New Netherland. A palisade (along the line of Wall Street) was erected across the neck of Manhattan in 1635.

In 1638 Director-General Kieft re-emphasized the ban on sexual relations between the Dutch and the Indians. (Nonetheless, in a colony where there was a distinct imbalance between men and women, there were many instances of illicit relations.) A year later he attempted to tax the Indians. Violent resistance to this taxation led to a punitive expedition by 50 Dutch soldiers and 20 sailors in 1640 and a general souring of relations. As a precaution, Kieft forbade the sale of alcohol to Indians and threatened huge fines and banishment from the colony for anyone breaking the ban.

Troubles with the Indians so disturbed the colony's leading merchants that Kieft found it politic to invite the commonalty to delegate twelve of their number to consult with him. Out of the wars with the Indians, the first tentative step towards popular government began in New Amsterdam. (The Twelve were haughtily dismissed after requesting further consultation in the management of the colony.) After much discussion, the Twelve reluctantly allowed Kieft to make an attack in 1642 against the Wecquaesgeek. The punitive expedition failed to find any Indians, but with further provocations and attacks, it was clear that both sides were girding for a battle. A lethal attack in February 1643 by Mohawk warriors on Tappans and Wecquaesgeeks near Fort Orange caused hundreds of the Algonquins to flee to the environs of New Amsterdam, where they congregated at Pavonia and Corlaer's Hook. Kieft seized this opportunity to deal once and for all with the Algonquins. What followed was a piece of frontier savagery, with native infants and children, as well as their parents, being hacked to death or drowned in a night attack. The next morning there was a wild hunt throughout the city for the survivors, who were unceremoniously slaughtered. In response, the Algonquin tribes collectively set about destroying the Dutch settlement. Outlying farms and villages were burned, and the settlers who had not fled to New Amsterdam for protection were killed. A peace treaty was signed in March 1643, but the colony was little more than a smoking ruin. The settlers, who had lost crops, cattle and their homes, blamed the thoughtless and arrogant Kieft for their ruination.

Stuyvesant

With the arrival on May 11, 1647, of Petrus Stuyvesant as Director-General, the Dutch commercial and colonial experiment in New Netherland was given another chance. He found a demoralized settlement, scarcely recovered from the devastation of the recent warfare with the natives; and he was instructed by the directors to make the enterprise profitable. A choleric son of a Reformed Church *dominie*, Stuyvesant had entered the service of the Dutch West India Company after a career in the army.

"The open country was stripped of inhabitants to such a degree that, with the exception of the three English villages of Heemstede, New Flushing and Gravesend, there were not fifty bouweries [farms] and plantations on it, and the whole province could not muster 250, at most 300 men capable of bearing arms."
A description of the colony in 1647, on Petrus Stuyvesant's arrival.

Bringing to administrative tasks the unbending expectation of a soldier, he wanted the colony to stand firmly to attention. A slovenly, drunken, dishonest community greeted him.

His approach to governance was autocratic. An adherent of the Dutch Reformed faith, Stuyvesant sought to uphold its teachings through the strict enforcement of Sabbath laws. He personally directed the persecution and torture of Quakers discovered in the colony, and pleaded with the directors in Amsterdam for permission to expel Jews who had arrived after the fall of the Dutch possessions in Brazil. He was jealous of his official prerogatives, quick-tempered, and aggressive. Forced to follow in the steps of Director-General Kieft and appoint a board of delegates (the Nine Men) to attend to the general welfare of the community, he resisted their attempt to secure independent municipal status for New Amsterdam, and imprisoned the leading author of a "Remonstrance" to the States-General which complained of the many failings of the company's policies and managers. In 1653 a form of municipal government was granted, against the wishes of Stuyvesant.

Stuyvesant was under constant pressure from the English from north and south, but he could scarcely muster more than two or three hundred soldiers to defend his domain. He tried to negotiate with the land-hungry English who were settling in Dutch territory after the surrender of the fur monopoly in 1639. Stuyvesant hoped to regularize a deteriorating position by encouraging trade links. Tobacco came to New Netherland from Virginia, fish from New England, dyestuff and salt from Curaçao, and cotton, liquor, luxury goods, and settlers from the United Provinces. New Netherland exported grain, timber, potash, and pelts.

The other facet of Stuyvesant's strategy for survival was internal. He sought to improve the moral climate of the settlement by enforcing religious orthodoxy. He complained to the directors of the profusion of taverns, brewers, and tapsters: "one full fourth of the City of New Amsterdam has been turned into taverns for the sale of brandy, tobacco and beer." He also sought to limit nighttime carousing by banning the sale of liquor after 9 p.m. The tendency of the commonalty of New Amsterdam to settle where they will, and to pass through the palisade wall at all hours, persuaded Stuyvesant to impose strict controls upon movement, and to require new housing to be built within the existing wall. These measures were needed for defense against the natives, and reflected his desire to impose closer controls on the inhabitants of New Amsterdam. He wanted to rule over a colony that was more compact, more godly, and more amenable to lawful regulation. His ordinances were ignored or evaded, and all he achieved was the growing disaffection of the inhabitants.

"The province of New Netherland, destitute of wealth, possessed a sweet tranquility that wealth could never purchase. There were neither public commotions, nor private quarrels; neither parties, nor sects, nor schisms; neither persecutions, nor trials, nor punishments; nor were there counsellors, attorneys, catchpolls, or hangmen." Washington Irving in *Knickerbocker's History of New York* (1809), a delightful comic spoof on the Dutch.

The fall of New Amsterdam

By the 1660s it was clear that the growing power of the English could not be finessed. Stuyvesant's dignified and legalistic protests at the encroachments by the English were ignored, and his commissioners rebuffed. In March 1664 King Charles II issued patents which bestowed virtually the whole of New Netherland to his brother, the Duke of York. In late August, four English men-at war arrived off Staten Island. After a couple of days of frantic discussion, it was clear that there was an insufficient number of soldiers to defend the colony. The British were willing not to disturb either Dutch property rights, or the pattern of Dutch commercial relations. The populace saw no point in protracted resistance, and on September 8th, Colonel Richard Nicolls, first Deputy-Governor of the English territory of New York, landed to begin a new chapter in the history of the city.

The arguments over why the Dutch failed were well-established years before the English frigates arrived. The reasons were clear: bad government; failure to build the population; incompetent commercial management; fraudulent use of company money for private profit; a high tariff which ruined legitimate trade; the arbitrary and high-handed behavior of the Directors-General and their close allies; the Indian wars provoked by Kieft; the heavy burden of taxation; the failure to maintain the schoolhouse, almshouse or orphan asylum, and so on. Poorly managed, discredited in the eyes of the settlers, the Dutch experiment ended because ultimately no one was prepared to lift a musket to defend it.

19th-century illustrations of scenes and characters in Dutch New Amsterdam from "Valentine's Manual."

A Schepen laughing at a
BURGOMASTERS JOKE.
FOR D.T. VALENTINES MANUAL
H.R.Robinson Lith. 51 Park Row

DIEDRICH KNICKERBOCKER.

PETER STUYVESANT,
Rebuking the Cobler.

A Dutch Settlement

With the arrival of French-speaking Walloon settlers (a carefully calculated move in the commercial and military rivalry between the United Provinces, England and France) aboard the *Nieuw Nederlandt* in 1624, New Netherland began its period as a Dutch colony. The Dutch West India Company claimed squatter's rights: they asserted that actual settlements alone were the basis of claims to title, regardless of Papal decrees or prior discovery. Since they had not discovered the territory, nothing would affirm their rights to the title of New Netherland more persuasively than a strong physical presence.

The Company gave settlers considerable assistance. In addition to free transportation, land for the colonists was allotted according to family size. Livestock could be purchased on favorable credit terms. Other than the fur trade, which the Company retained as an absolute monopoly, the settlers were allowed to engage in a range of economic activities. The right to allocate land, decide what crops to plant and where to locate the colonists was left to the Company's representative.

We know little about the experience of these first settlers. The threat of Indian attacks caused Peter Minuit, the Company's first Director-General (appointed in 1626), to evacuate the outlying settlements to New Amsterdam. Amsterdam engineer Crijn Fredericxsz had brought with him the Company's plans for a substantial fort when the first settlement was established in Manhattan in 1625, but Minuit found the colony in so deplorable a condition that construction had to be delayed. Livestock and settlers were also poorly provided for. Minuit purchased the island from the Indians, and ordered materials for the intended fort diverted for use in the erection of 30 houses.

Minuit's New Amsterdam was a rough trading outpost. Fortification consisted of a blockhouse surrounded by a palisade wall. For a population of 270 there were 30 log houses, a stone-walled counting house (where the Company's pelts were stored), and a mill. Farmers built houses, barns, and sheds. The paths they traveled to the Company's stores and offices near the fort began to define a pattern of streets and roads.

The costs of the first colonial expeditions were high, and the fur trade was the only export which promised a return on the Company's investment. Furthermore, the military disaster of the recent Dutch attempt to oust the Portuguese and Spanish from Brazil made the Company wary of the enterprise. Labor was scarce, and although

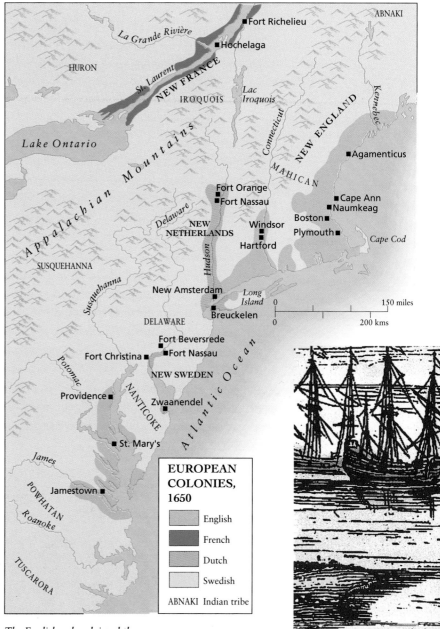

The English, who claimed the whole of the North American coastline, protested the activities of the Dutch West India Company in 1622 through diplomatic channels, and refused to acknowledge Dutch rights to the colony. By 1650, the colony was under the autocratic rule of Director-General Petrus Stuyvesant, who was under constant pressure from the English settlements to the north and south of New Netherland. Five years later he took military action against the weakest of the other colonies, the Swedish.

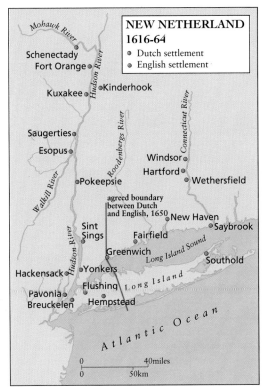

NEW NETHERLAND 1616-64
- Dutch settlement
- English settlement

Anxious to boost a dangerously underpopulated colony, in 1629 the Dutch West India Company granted patroonships, large estates to investors who would agree to settle 50 colonists within four years. Only one of the original patroonships, Rensselaer, avoided Indian attacks, and was a success. In the 1640s the Dutch granted charters for English settlements at Newtown, Hempstead, Gravesend, Flushing, then to the Dutch at Breuckelen (Brooklyn), and shortly afterwards to the Dutch at Beverwyck and Midwout.

This early view of Manhattan (below) shows a small cluster of buildings adjacent to the fort and mill. The company store, brewery and house of the fiscal were all located here. A road following the shoreline of the East River ran north of the ditch and palisade at Wall Street, to the farms which had been granted to settlers, where most of the colony's food was grown.

the Company guaranteed to supply basic needs, costs were high. The disaffected Walloons and their families began to return to the United Provinces in increasing numbers.

New Netherland languished amid the many distractions of imperial and commercial rivalry in the 1630s and the growing threat of war between the United Provinces and England. When Wouter Van Twiller was appointed Director-General in 1633, the Company sent with him a party of skilled workmen (masons, brick layers, carpenters) to reconstruct the fort and build a wharf, additional warehouses and houses. Slaves were imported from the West Indies to work on the fort, and a site was selected (on the East River) where they could be housed. They were soon used to tend the livestock, work on the farms, and perform other manual labor around the warehouses and docks of the Company. Unlike the practice elsewhere in the Dutch empire, slaves in New Netherland could eventually be granted manumission. This half-freedom granted them, after the payment of an annual sum, the freedom to own property, travel within the colony and marry.

New Amsterdam 1630-40

By the mid-1630s New Amsterdam had a flour mill, two saw mills, a shed for shipbuilding, goat pens, a local midwife, a church, and a bakery.

The population of the colony (Manhattan and surrounding farms) was estimated to be between 400 and 500 by 1643. The Dutch West India Company was anxious to attract settlers, and granted charters (allowing considerable local autonomy) for English settlements at Newtown (1642), Hempstead (1644), Gravesend (1645), and Flushing (1645), then granted land for Dutch settlements at Breuckelen (1646), Beverwyck (1652), and Midwout (1653).

French-speaking Walloons were no longer the majority; by 1643 18 different languages were spoken in the colony. Nevertheless, the commanding positions in New Netherland society were exclusively reserved for the Dutch, and their values were technically enforceable by law, if not always rigorously in practice. All officials took an oath affirming the primacy of the Reformed Church, and non-conforming religions were banned.

The colony was often unruly. The Directors-General made sporadic attempts to enforce Sabbath-observance, and banned the sale of intoxicating liquor after 9p.m. Anyone who worked on the Sabbath could be fined; active amusements such as boating, bowls, card-playing or dancing were more heavily penalized. Nonetheless, such enforcement of public morals was haphazard.

The pastor Michaëlius, who had previously served on the West coast of Africa and in Brazil, observed that "The people, for the most part, are rather rough and unrestrained....". The consumption of home-brewed beer and imported Holland gin was the main distraction in this remote commercial trading station.

New Amsterdam was a corrupt, mismanaged company town. New settlers were outraged to find prices in the Company store were higher than in Amsterdam. The local management, dominated by the Directors-General, derived no part of their authority from the settlers. It was widely assumed that they pursued personal

In the perspective map below, Long Island can be seen in the foreground, Manhattan in the middle distance and New Jersey in the background. Manhattan is merely a small settlement, and further north only the occasional farmstead or orchard disturbs the virgin land. Daily life in New Amsterdam was preoccupied by commerce and farming. A tobacco plantation with two slaves, belonging to the former Director Wouter van Twiller at Saponikan (near Greenwich Village), was rented for five years to an Englishman, Thomas Hall, in 1641. An annual payment of 750 lbs of tobacco (reduced if one of the slaves died during the lease) and the construction of a 50 foot-long barn, were stipulated in the contract signed in New Amsterdam on November 30, 1641.

In the 1630s the town centre of New Amsterdam (right) consisted of the market place, brewery, church and mill, with the Heerewegh (Broadway) leading diagonally from it. An early pattern of streets and roads was established from the paths farmers traveled to company buildings near the fort.

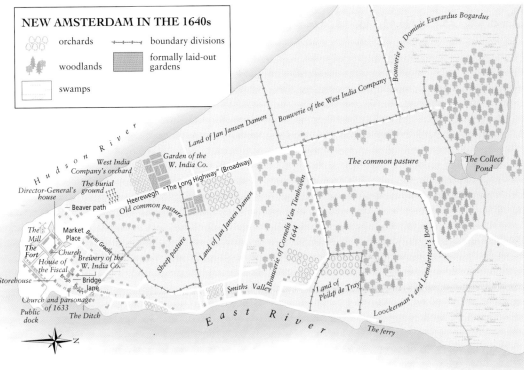

NEW AMSTERDAM IN THE 1640s

- orchards
- woodlands
- swamps
- boundary divisions
- formally laid-out gardens

At the foot of Visscher's 1651 map of New Amsterdam is a drawing of the port (seen below right); it includes a gallows welcoming a ship arriving at port. It was a reminder that despite the neat appearance of small row houses fronting kitchen gardens and the tidily-named Dutch streets, New Amsterdam was a thinly populated, uncomfortable and muddy place with few creature comforts and much lawlessness.

interest first, and Company policy second. The fort fell into decay, few public facilities were provided, and the rampant abuses of power were largely without redress. Attempts to restrict the trade in guns and alcohol to the Indians were deeply resented and subverted by traders. Smuggling destroyed the Company's fur trade monopoly, which was abandoned in 1639.

The rapidly expanding population consisted largely of fur traders seeking a quick fortune. The frankly commercial spirit of the colony encouraged the entire population to look after their own interests, and to evade where possible the heavy-handed regulations of the Company.

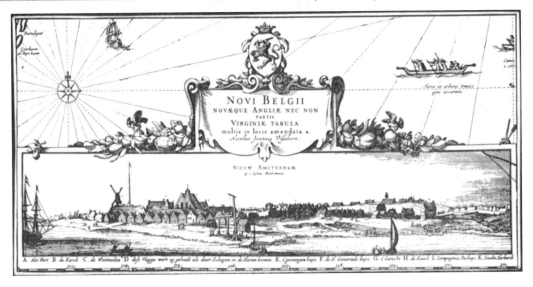

Extending the Dutch Presence

The Dutch West India Company reserved the land of Manhattan Island for Company use. Special plots of land were reserved for the conduct of Company business. The weighhouse, counting house, Stadt Huys (built in 1642 on the shoreline on what was then simply known as Waterside) and other Company properties dominated New Amsterdam.

Other plots were allocated to house Company employees and those who had received permission to settle on the island. Between 1630 and 1644, 173 immigrants came to New Netherland. One-third arrived as members of households, and these families generally remained to form the stable population of the colony, whereas the single men moved on. Contracts for apprentices or servants expired at age 21, further adding to the transience of those without family ties.

Early land grants refer vaguely to a "lot east of the fort" (on the present Bridge Street), or to a "lot on the ditch, bounded by a trench in the marsh" (on the north side of Beaver Street). Mapping property boundaries was becoming an urgent necessity.

Above Wall Street, the line of the original defensive palisade, the island soon assumed a now unfamiliar, miscellaneous pattern of holdings outlined by grants and property transactions. The defining shape for the island was the lane which continued *De Heere Straet* (Broadway) north beyond the wall. Most Dutch settlers preferred to live in farms and houses scattered across New Netherland, and resisted pressures to live together in villages. Native raids of the 1640s largely destroyed small settlements at Bloemendael (Bloomingdale village), and Haarlem (re-settled in 1658). Company officials took large landholdings on Long Island and at what became New Amersfoort (now Flatlands), also buying Nut Island (Governor's Island), and two islands in Hellgate, in 1637.

By 1639 Dutch plantations thinly lined the East River. Other land purchases from the Indians in the 1630s extended the Dutch presence on the western end of Long Island. In 1642 three Long Island villages, bought in the 1630s, were amalgamated to form Breukelen. Dutch settlers first bought land in Queens in 1635; Jonas Bronck was the first settler in the Bronx; Staten Island, granted in 1630 to Michael Pauw, was difficult to settle because of Indian raids: the first permanent European inhabitants settled Oude Dorp (Old Town) in 1661.

Virtually nothing remains of Dutch New Amsterdam except for the irregular layout of lower Manhattan's streets and the remnants of some Dutch street-names. This engraving (above), made in the mid-19th century, shows the last Dutch house then still standing on Broad Street. Dutch settlers had brought the step-gabled style of vernacular architecture to New Amsterdam. It was soon to be supplanted by the more classical facades of 18th-century Britain.

CITY TAVERN, NEW AMSTERDAM, AFTERWARD "THE STADT HUYS," BUILT IN 1642.

The Stadt Huys (left) was located overlooking the Great Dock on the waterfront, facing the East River. It was built as the City Tavern in 1642 to house the increasing number of seamen – many of them English – calling at New Amsterdam. It served as the City Hall from 1653 to 1667. The prominently placed double stocks were for the humiliation and punishment of minor wrongdoing.

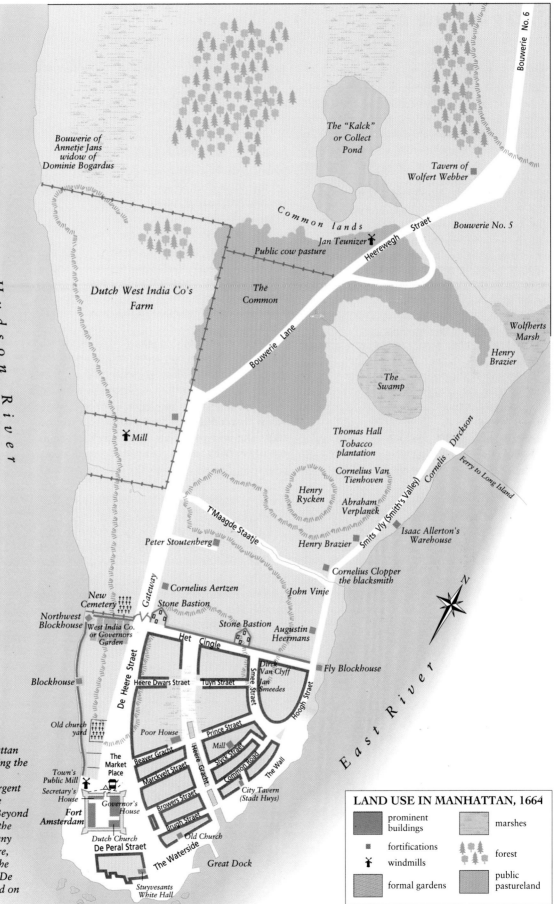

Bouwerie No. 6

Bouwerie of
Annetje Jans
widow of
Dominie Bogardus

The "Kalck"
or Collect
Pond

Tavern of
Wolfert Webber

Common lands

Bouwerie No. 5

Public cow pasture

Jan Teunizer

Heerewegh Straet

Dutch West India Co's
Farm

The
Common

Wolfherts
Marsh

Henry
Brazier

Hudson River

Bouwerie Lane

The
Swamp

Mill

Thomas Hall
Tobacco
plantation

Cornelius Dirckson

Ferry to Long Island

Cornelius Van
Tienhoven

Henry
Rycken

Abraham
Verplanek

Smits Vly (Smith's Valley)

T'Maagde Staatje

Peter Stoutenberg

Henry Brazier

Isaac Allerton's
Warehouse

Cornelius Clopper
the blacksmith

John Vinje

Cornelius Aertzen

New
Cemetery

Gateway

Stone Bastion

Northwest
Blockhouse

West India Co.
or Governors
Garden

Stone Bastion

Augustin
Heermans

Het   Cingle

Dirck
Van Clyff
Jan
Smeedes

Fly Blockhouse

Blockhouse

Heere Dwars Straet

Tuyn Straet

Smee Straet

Hoogh Straet

East River

De Heere Straet

Old church
yard

Poor House

Prince Straet

Mill

Heere Gracht

Suyck Straet

Beaver Gracht

Common Road

The Wall

Town's
Public Mill

The
Market
Place

Marckvelt Straet

City Tavern
(Stadt Huys)

Secretary's
House

Browers Straet

Governor's
House

Fort
Amsterdam

Brugh Straet

Dutch Church
De Peral Straet

Old Church

The Waterside

Great Dock

Stuyvesants
White Hall

N

As the settlement of Manhattan
became established, surveying the
city and creating maps of
property lines became an urgent
necessity. Early grants were
vague in their definitions. Beyond
the present Wall Street lay the
cemetery, a mill, the company
farm and public cow pasture,
marshland, and forest. At the
tavern of Wolfert Webber, De
Heere Straet (Broadway) led on
to Haarlem and the north.

LAND USE IN MANHATTAN, 1664

prominent
buildings

marshes

fortifications

forest

windmills

public
pastureland

formal gardens

Stuyvesant's City

When Peter Stuyvesant arrived as Director-General in 1647, New Amsterdam was still prostrate from the devastations of the Indian wars. The so-called fortress, he observed, was "more a molehill than a fortress, without gates, the walls and bastions trodden under foot by men and cattle." Trade languished and immorality, drunkenness and card-playing prevailed. He began a series of improvements which year by year changed the shape of the city. He ordered bulkheads built along the waterfront. (As late as 1651, the buildings on the waterfront faced a muddy shoreline.) In 1648 he ordered the building of the first pier at Schreyer's Hook on the East River. A Latin school was opened in the 1650s, along with other improvements: a weighhouse was constructed at the East River wharf, and bridges were built across the canal.

He took seriously the need to defend the city, and at a meeting on March 13, 1653 with the Council, Burgomasters and Schepens of the city, a defensive strategy was promulgated. The population was too large to be defended within the fort. It was decided to build a high stockade and small breastworks to surround the city. Those living in the villages at some distance could not be defended, and there was no thought to attempt it.

New Amsterdam in 1660 faced east, towards the ships at anchor in the East River. Visual representations of the city, such as Visscher's, portray the settlement as though viewed from the yard-arm of a ship in the river. In the distance was the wind-driven sawmill, the roofline of the city's church, and the less than imposing walls

of the fort. At the very tip of the island, facing the weighhouse pier on *De Peral Straet*, stood Stuyvesant's mansion and gardens, purchased in 1658. For many years it was the finest residence in the city. The busy commercial structures along *De Peral Straet* were the commercial center of the city: the weighhouse, with its jutting pier; the taverns; bakeshops; hatter's shop; warehouses and the company pack-house. *De Peral Straet* was also the home of Dr. Kierstide, New Amsterdam's first resident physician.

There were four principal streets which wheeled, as though by precise drill, towards the north. *De Heere Straet* extended from Fort Amsterdam to the wall. It was paralleled by the *Heere Gracht*, built on either side of a ditch which descended from boggy land beneath the wall. The ditch was cleared, and perhaps humorously called a canal. At high tide small boats could carry goods three blocks into the heart of the city; at low tide, it was a foul-smelling open sewer. Lining *Heere Gracht* were the homes of burghers and several taverns and breweries.

When plans of the city were sent to the directors in Amsterdam, the Director-General was admonished for allowing so much of the available space within the wall to be used by gardens. They believed that a more compact use of available land would be more economical, and perhaps also more amenable to control. The city had a population of 1,500 when the English took control in 1664.

The wall and defensive ditch (above) were constructed with funds raised by an assessment upon the inhabitants. The wall was fortified by blockhouses on the east and west shorelines, and stone bastions faced northwards. The Castello Plan (right) is a copy made in about 1670 of a Dutch survey of the city drawn in 1660. The plan was used to allocate land for new arrivals. Beyond the canal, Heere Gracht (below), the more densely built-up streets gave way to areas of larger gardens and houses set on more generous plots of land.

NEW AMSTERDAM, 1655

	land granted prior to 1649
	land granted after 1650

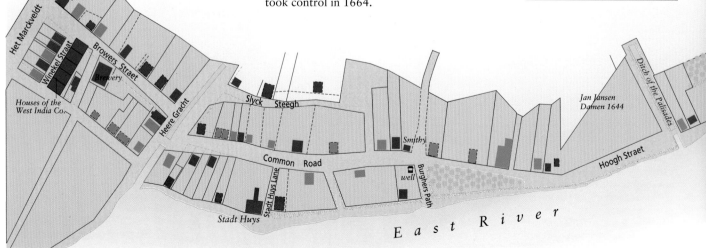

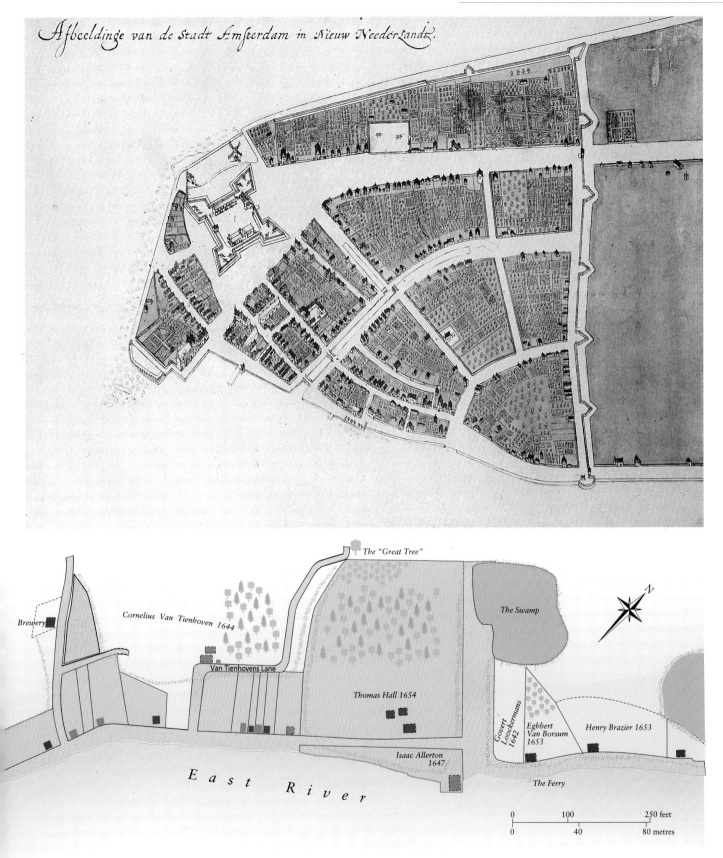

Afbeeldinge van de Stadt Amsterdam in Nieuw Neederlandt.

The "Great Tree"

Brewery

Cornelius Van Tienhoven 1644

The Swamp

Van Tienhovens Lane

Thomas Hall 1654

Govert Loockermans 1642

Eghbert Van Borsum 1653

Henry Brazier 1653

Isaac Allerton 1647

The Ferry

E a s t   R i v e r

N

0	100	250 feet
0	40	80 metres

Chapter 3 British New York 1664–1783

Under British rule, life in New York was dominated by merchants, lawyers, traders, and public officials. It seemed to visitors that New York was more heterogeneous than other colonies and that its inhabitants, coming from diverse places, worshipped in a confusing array of faiths. New Yorkers were noted for dressing more gaily, and with greater ostentation, than people in Boston or sober Philadelphia. The city's coffee-houses, taverns, and clubs were well-patronized. There were 17 taphouses in New Amsterdam in 1647, but no printing press, no newspapers, and no public libraries. As the port grew, so too did the number of taverns and the legion of bawdy women who haunted the city's streets. At night the customers poured out into the streets, full of carousing and drunken merriment. A small, compact community throughout British rule, few residents were not within earshot of the noise of their drunken revelry. The existence of a "Mob," and the danger of serious disorder and riot, was seldom far from the thoughts of educated and respectable New Yorkers.

The English seizure of power 1664
In 1664 New Amsterdam became a proprietary colony named after James, the Duke of York. Although the first British governor, Richard Nicolls, clearly intended to rule on the same autocratic basis as the Dutch West India Company, the terms of surrender were calculated to reassure Dutch merchants and landowners that their interests in New York would be safe. Nicolls continued the Dutch system of local government, and the pattern of landgrants and patroonships was confirmed, solidifying the ties between the new English rulers and the wealthier Dutch inhabitants in the colony. With the outbreak of the second Anglo-Dutch war in 1665, trade with Amsterdam was cut off. The break of trading links marks the true beginning of the Anglicization of New York. What may have seemed no more than a temporary wartime dislocation was, in fact, an expression of the longterm mercantile strategy of the British Empire to exclude foreign merchants from trade with the colonies.

Nicolls and his successor, Colonel Francis Lovelace, were conscientious and tolerant colonial rulers, anxious to secure the loyalty and security of the Duke's colony. They began the gradual process of integrating the new colony into the pattern of English colonial government, law, and economic activity. Communications were improved. The first inter-colonial post was carried between New York, Hartford, and Boston in January 1673. Jews and Quakers were no longer actively persecuted.

"Here is one very considerable Town, first built by the Dutch and called New-Amsterdam, which name is now changed to New-York: It is well seated both for Trade, Security and Pleasure, in a small Isle called Mahatan [sic]... The town is Inhabited by the English, and Dutch, and hath a considerable Trade with the Indians, for the skins of Elks, Deer, Bears, &c. Also for those of Bever, Otter, and other Furrs; and doth likewise enjoy a good Trade with the English." Richard Blome, an English traveler, 1672.

Dutch rule restored 1673

Word had reached the city the previous year that a third war had begun between the Dutch and the English. The underlying feeling of the Dutch inhabitants of New York was suggested by the enthusiasm which swept over the city when, in July 1673, a Dutch fleet of 23 vessels, carrying 1,600 armed men, arrived off Sandy Hook. While Fort James held out for an afternoon under Dutch barrage, a force of 600 troops were landed elsewhere on Manhattan, where they were warmly greeted by 400 armed Dutch burghers. The English garrison quickly surrendered, and the second era of Dutch rule began. The city was renamed New Orange, and the old Dutch forms of municipal government were reintroduced. Unbeknownst to the inhabitants, the Dutch and

City Hall and Great Dock, 1679. The existing wharf at the foot of Whitehall had been extended to form the Great Dock in 1676.

English had quickly negotiated away the war in February 1674. The English regained New York in exchange for Surinam. Word did not reach New Orange until June, and the new English governor, Major Edmund Andros, did not reach the city until October.

Libertyes and Priviledges

Governor Andros banned the use of Dutch ships for the colony's trade, and oaths of loyalty were required of all inhabitants. The policy of integration was strengthened. A new road between New York and Harlem was ordered to be laid out, and a ferry service was opened at Spuyten Duyvil, which connected the city with the country to the north. A tax was raised to repair the fort. It was a time of peace and tax and excise collectors were sent to every colony. In every sphere of life the prerogatives of the Crown

"...I cannot but suspect they would be of dangerous consequence, nothing being more knowne that the aptness of such bodyes to assume to themselves many priviledges which prove destructive to, or very ofte disturbe, the peace of the government wherein they are allowed."
The Duke of York, writing to Governor Andros about demands in the colony for the summoning of "General Assemblyes," 1676.

were being reasserted. The governor strengthened his position through the power to make grants of land, and to award monopolies of trade. A "bolting" monopoly (which involved the sifting and packing of flour and biscuit for export) was granted to millers and flour merchants in New York in 1678, and did much to reinvigorate industry and trade in the city.

In 1682 Colonel Thomas Dongan, a Catholic Irishman who had served under Louis XIV, succeeded Andros as governor. Dongan granted a "Charter of Libertyes and priviledges" allowing an election to be held for an Assembly which would deliberate with the members of the Council (appointed by the Governor) and the Governor himself. The Dongan charter divided the province of New York into counties: New York (Manhattan), Kings (Brooklyn), Richmond (Staten Island), and Queens. On October 30, 1683, the first Catholic Mass was held in New York, arousing the deepest suspicions among the Dutch, whose visceral hatred of Catholics was bred during their brutal struggle for independence against Spain. Presbyterian merchants were equally fearful of the Duke's intentions. The death of Charles II

New York in 1766-67, surveyed by Lieutenant Bernard Ratzer.

in 1685 brought the Duke of York to the throne as James II, and transformed New York from the Duke's proprietary colony to a royal province. He declined to approve the charter granted by Dongan, and at once sought to amalgamate all of the colonies north and east of the Delaware River into a Dominion of New England. The king sent Andros to Boston as governor-general. Captain Francis Nicholson was sent to New York as lieutenant governor. The failure of the Dongan Charter, and the refusal of the king to confirm any of the acts of the Assemblies of 1683, 1684 or 1685 left the Crown, through the governor, with unabated royal prerogative in the city. The governor appointed every official, down to the clerk of the market, and wielded immense power to favor his supporters.

The Glorious Revolution and Leisler

Word of the invasion of England by William of Orange and of the forced abdication of James II arrived in Boston on April 26, 1689. Andros was arrested and kept in prison to await the final outcome of the "Glorious Revolution." News of the fall of Andros reached New York at the end of May. The militia, led by Jacob Leisler, seized control of Fort James in the name of William of Orange. Leisler had been a leading figure in the colony's commercial life for more than a decade. He had come to New Amsterdam in 1660 and prospered. In 1673 he was assessed to be the richest man in New York.

The English merchants and landowners in the colony and the Dutch who had joined them at the trough of preferment violently opposed Leisler. Through trade, land transactions, financial ventures, and dynastic marriages, they formed a close-knit aristocracy surrounding the governor. They had much to lose if Leisler were to overturn the social order upon which their considerable wealth was based.

Leisler's supporters were mainly drawn from Dutch artisans, merchants, and laborers who perceived the steady Anglicization of New York as a threat to their communal life. They were prosperous men, if not of the first rank. Leisler sought to hold the province in the Protestant interest until a new governor could be sent. He refused to accede to the new Governor's representative, Major Richard Ingoldsby. The partisan feelings aroused by his actions, and his subsequest arrest and execution for treason, divided New York politics for decades.

The development of the colony

New York did not suffer as badly as Boston from the high taxation and social costs of the warfare against the French territories to the north, and, like Philadelphia, it benefitted from a rich and productive agricultural hinterland. But it lagged behind both cities in population, and at various times New York shipping struggled to compete with its rivals. A system of corruption and bribery linked city merchants and traders with the Governor, who turned a blind eye to the many "pyrate" expeditions which preyed on the shipping of other states.

Funds to support the government were raised by the Assembly from duties on imports, and an excise on the retail sale of liquor. The Assemblies sought to restrain the Governor's exercise of Crown prerogative through the control over revenue. Out of exasperation at the corruption and incompetence of Governor Lord Cornbury, the Assembly in 1709 agreed only to grant excise for one year at a time, and to reduce the Governor's salary list by 40 percent. Taxation was to play a key role in the political struggle between the colony and its governor.

Between 1715 and 1719 Governor Hunter settled most of the colony's outstanding financial problems, and established the basis for cooperation and conciliation which lasted for nearly 20

Seal of the City of New York, 1686.

FORT GEORGE IN 1740.

After the British had taken power in New York, Fort Amsterdam was patriotically renamed Fort George.

years. Under British rule New York made significant economic advances, perhaps best illustrated in the transformation of Wall Street from a little-frequented path, lined with small houses and large gardens, on the perimeter of the city in 1664, to the heart of its commercial life. The first permanent pavement in New York was laid in Wall Street in 1693, and the wharf at Wall and Pearl Street was constructed in 1694. The increasing commercial role of Wall Street was confirmed when the new City Hall, replacing the Stadt Huys, was erected on the "upper" street at the intersection of Wall and Broad Streets. Trinity Church was

"*Neither their Streets nor houses are at all Regular Some being 4 or 5 Story high & Others not above two... many of 'em Spacious Genteel Houses. Some are built of hewn stone Others of English & Also of the Small white Hollands Brick, which looks neat but not grand... The Streets are very Irregular & Crooked & many of 'em much too Narrow they are Generally pretty well paved which adds much to the decency & Cleanness of the place & the Advantage of Carriage.*" James Birket, an English visitor, 1750.

erected in 1696 at Broadway and Wall. Within a decade the Market House at the eastern end of Wall Street had been completed, and the Coffee House at Wall and Water Streets opened. The First Presbyterian Church was erected in 1712 on a lot west of City Hall. Bayard's sugar house was an imposing commercial building on Wall Street by the 1730s. A slave market existed at the foot of lower Wall Street from 1731.

New York and the Revolution

At the conclusion of the French wars in 1763, the British government attempted to raise revenues from the colonies through a tax in 1764–65 on sugar, paper, and legal documents. These measures were greeted with a storm of protest, boycotts, and noncompliance, which forced parliament to repeal the Stamp Act in March 1766. When parliament passed graduated duties on tea, printers' ink, glass, and other imports, New York merchants agreed in April 1768 to comply with a general boycott of British goods which had begun in Boston. The simmering sources of discontent were deepened when the news arrived in May 1773 that the East India Company had been given a monopoly of the sale and distribution of its low-priced tea. American smugglers, whose price would be undercut, were outraged. Tea merchants saw the likely ruin of their prosperity in such a virtual monopoly. Boston merchants tossed barrels of the tea into the harbor, for which the port of Boston was ordered closed until indemnification was paid. New York staged its own tea party, and at a mass meeting on July 6, 1774, decided to send deputies to the Continental Congress to be held in Philadelphia.

Armed conflict, begun at Lexington and Concord on April 19 1775, was not followed by moves toward political independence until the following year. On May 10, 1776, the Continental Congress instructed all colonies which had not done so to establish republican state governments. The Fourth Provincial Congress of the colony of New York met at City Hall in New York on July 9th, and on the next day transformed itself into a convention of the representatives of the State of New York. A new constitution for New York State was adopted in April 1777, and New York was the second state to ratify the Articles of Confederation in February 1778. One third of all the military engagements of the war took place on the soil of New York.

Edward Hyde, Lord Cornbury, Governor of New York, 1702-08. He was notorious for appearing in public dressed in his wife's clothes. New Yorkers were finally forced to petition the Queen for a new governor.

Dutch Streets and English Streets

Governor Dongan lamented in 1687 that few English, Scottish or Irish families had emigrated to New York since the colony was taken from the Dutch in 1664. Land was cheap in nearby New Jersey and in Pennsylvania, and the Dutch patroonships and the great manors created by English land-grants made the colony less attractive to immigrants. The Dutch remained the dominant group within the population, but were losing ground. With the arrival of French Huguenots and other immigrants after 1685, they constituted only 60 percent of the white population by the turn of the century. The English and French began to form a new commercial elite, and were twice as likely as the Dutch to be among the leading merchants of the city. While the Dutch were heavily represented among the blacksmiths, carpenters, coopers, shoemakers, and leatherworkers, the family and ethnic ties of the English and French gave them commercial advantages in the West Indies trade.

The changing pattern of wealth in New York is revealed in the emergence of significant differentiation among streets. By 1703, wealthy English and Huguenot merchants were concentrated in the city's commercial dockside areas, while craftsmen and tradesmen lived elsewhere.

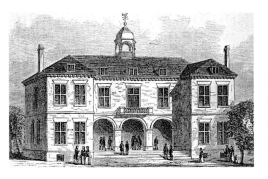

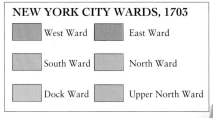

The charter granted by Governor Dongan in 1683 divided the city into the wards shown below. Dock Ward, closest to the harbor and inhabited mainly by English and French, was the richest. The poorest was North Ward, 78 percent of whose inhabitants were Dutch. The ethnic composition of the city changed on crossing Prince Street. City Hall (left) in 1700.

NEW YORK CITY WARDS, 1703

- West Ward
- South Ward
- Dock Ward
- East Ward
- North Ward
- Upper North Ward

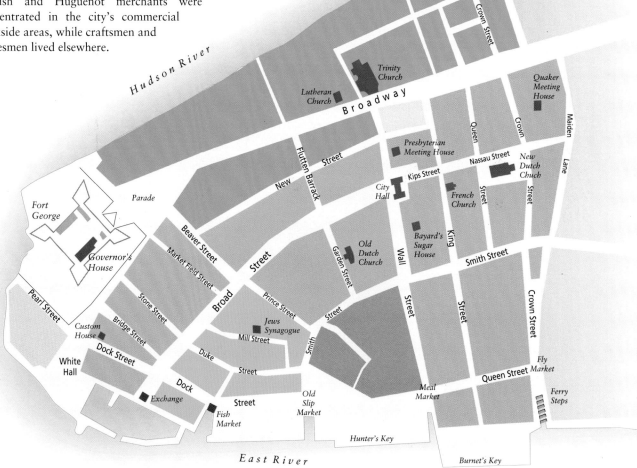

In 1703 the wealthy English and Huguenot merchants lived on Waterside (renamed Dock Street), Queen Street, Bridge Street, and Pearl Street, as did the major Dutch merchants; their homes either faced East River, where the ships lay at anchor, or were nearby. The city's wealthiest inhabitants were concentrated in Dock Street, Bridge Street and Stone Street. Merchants, masters and shipwrights were heavily represented on Queen Street and Smith Street; brickmakers and carpenters on Broadway; bolters on Broad and Bridge Streets and carmen in the Upper North Ward and Broadway. The Dutch formed large majorities in the Upper North Ward (above Wall Street), Smith Street, Broadway (West Ward), New, Queen, Broad, Stone, and Beaver Streets. The English and French were in the majority on Queen Street (south of the Wall), Pearl, and Dock Streets (Dock Ward).

In 1700, there was little sign in New York of the separation of commercial and residential districts. Artisans, shopkeepers, and wholesalers lived above their place of business, which often sprawled into the sidewalk and street (below).

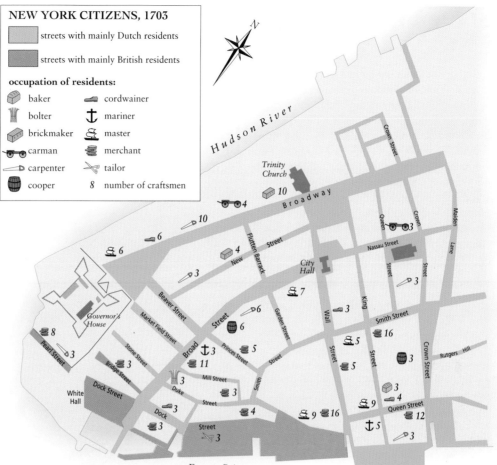

NEW YORK CITIZENS, 1703

- streets with mainly Dutch residents
- streets with mainly British residents

occupation of residents:

- baker
- bolter
- brickmaker
- carman
- carpenter
- cooper
- cordwainer
- mariner
- master
- merchant
- tailor
- 8 number of craftsmen

Huguenots and Jews

Many of those who emigrated to New York came as a result of religious persecution. Settlement in the colonial territories of the great trading empires, although still fraught with religious restrictions and persecution, afforded the best alternatives to zealotry.

Protestants in France (Huguenots) had endured years of religious persecution. Huguenots survived the massacre of Saint Bartholomew's day in 1572 and in 1598 won from Henri IV the Edict of Nantes, which protected their rights of worship. When the Edict was revoked in 1685, some 200,000 Huguenots emigrated to England, the Netherlands, Germany and elsewhere. Small groups came to the New World, and established the communities of New Paltz in Ulster County and New Rochelle in Westchester County.

The French presence in New Amsterdam had an important impact on the colony. The first schoolmaster to arrive in New Amsterdam in 1637, was Dr. La Montagne, a Frenchman. (He was said to have to take in washing to make ends meet). Between 1648-58 all public documents were issued in English, Dutch, and French. By 1656 town proclamations were normally delivered in Dutch and French. The French Church was founded in New Amsterdam in 1659.

When the Sephardic Jewish community was expelled from Spain and Portugal in 1492, many found a welcome haven in Holland, and Dutch colonies elsewhere. Following the Dutch seizure of coastal territory in Brazil in 1633, Jewish traders settled in Pernambuco. In 1654, the Portuguese re-conquered Pernambuco, and a party of 27 Jews arrived, penniless refugees, in New Amsterdam. Stuyvesant and his Council did not want to admit the Jews, but the directors in Amsterdam reminded him that there were substantial numbers of Jewish investors in the company itself. They were allowed to remain. In time, Jews won the right to own real estate, engage in trade, and to acquire burgher rights.

After the British took the colony in 1664, Jews prospered in colonial New York. A small plot was acquired outside the wall in 1656 for a burial ground and in 1682 a larger burial ground, south of Chatham Square, was opened. The first Hebrew School was founded in 1728. A synagogue on Mill Street was dedicated in 1730.

When the British captured New York in 1776, the majority of the Jewish community left for Philadelphia, unwilling to collaborate with the British. However good things had been under British rule, they felt that the new republic would be even better for their co-religionists.

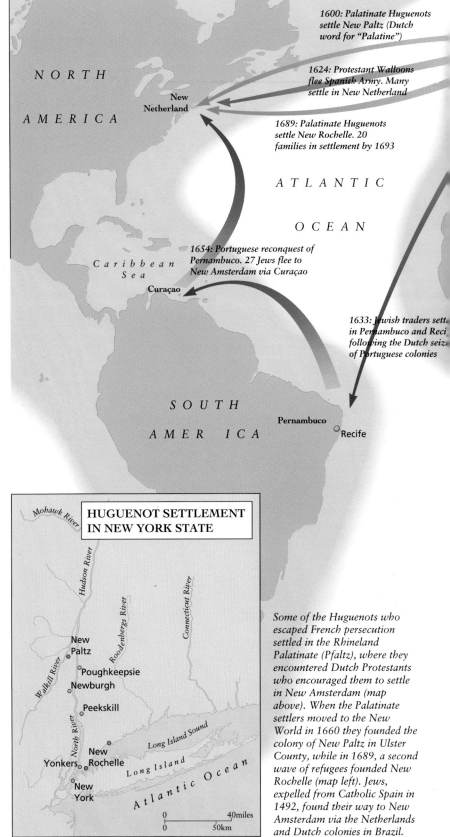

1600: Palatinate Huguenots settle New Paltz (Dutch word for "Palatine")

1624: Protestant Walloons flee Spanish Army. Many settle in New Netherland

1689: Palatinate Huguenots settle New Rochelle. 20 families in settlement by 1693

1654: Portuguese reconquest of Pernambuco. 27 Jews flee to New Amsterdam via Curaçao

1633: Jewish traders settle in Pernambuco and Recife following the Dutch seizure of Portuguese colonies

NORTH AMERICA

New Netherland

ATLANTIC OCEAN

Caribbean Sea

Curaçao

SOUTH AMERICA

Pernambuco

Recife

HUGUENOT SETTLEMENT IN NEW YORK STATE

Mohawk River

Hudson River

Roodenbergs River

Connecticut River

Walkill River

North River

New Paltz

Poughkeepsie

Newburgh

Peekskill

Yonkers

New Rochelle

New York

Long Island Sound

Long Island

Atlantic Ocean

| 0 | | 40miles |
| 0 | | 50km |

Some of the Huguenots who escaped French persecution settled in the Rhineland Palatinate (Pfaltz), where they encountered Dutch Protestants who encouraged them to settle in New Amsterdam (map above). When the Palatinate settlers moved to the New World in 1660 they founded the colony of New Paltz in Ulster County, while in 1689, a second wave of refugees founded New Rochelle (map left). Jews, expelled from Catholic Spain in 1492, found their way to New Amsterdam via the Netherlands and Dutch colonies in Brazil.

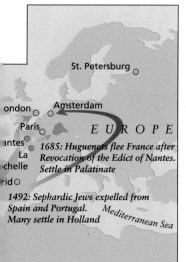

JEWISH AND HUGUENOT IMMIGRATION, 1492-1686

- Huguenot movements
- Jewish movements
- Protestant movements
- Huguenot settlement
- Palatinate

1685: Huguenots flee France after Revocation of the Edict of Nantes. Settle in Palatinate

1492: Sephardic Jews expelled from Spain and Portugal. Many settle in Holland

Huguenots survived the massacre of Saint Bartholomew's Day in 1572 (above), and won from Henri IV the Edict of Nantes, which established Protestantism in 200 towns, and guaranteed the Huguenots' rights of worship. It was revoked in 1685.

The French Church was founded in New Amsterdam in 1659 (map below), but French worshippers were absorbed into the Anglican communion, and it was not until 1796 that the French Church of the Holy Spirit was opened (right). Jewish immigrants held religious services in a room in Beaver Street in 1673, and a map of 1695 shows a synagogue on Mill Street.

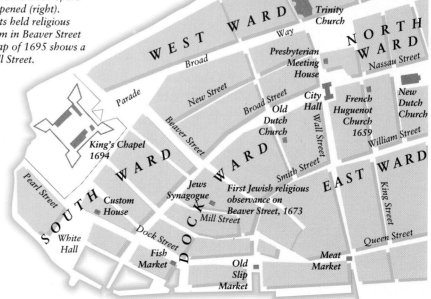

Peter Kalm attended synagogue in New York in 1748:
"...there are many Jews settled in New York, who possess great privileges. They have a synagogue and houses, and great country seats of their own, property, and are allowed to keep shops in town. They have likewise several ships, which they freight, and send out with their own goods. In fine, they enjoy all the privileges common to the other inhabitants of the town and providence."

African-Americans in New York

African-Americans were brought to New York as slaves well before any Roman Catholics lived in the city, and decades before the first Jews arrived from Curaçao. Under conditions that were disorienting, brutal and cruel, they survived. A free black community, of which very little is known, began in 1644, when 11 blacks were freed and given plots of land to farm. (The right to own land was removed from free blacks in 1716, after a slave revolt.)

In New York County, slaves were employed largely as domestic servants, or at artisanal trades which they came to practice in increasing numbers. Slave-holders constituted a broad

After the revolt of 1712, the fear of slave unrest brought legislative efforts to tighten the control of slaves. In 1741, in a heightened atmosphere of fear due to a series of robberies and unexplained fires over six days, including the burning of Fort George, another slave conspiracy was discovered. The trail of investigation led to John Hughson, a white alehouse keeper and receiver of stolen goods, and to two slaves, Caesar and Prince, who had been found with goods stolen from the properties set on fire. In the trial, which dominated the city for months, a tale of conspiracy, theft, arson, and murder was slowly unfolded, amidst hysterical accusations.

cross-section of the community, with the wealthiest landowners owning the largest number of slaves. The average slave-holding in New York was about two adult slaves. New York had the highest proportion of slaves of any of the colonies north of Virginia.

Resistance to slavery was a daily, local occurrence, of which little record survives other than the whippings and other punishments inflicted upon slaves by their masters. The first slave revolt occurred on April 7, 1712, when a fire was started at the home of Peter Van Tilburgh by slaves "evidently meant as a signal for a general revolt." A band of armed slaves killed nine white men who rushed to put out the fire. Armed soldiers were sent to quell the uprising, and the rioters fled. Some killed themselves rather than be taken captive. Thirteen slaves were hanged; one was left to die by starvation in chains; three were burned; another was burned over slow fire for eight to ten hours; and the body of another was broken at the wheel.

Hughson kept a "disorderly house" where he served large parties of blacks and where dancing and fiddling were customary. Boarding with Hughson and his wife was a 16-year-old indentured servant named Mary Burton, whose testimony unravelled the conspiracy. The accused slaves testified that Hughson swore them with an oath to steal their owner's weapons, burn the fort, kill all the white people and steal their goods.

The toll of the 1741 revolt was heavy: four whites were hanged, 13 slaves were burnt at the stake, 18 slaves were hanged, and 70 were transported to the West Indies and elsewhere.

The slave-market (above) appears on a 1730 map of New York, on the East River and Wall Street. As late as 1790, one in every five households owned at least one slave.

In 1991, human bones were found between Reade and Duane Streets. This was the site of the burial ground used by blacks from 1710-1790 (above), known as the "Negroes Burial Ground"

From 1640, manumitted or "half-free" slaves, were granted lots from 1-20 acres near the Collect Pond. The "Negro lots" formed the basis for the first free black settlement in the city.

slave market

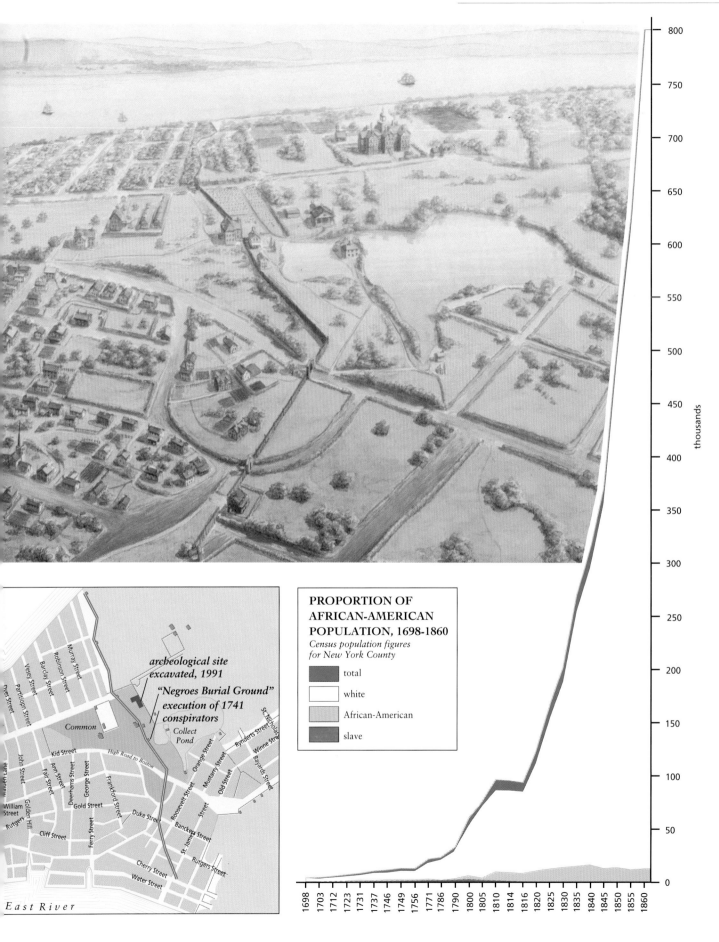

East River

archeological site
excavated, 1991

"Negroes Burial Ground"
execution of 1741
conspirators

Common

Collect
Pond

High Road to Boston

Murray Street
Robinson Street
Barclay Street
Vesey Street
Partition Street
rtyes Street

Kid Street
John Street
Ann Street
Fair Street
Deerhams Street
George Street
Frankford Street
Gold Street
William Street
Golden Hill
Rutgers
Cliff Street
Ferry Street
Duke Street
Banckett Street
St. James Street
Cherry Street
Rutgers Street
Water Street

Roosevelt Street
Orange Street
Mustary Street
Old Street
St. Nicholas
Rynders Street
Bayards Street
Winne Street

**PROPORTION OF
AFRICAN-AMERICAN
POPULATION, 1698-1860**
*Census population figures
for New York County*

total

white

African-American

slave

thousands

800
750
700
650
600
550
500
450
400
350
300
250
200
150
100
50
0

1698 1703 1712 1723 1731 1737 1746 1749 1756 1771 1786 1790 1800 1805 1810 1814 1816 1820 1825 1830 1835 1840 1845 1850 1855 1860

A British Colonial Port

Commercial needs determined the development of New York. As trade expanded, merchants needed more places to store goods and larger premises to conduct business. The existing wharf at the foot of Whitehall was greatly extended to form the Great Dock in 1676, but it was soon inadequate for the needs of the city's trade. The process of filling and building upon tide-lots was already well advanced by 1730. Wharves, named after the merchants or shipowners, began to line the East River, from Cruger's at the Old Slip Market to Hunter's, Burnet's, Lyons', Schermerhorn's, Livingston's and Ellison's which lined Queen Street to Peck's Slip.

A new city wall and gates were built south of the Collect Pond, and land which had formerly been orchards, pastures and commons was laid out for commercial and residential use. William Street and Nassau Street were extended into what had been the estates of Jacob Leisler, west of Beekman's Swamp. The filling-in of swamps had been achieved by the granting of land on condition that it be drained and filled. Jacobus Roosevelt bought, drained and laid out streets on what had been Beekman's Swamp west of Peck's Slip in 1734. Outside the city wall there were farms owned by Rutgers, Lispenard, DeLancey, Lady Warren and Bayard, as well as a few factories. Harrison's brewery lay on the banks of the Hudson.

By 1769, the streets west of Broadway had been fully laid out, but were by no means as heavily built-up as those along the East River. Construction in mid-century brought the Collect or Freshwater Pond virtually within the built-up urban area, and extended the city far to the north of Wall Street. In the early part of the century older inhabitants might still retain vivid recollections of the early Dutch governors, and of a settlement which might be crossed in a brief walk, but by mid-century memories of Dutch rule had largely faded.

The cosmopolitan nature of New York made the continued use of the Dutch language difficult. It was probably retained for domestic use in a dwindling number of families, but endured significantly into the next century only in rural areas and the insular community of Albany. The

The Growth of Manhattan

The 18th-century building boom depicted below displaced the monuments of the Dutch era. New buildings on the quays and wharves transformed the streets lining the shores of the East River. Shipyards were now located at the upper reaches of the city. The substantial gardens of the early years of British rule were disappearing, and shade trees on Bowling Green and Broadway took their place. Public buildings sprouted on former common land.

Dutch flavor of New York City was preserved more in the surviving stepped gable-end houses (which already looked old-fashioned by comparison to the larger, Palladian buildings erected by the English) than in conscious attempts to retain an ethnic identity. The great Dutch fair, the Kermis, which began on the Monday after the Feast of St. Bartholomew on 24th August, long remained the most popular city holiday.

The view up Wall Street was one of the most popular images of the city's commercial development. The First Presbyterian Church (steeple on right) and much of the other real estate in this 1829 engraving perished in the Great Fire of 1835.

By mid-century streets west of Broadway were fully laid out (below). New docks and warehouses lined the Hudson above Trinity Church, and above Columbia College lay the city's pleasure grounds, Ranelagh and the Vauxhall Gardens, located on the Bowery Road.

New York and the American Revolution

Electrifying news of the defeat of the British in battle at Lexington and Concord reached New York on 23rd April 1775. To celebrate the event, a patriotic mob broke into the Arsenal on the Hudson River and stole 600 muskets. By June, however, the British were prepared for a renewed campaign against the rebels. New York was an obvious target, highly vulnerable to British seapower.

General Charles Lee, sent by Washington to New York in January 1776, secured the East River with forts on both banks from the Battery to Hell Gate. The defensive key to the city lay on Brooklyn Heights, which Lee surrounded with interlocking entrenchments between Wallabout Bay and Gowanus Creek. Washington's army arrived in New York on 13th April 1776. His engineers extended Lee's line one mile south and east of the Heights. Fort Washington was constructed on the high ground on the northern end of Manhattan. Under the command of General Sir William Howe, British forces landed on Staten Island at the end of June, enthusiastically greeted by the city's Tories.

Howe delayed his move until 22nd August, when he crossed the Narrows and landed at Gravesend Bay with 15,000 troops. On the night of the 26th he led 10,000 men through Jamaica Pass, and at dawn on the 27th the American forces were driven back to Lee's first line of entrenchments on the Heights.

British soldier

New York, with its substantial number of Tories among the city's merchant class, was a potential British base (given their superior naval power). It would give the British a stronghold from which to carry on the war against the rebels after their defeat at Lexington and Concord in April 1775. British troops under General Sir William Howe first clashed with patriot troops under George Washington (top right) at Brooklyn Heights, on August 27th, 1776 (right). Washington's troops were routed, but the tables were turned at Harlem Heights on September 16th.

American soldier

On the night of the 29th, Lee's 9,000 troops and all stores and equipment were ferried in small boats to Manhattan. It was a skilled maneuver, carried out in silence in rain and fog. The British only discovered the next morning that the rebels had decamped.

Howe waited two weeks before launching an attack across the East River on September 15th. At 11 a.m., five frigates opened fire. Sir Henry Clinton's division of Light Troops and Reserves was rowed across from Newtown Creek to Kip's Bay and Turtle Bay, in 84 boats. Defending troops, consisting of ill trained militia, fell back; British troops pushed rapidly forward to the west and north. Washington tried and failed to rally the panicking troops. Success came when Major Aaron Burr led Silliman's brigade past British patrols through lanes and woods on the west side to safety at Harlem Heights.

George Washington, 1732-99, probably did more than any other man to secure American independence. An experienced soldier, he became commander of the Continental Army in 1775, leading his troops to eventual victory. From 1789-96 he served as the first President of the USA.

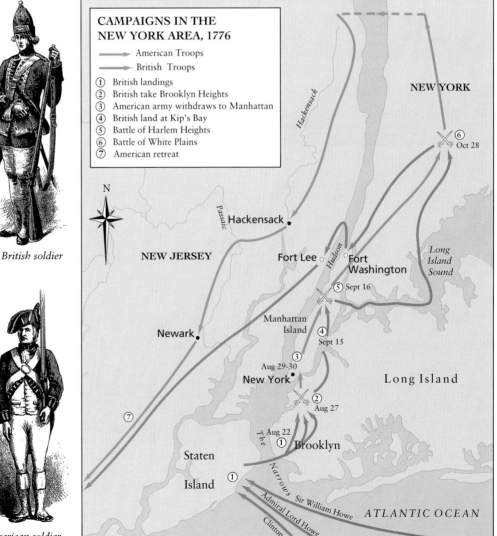

The British troops halted just beyond McGowan's Pass at the northern end of Central Park. As the bugler of the British Light Infantry insultingly sounded the fox chase, American troops poured down from Harlem Heights and a flank attack caused a hasty British retreat.

There were heavy casualties: 171 British troops were killed and wounded, and about 130 Americans out of some 9,000 men fit for duty. The bloody nose inflicted on Howe could not affect the fundamental military reality that New York could not be held. On October 16th, Washington evacuated the city, leaving 2,000 troops behind to defend Fort Washington as he headed north towards White Plains.

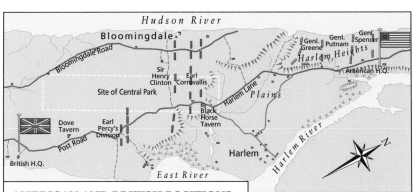

AMERICAN AND BRITISH POSITIONS, SEPT. 16 - OCT. 12, 1776

▬ American troops
▬ British troops

Having succeeded in establishing themselves at the northern end of Central Park on September 15th, the British troops were lured the next day into advancing to Harlem Cove, after Washington had sent forward Lt. Col. Thomas Knowlton with 120 Connecticut Rangers to skirmish with a British advance party (left). The Americans, who had retreated to Harlem Heights, then poured down upon them in a flank attack, causing the British to retreat through a field of buckwheat and an orchard. Washington disengaged in the afternoon, fearing the arrival of British reinforcements. New York City remained under British military occupation from September 12, 1776 until November 25, 1784.

THE BATTLE OF HARLEM HEIGHTS, SEPT. 16,1776

→ American troops
→ British troops

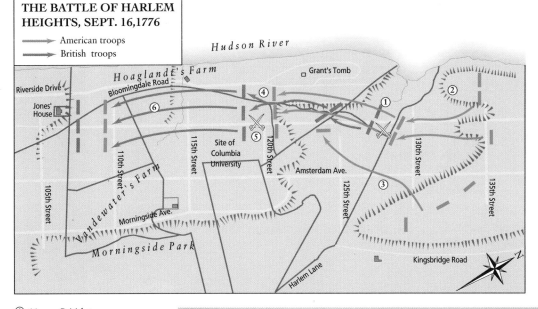

① 11 a.m. British troops move forward

② American troops descend from Harlem Heights

③ Flank attack

④ British retreat through Buckwheat Field

⑤ 12 p.m. Main Action. Troops disengage at 1 p.m.

⑥ British troops retreat

A British view of the attack on Fort Washington on November 16, 1776. The British vessels are heading south down Harlem River. During the American Revolution, the American eagle (below) became a symbol of fierce independence and liberty.

Occupation 1776–1783

THE GREAT FIRE, 1776

extent of fire damage

Map labels:

Hudson River

1 Broadway General Howe's HQ

Trinity Church (destroyed by fire)

Pearl Street / Whitehall / New Street / Beaver Street / Market Field Street / Stone Street / Bridge Street / Dock Street / Flatten Barrack

Broadway

Crown Street / Cortlandt Street / Dey Street / Partition Street / Vesey Street / Barclay Street / Church Street / Murray Street / Warren Street

B

Bayard's Sugar Mill, where patriot POW's were held in appalling conditions

8 Broad Street / Dock Street / Duke Street / Mill Street / Smith Street / Princes Street / Garden Street / Wall Street / King Street

A / C / F / 5 / Jane Street / Maiden / John / Fair / Nassau street

Brtidewell (built 1775). Patriot POW's were also held here, and on prison ships in the harbor

The Common

Smith Street / Queen Street / Crown Street / Rutgers Hill / William Street

6 / 7

3 / D / Golden Hill / Cliff Street / Beekman Street / George Street / Gold Street / King Street / Princes Street / Frankfort Street / Chatham Street / Palisades

East River

4 / Queen Street / E / Ferry Street / Vandewater Street / Cherry Street

Peck's Slip

The experience of New York City during the Revolutionary War was unique. It was the only American city to remain under British occupation for virtually the entire struggle, and it suffered more physical damage than any other city. Its inhabitants also experienced a striking symmetry of fortunes. At the prospect of war in October 1775, many loyalists – supporters of the link with the British crown – fled the city. When the British army arrived the next summer, there was a frantic flight of patriots – those who sought independence – from the city. Thus the population rose and fell dramatically throughout the war. Nonetheless, local farmers and merchants maintained extensive trading links with the British occupying forces, even while they lay in the harbor awaiting orders to land.

The city fared poorly under military occupation. On September 21, 1776, a fire began near Whitehall. A quarter of the city was destroyed, including Trinity Church, the Lutheran Church, and over 1,000 houses. A further fire followed in August 1778, and the explosion of 260 lbs. of gunpowder on an ordnance ship in the East River caused a great deal of damage to property. It proved impossible to reconstruct many of the burnt-out buildings during the war.

On November 16, 1776 General Sir William Howe captured the Fort Washington garrison, taking 3,000 prisoners, plus their equipment and cannons. American prisoners-of-war were held in appalling conditions in the city prison in New York and in prison ships in the harbor. Howe ordered the fortification of the city against an American attack, and New York City remained the principal base for British military operations in North America. Throughout the war the city was surrounded by patriot forces, thus denying the British easy land communications with other colonies. Both sides participated in a vicious guerilla war, engaging in cattle-rustling, thievery, abductions, and the systematic burning of crops.

In 1776 Howe appointed a loyalist military force, led by Oliver De Lancey, who had volunteered to raise three battalions of 500 men each. The former Governor of the Province was appointed commander of Provincial Troops in April 1777, and led a campaign to harass the patriotic forces. Such tactics did much to sway the substantial number of Americans who had remained neutral towards the side of the patriots. The armed loyalists were never very numerous, and a British garrison was needed to

New York under British Occupation (above): **A** *Old Dutch Church;* **B** *Presbyterian Meeting House;* **C** *New Dutch Church;* **D** *Baptist Meeting House;* **E** *St. George's Chapel;* **F** *Quaker Meeting House. Secular and military use:* **1** *Fish Market;* **2** *Old Slip;* **3** *Fly Market;* **4** *Peck's Market;* **5** *Oswego Market;* **6** *Powderhouse;* **7** *Upper Barracks;* **8** *Prison.*

During the British occupation, an ordnance ship explosion and fires in 1776 and 1778 (map above) damaged a substantial part of the city. The rebuilding had to wait for the end of the revolutionary war (see page 56).

A facsimile of a British Headquarters map of New York and the surrounding country in 1782 (above).

During the war and occupation, a Scottish officer, Captain Archibald Robertson, drew a series of views of New York and its environs. The watercolor (below) depicts the British fleet at anchor in Upper Bay, between Long Island and Staten Island in 1776, immediately prior to the British occupation of the city.

defend the city against continual armed raids by the patriots. In July 1779, 600 American troops recaptured Stony Point; the entire British force was either killed, wounded or taken prisoner.

Returning Loyalists found New York "a most dirty, desolate, and wretched place." Loyalists from many colonies sought refuge in the capital of Tory America, and the city's population expanded from 17,000 to 30,000. Many of the patriots who had fled were Dissenters, and their abandoned churches were used by the British as prisons, stables, hospitals, and riding schools.

The city's taverns and brothels were busy. Milliners and dressmakers did boomtown trade. The occupying powers reopened John Street Theater, renaming it the Theater Royal. Horse-races, bull-baiting, bowling and golf matches were held in Brooklyn during the occupation, and cricket was played near the Jews' cemetery. There was no shortage of newspapers during the occupation as loyalist printers relocated to New York, while patriot printers moved to New Jersey and upstate New York.

No major military action took place in New York until the end of the war. Cornwallis surrendered at Yorktown on October 19, 1781, but British troops did not finally depart until November 25, 1783. On that day Washington made his ceremonial entry into the city, and gave his farewell address to his troops at Fraunces' Tavern. "Evacuation Day" was celebrated for decades as a patriotic holiday in New York.

At the end of the war, the Loyalists petitioned the King for resettlement in Nova Scotia, the West Indies or England. Some 460 families left for Nova Scotia in the autumn of 1782. A further 8,000 loyalists left soon after. Similar departures were made from Boston, Philadelphia, Savannah and Charleston. In all, about a third of the city's population departed with the British garrison. New York became a bargain-hunter's paradise, as loyalists and British forces sold their goods and packed up to leave the city.

PART 2

"... one of the first objects which claimed their attention was the form and manner in which the business should be conducted; that is to say, whether they should confine themselves to rectilinear streets, or whether they should adopt some of those supposed improvements by circles, ovals, and stars, which certainly embellish a plan, whatever may be their effect as to convenience and utility. In considering that subject they could not but bear in mind that a city is to be composed principally of the habitations of men, and that straight-sided and right-angled houses are the most cheap to build and the most convenient to live in. The effect of these plain and simple reflections was decisive."
Remarks of the Commissioners for Laying out Streets and Roads in the City of New York under the Act of April 3, 1807.

New York from Governor's Island, 1820

Chapter 4 Rebuilding the City 1783–1825

On April 30, 1789, Washington was inaugurated as President of the United States in New York. The contribution of New York to the new republic lay in its wealth, its trading prowess, the prosperity of its agriculture, and in the intelligence, agility and determination of two New Yorkers, Alexander Hamilton, only 32 in 1787, and John Jay, ten years his senior. As Secretary of the Treasury under Washington, Hamilton was the preponderant influence upon the government in the 1790s; Jay's Treaty of 1794 ended a series of frontier and economic disputes with Great Britain. New York commercial interest had achieved its chief goals: the Federalist party was in power, the trading relationship with England was secure, and a stable political and financial system had been created. New York's leaders greeted the new era with delight and self-satisfaction. For the next 25 years the nation was ruled, whether by Federalists, Anti-Federalists or Republicans, by the generation that had declared independence, fought the British and written the Constitution. Despite the seismic transfer of power when Thomas Jefferson was elected president in 1800, there remained a shared language of public discourse. It was 125 years since the British had seized control

View of the City and Harbor of New York (date depicted 1794) by Charles-Balthazar-Julien Fevret de Saint Mémin. The figures in the foreground are walking down Clinton Street, a rustic country lane.

of New York, ending Dutch rule. The men of 1789 in New York stood mid-way between Petrus Stuyvesant and the crowds flocking into the Armory Show in New York in 1913. They inaugurated the beginning of the modern era, a period of rapid growth of the city, and of great physical change.

Population

When the British Army and their loyalist allies evacuated New York in 1783, the population of the city was 12,000. The demobilization of the revolutionary army, and the return of many patriots who had fled the city when the occupation began, caused the population to more than double between 1783 and 1786. Nonetheless, Philadelphia remained the new republic's largest city, and was not to lose its place for two decades. When the first federal census was completed in 1790 Philadelphia, with a population of 42,520, substantially exceeded New York City at 33,131. Rapid population growth over the next three decades largely explains the dramatic physical expansion of the city. New York's population outstripped "natural" growth, and was enhanced by a flood of migrants into the city from New England.

The second Trinity Church, 1788.

In 1790, the population of New York included 3,470 African-Americans, of whom 2,369 were slaves. Nineteen percent of the city's white households were slave-owners in 1790. Among their number was Alexander Hamilton, along with John Jay a member of the Manumission Society. When Hamilton suggested that members of the Society begin by freeing their own slaves, he was solidly voted down by the New York humanitarians, believers in gradualism. Hamilton remained a slave-owner until his death in 1804. The "Gradual Manumission Act" of 1799 freed the children of slaves born after July 4 of that year. Slaves born before 1799 were not finally freed until 1827. It was a gradual process, and as New Yorkers became less fearful of emancipation slaves were able to negotiate the date of their freedom – often after a period of indentured service. By 1810, New York City had the largest community of free blacks in America. By 1820, there were only 518 slaves in the city.

With a declining proportion of inhabitants of Dutch background in 1790, and a population in the city of between 2,000 and 2,500 from Germany, the approximately 5,000 Irish living in New York constituted the most rapidly growing immigrant group after the English. The Irish dispropor-

"I,——, do hereby solemnly without any mental reservation or equivocation whatsoever, swear and declare, and call God to witness (or if the people are called Quakers, affirm) that I renounce and abjure all allegiance to the King of Great Britain."
The beginning of the New York loyalty oath, passed March 26, 1781.

Unlike other great capital cities, New York lacked imposing vistas to set off its major buildings. Broad Street is a case in point. Originally the location of a canal lined with commercial structures, as the street grew in financial importance a new City Hall was erected in 1701 (replacing the old Dutch Stadt Huys on Pearl Street) at the intersection of Broad and Wall Streets. It was remodeled by the addition of a Doric portico by Major Pierre Charles L'Enfant (seen from Broad Street, left, in 1796), and renamed Federal Hall. The Congress of the United States sat in this building from 1785 to 1790, and the inauguration of George Washington as first president took place on the balcony on April 30, 1789.
In 1842 the Federal Hall was demolished to make way for a Doric temple of Massachusetts marble housing the United States Custom House. It served as a U.S. Sub-Treasury from 1862 to 1925. It is now the Federal Hall National Memorial, with John Quincy Adam Ward's equestrian statue of Washington facing Broad Street and the New York Stock Exchange.

tionately experienced the conditions which became so characteristic of urban life: poverty, overcrowded housing conditions, political prejudice, religious discrimination. Irish immigrants were living in conditions which made them particularly susceptible to the yellow fever epidemics which spread through the overcrowded city. A majority of the victims of the 1795 epidemic in New York were from Ireland. Carrying antibodies from Africa, slaves were largely immune to the New York yellow fever.

Rebuilding after the fire of 1776
Returning to the city in 1789 after several years in France, a New Yorker found the city "a neglected place, built chiefly of wood, and in a state of prostration and decay... there was silence and inactivity everywhere...." Colonial Broadway, destroyed by the fire of 1776, was still a decaying ruin. The 1,000 houses destroyed by fire, and the general harm done to the fabric of the city during seven years of British military occupation, left the returning inhabitants with a massive effort of reconstruction. Many of those who had survived the occupation lived in "Canvas Town," shanties and huts made of old ships' canvas and spars erected in the burnt-out areas. Virtually the entire merchant class had left with the British, and a new class of "patriot" merchants soon established their dominance. They set about the process of rebuilding the disrupted commercial links upon which the city's prosperity rested. New York's merchants were going to be a force to reckon with in ports across the world.

During the administration (1784–89) of James Duane, the first post-revolutionary mayor of New York, five commissioners were appointed, under the terms of a law of 1784, to supervise the rebuilding of the burnt-out district west of Broadway, below Barclay Street. Fort George was levelled in 1788 to make room for a proposed presidential mansion, but it was not completed before the federal government moved to Philadelphia. It became the residence of the state governor, then served as the custom house. Among the changes made to the street plan was the widening and paving of Greenwich Street (which connected the city to the village of Greenwich), and the tidying of the existing streets to ensure their intersections were clear and straight.

Docks and wharves

For visitors and immigrants to New York, the city's busy wharves made an indelible impression of commercial bustle. It was the wharves which defined the city and shaped perceptions of its overwhelmingly commercial orientation. The city's livelihood depended upon the efficiency of its wharves and in the decade after the evacuation, wooden sheds and storehouses had been erected along the East River which made the dock areas crowded, ramshackle and confused. Due to the hodge-podge of grants dating back to Dutch days, and changing water rights granted by the state legislature to the Common Council, and promptly sold to private parties for dock construction, property rights in the area between high-water and low-water marks were uncertain. In 1798, the Common Council was authorized by the state legislature to tidy up the problem and to rebuild the docks and wharves from Whitehall Slip to the Fly Market.

Streets

The city had been built up to about Roosevelt Street in 1776, and to the west of Broadway building had gone a little beyond Chambers Street. By the time of Washington's inauguration, the built-up streets on the east reached the present Broome Street and on the west, Reade Street. By 1796, the outer limits had extended to the present line of Houston Street. On streets which were naturally low, running to the Collect Pond and its outlet brook into the East River, there were muddy alleys, lined with decayed, foul-smelling frame buildings which had sunk due to erosion, and where wet weather regularly produced flooding. These were the streets in the vicinity of Peck's Slip where the city's poor and new immigrants lived. The inevitable deaths in these streets from the yellow-fever epidemics between 1797 and 1803 were buried in a potter's field at the present site

"Bales of cotton, wool, and merchandize; barrels of potash, rice, flour, and salt provisions; hogsheads of sugar, chests of tea, puncheons of rum, and pipes of wine; boxes, cases, packs and packages of all sizes and denominations, were strewed upon the wharfs and landing-places, or upon the decks of the shipping. All was noise and bustle. The carters were driving in every direction; and on board the vessels, were moving their ponderous burthens from place to place." John Lambert, a British visitor to New York in 1807.

"It may to many be a matter of surprise that so few vacant spaces have been left and those so small, for the benefit of fresh air and consequent preservation of health. Certainly if the city of New York was destined to stand on the side of a small stream such as the Seine or the Thames, a great number of ample places might be needful. But those large arms of the sea which embrace Manhattan island render its situation, in regard to health and pleasure as well as to the convenience of commerce, peculiarly felicitous." Remarks of the Commisssioners for laying out streets and Roads in the City of New York, under the Act of April 3, 1807.

of Washington Square.

In March 1787, the state legislature authorized the Common Council to lay out new streets and improve existing ones, funded by levies upon the owners of lots or houses which benefitted from the work. Paving ordinances of September 1788 required the owners of lots facing the public slips to pay for the paving of nearby streets. Once outside the most heavily commercial areas near the docks, most city streets were unpaved. There were no sewers, and no drainage for rainwater; open sewers were a common feature. Pigs wandered at random, foraging for food.

In 1795 and 1796 the Common Council decided to construct two outer streets which would ease traffic, and improve the amenity of the waterfront. Existing waterlots were condemned and by 1796 South Street and West Street, each a handsome 70 feet wide, were laid out and graded.

"In Harlem Lane," a pen and ink drawing by Archibald Robertson. The view is located at the present-day intersection of Eighth Avenue and 120th Street.

The great thoroughfares

The attention given to Broadway and to Wall Street in the 1780s testifies to their rise to social and economic importance. Broadway, the city's premier showcase, was graded, and an arched bridge was placed across the Collect Pond outlet at the present location of Canal Street, enabling the street to continue northwards to Bloomingdale and the Kingsbridge Road.

Various improvements were ordered for Wall Street in 1786, and by the end of the century it was the home of many banks and insurance companies, as well as the wealthiest and most fashionable New Yorkers. Attractive two- and three-story redbrick houses in the Federal Style lined Wall Street, Broad Street, lower Broadway, Greenwich

"There are several extensive book stores, print-shops, music-shops, jewellers, and silversmiths; hatters, linen-drapers, milliners, pastry-cooks, coachmakers, hotels and coffee-houses. The street is well paved, and the foot-paths are chiefly bricked."
A late 18th-century visitor to New York.

Street, and the Battery. It was the fashion to paint houses red, gray or cream, with the mortar joints picked out in a contrasting color.

Federal Hall and City Hall

With the adoption of the new constitution in September 1788, New York City was to be capital of the new state of New York, and temporary capital of the nation. To serve as Federal Hall, City Hall was lavishly refurbished, at the cost of $65,000 (paid for by the proceeds of a lottery) under the direction of Major Charles L'Enfant. When the first Congress met at Federal Hall on 6 April 1789, Washington was declared the first president of the United States. Washington lived at a house located on the corner of Cherry and Dover streets until February 1790. He then resided at the Macomb mansion at 39 Broadway until August, when New York ceased to be the federal capital.

A new City Hall was proposed in May 1800. The design competition was won by the French emigré engineer Joseph Mangin and the Scotsman John McComb, who supervised the work. Construction continued from 1803 to 1812. It was so clearly at the northernmost edge of the city that economies were taken with the materials used for the rear of the building, faced with brownstone, cheaper by far than the handsome Massachusetts marble used for the rest of the building. Even so, it cost $500,000 to build. The old Federal building on Wall Street was sold at auction for $450.

The Bridewell (below), named after the house of correction in the London parish of Bridewell, was built on a site west of the present City Hall in 1775. It was used as a military prison during the British occupation. It ceased to house prisoners in 1814, but remained a place of detention for debtors and persons held for trial. It was replaced by the Tombs, on the site of the Collect Pond, in 1838.

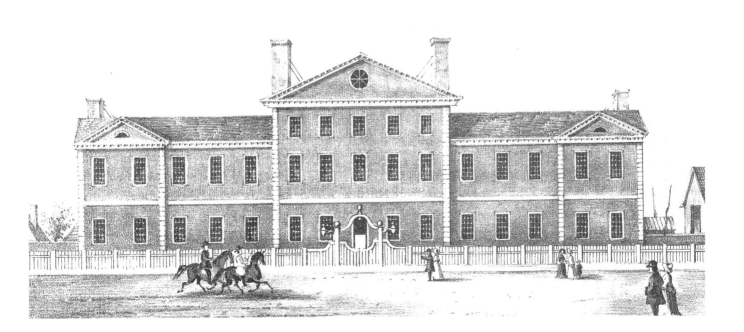

The End of Loyalist New York

At the end of the war in 1783, an estimated 100,000 New York loyalists, including most of its property-owners, went into exile. The city's leading merchants and landowners, who had been overwhelmingly loyal to the Crown, departed, as did the leading figures of the Anglican communion. The fate of the New York Tories in the postwar settlement had a larger effect on the history of New York than on any other colony.

Tories in New York were disfranchised in March 1778. In October 1779, Tory lawyers were barred from practice. Loyalist property was

Federal Hall, capital of the new republic.

Property ownership changed dramatically in New York after the revolution, as loyalists were exiled and their property forfeited. The enormous DeLancey estate (below), was a good test case for the democratic outcome of the revolutionary struggle. Wealthy lawyers and the trading classes benefitted most from the redivision of land (map right).

declared forfeit. The highwater mark of anti-loyalism was a law passed in 1784 which barred all loyalists who had been office-holders under the British, served in the British army, abandoned the state during the war, or who had joined the British, from voting or holding office. An estimated two-thirds of all of the inhabitants of the City and County of New York lost the right to vote.

Alexander Hamilton, who had held talks with New York loyalists before the British evacuation, became the chief advocate for moderation: "make it the interest of those citizens, who, during the revolution, were opposed to us to be friends to the new government, by affording them not only protection, but a participation in its privileges, and they will undoubtedly become its friends."

The advocates of moderation successfully halted further persecution of the loyalists, and most of the measures of the 1784 law were repealed two years later. In 1792, all banished Tories were permitted to return, but they were required to accept the state's title to their confiscated property.

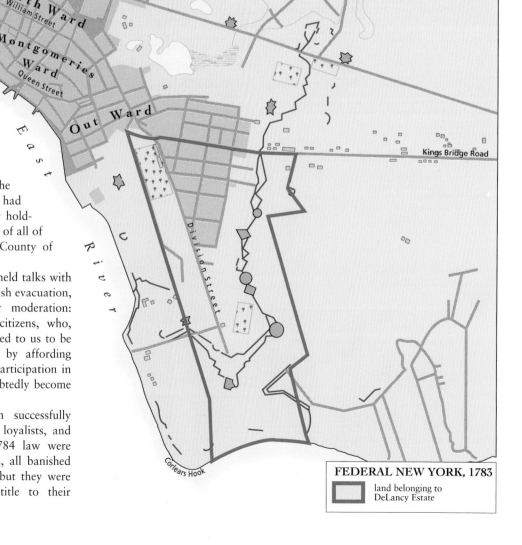

FEDERAL NEW YORK, 1783

land belonging to DeLancy Estate

East DeLancey Farm, divided from the West Farm by Clinton Street, was purchased by leading mercantile, landowning and legal families, as was much of the West Farm; the latter also went to 69 self-designated "gentlemen." The four blocks bounded by Essex, Grand, Attorney and Broome Streets, were subsequently purchased by carpenters, tobacconists, masons, butchers, teachers, brewers, and a boat-builder. The smallholdings formed the sinews of postwar city development, and mechanic and merchant lived side by side on the former DeLancey estate. The DeLancey mansion (below), situated on the southeast corner of Broad and Pearl streets, later became the Fraunces Tavern.

Although much of the old city had been destroyed in the fire of 1776, Broad Street (below right), drawn by George Holland in 1797, was still a jumble of old and new. A Dutch gabled house, dated 1698, rubs shoulders with 18th-century churches and houses.

PURCHASERS OF THE DELANCY FARMS:

- William Beekman
- Abraham Cannon
- John Delamater
- William Denning & Adam Gilchrist
- Nicholas Fish
- George Fisher
- Nicholas Gouverneur
- Isaac Gouverneur
- Joseph Hallett
- John Lawrence
- Morgan Lewis & Henry Livingston
- Henry Livingston
- Philip Livingston
- Philip Livingston & Nicholas Fish
- Jonathan Lawrence & George Fisher
- Dominick Lynch
- Janet Montgomery & John Delamater
- Daniel Phoenix & Joseph Hallett
- John Quackenbos
- Isaac Roosevelt, Henry Kip & John Lawrence
- Henry Tiebout
- Marinus Willett & John Lamb

The DeLancey family, who owned substantial property on Manhattan, were ultra-loyalists and their fall was dramatic. Their main estate was sold off by the Commissioners of Forfeiture in lots the size of city blocks. The East DeLancey Farm, with over a mile of valuable waterfront, fell to 15 leading mercantile, landowning and legal families. The West DeLancey Farm was occupied by many sitting tenants given no prior right of purchase. There were 175 purchasers, including 69 self-designated "gentlemen," as well as merchants, lawyers, and attorneys. With a second round of property sales, however, a different pattern emerges, with purchases by house-carpenters, tobacconists, butchers, teachers, masons, brewers, and a boat-builder.

There were more property-holders in post-revolutionary New York, but those who had come best out of the dissolution of loyalist estates were unquestionably the merchants, lawyers, and wealthy families in trade. The loyalist aristocracy had been displaced, but the wealthy still remained in control.

Capital of Commerce

When the British left New York in 1783, taking with them the city's commercial leaders, there was a temporary recession. The economic recovery was led by rising prices. Wheat, one of New York's most important exports, which fetched 75 cents a bushel in 1785, rose to $2.10 by 1800. Speculators in real estate were encouraged by the rising cost of improved land near the city.

The Bank of New York opened on Pearl Street in March 1784. To the city's anti-Federalists and Republicans, the bank was a threat and the legislature was persuaded to charter a corporation, the Manhattan Company, ostensibly to improve the city's lamentable water supply. In the small print of the bill lay powers to engage in banking activities. Banking rivalry did much to spur rapid economic growth.

By 1789, New York had become the leading center for speculation in all forms of securities. Risk-taking and the development of complex financial instruments were much admired. Alexander Hamilton, leader of the New York Federalists, successfully created a national financial system which would secure the adhesion of the wealthy to the new federal union. The main planks were the assumption of state debt, the creation of a national bank, and the reliance upon excise tax for most government revenue.

With Hamilton's program installed by 1791, stock quotations appeared in the press, and security transactions largely became the preserve of specialist brokerage firms. Combining to set standard fees, these brokers opened a stock exchange at 22 Wall Street in 1792, and moved to the Tontine Coffee House in 1793.

By 1805, Broadway had become the home of many elegant shops, especially in the drygoods retail trade. Pearl Street was close enough to the

docks to act as center for the wholesale dry goods trade. Fashionable New Yorkers relied upon the bootmakers, hairdressers, jewelers, and perfumeries located there. Water Street, Front Street, and South Street were lined with grocery warehouses. Wall Street had become the preferred location of banks, insurance offices, exchange brokers and auctioneers.

For transport most people depended upon the livery stables for travel within the city, and the stage lines for travel elsewhere. The city leased ferry rights to private operators for fixed periods of time, setting rates and conditions of carriage. Travel from New York to Liverpool took on average 23 days, and 40 to make the return journey. The very best ships could make the outward journey in 16 or 17 days.

As commerce expanded, post-revolutionary New York (below) developed into a fashionable shopping city, and the leading center for speculation in securities. Merchants no longer lived near their waterfront commercial premises, preferring to live in the more fashionable residential districts to the north of the growing city. Livery stables charged one shilling for travel within one mile of City Hall. Stages for Albany, Boston and Philadelphia left from Fraunces Tavern; the Albany route took two or three days in summer, four or more in winter.

The New Exchange on lower Broad Street (below) replaced a group of Dutch gabled structures seen in the drawing on page 61. The Exchange was the meeting place of the city's merchants.

"*From Bristol we went to Trenton . . . but over a very rough road, so much so that having never been in such I thought my bones would be jolted out of my skin – . . . From there we went to Brunswick 16 miles but this road was worse than any before – It was so bad that for 8 miles we were in danger of breaking down or being overturned every minute and had it not been for the Skill of the Driver, of which by this time I was convinced, I expected to have a leg or an arm broke before night – I was so much amused with a waggoneer whom we met at the top of a Hill just at the commencement of this very bad road & who had got with great difficulty thro' it – He asked us if we were going to Brunswick, if so says the waggoneer shaking his Head the Lord Pity you.*"
From the diary of James S. Glennie, who travelled from Philadelphia to New York, December 1810.

In the 1780s Broadway (above) was graded, and an arched bridge was placed across the Collect Pond outlet at the present location of Canal Street, enabling the street to continue northwards. Broadway was the city's premier shopping and commercial showcase. The Coffee House (right) was the meeting place of the city's merchants. The steam frigate Fulton the First *was built in New York, at Corlear's Hook, and launched in 1814 (below). Robert Fulton, the designer, was a pioneer of steamship navigation.*

The Informal City 1783 – 1825

Taverns played an important role in New York politics. Mechanics (the term included master workman, journeyman and apprentice) hungered for political intelligence, and enterprising landlords made newspapers available in their taverns. Taverns were to be found in every area of the city, many of venerable age, each marked by a distinctive sign, such as the Spread Eagle at Whitehall and the King's Head on Pearl Street. They offered rooms for guests as well as for banquets, auctions, and political meetings.

Coffee Houses were cherished by merchants. They were the location of the growing market in shares and securities and served as the principal meeting places for public auctions of goods newly arrived in the city.

Many taverns had gardens in which puppet shows, concerts and musical entertainments were offered. They were competing with showmen, such as Dr. King, who held an exhibition at 28 Wall Street of a male and female orang utang, sloths, baboons, monkeys, porcupines, and other natural curiosities, and Mr. Bowen's waxworks exhibition on Water Street, which included representations of the President, the royal family of Britain, the Bishop of New York, and edifying biblical scenes. Theatrical life in America, which had stopped in 1774, resumed after the war. The theater grew ever more popular. The Park Theater contained a coffee-room and could seat an audience of 2,400. Its vaulted dome was even adorned by a large glass chandelier.

The city fathers sought to repress the popular amusements provided by the taverns. In 1788, tavern-keepers were threatened with fines and imprisonment for allowing cock-fighting, gaming, card-playing, billiard tables, shuffleboards or dice in their establishments. Those making substantial winnings at cards were threatened with confiscatory fines, fraud at cards was to be repressed by corporal punishment, and for drunkenness there was either a fine or two hours imprisonment in the stocks. Applicants for liquor licenses were required to give a bond of £50 not to keep a disorderly house.

The first of New York's great hotels, the City Hotel, was opened in 1794. It proudly filled the entire block on lower Broadway bounded by Thames and Cedar Streets. The ground floor along Broadway was converted into shops. New Yorkers became passionate devotees of dancing, and the exclusive City Assemblies were held at the City Hotel. An English visitor noted that "none but the first class of society can become subscribers to this assembly."

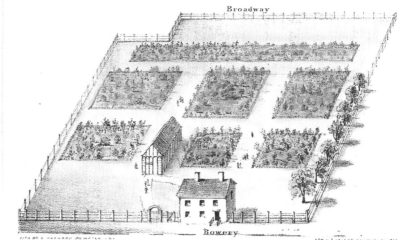

VAUXHALL GARDEN 1803

VIEW OF PARK ROW. 1825.

In the summer, Vauxhall Gardens (above) was a favorite resort. Located on the Bowery Road, it was a delightful park with gravel walks, shrubs and trees. There was a small theater and fireworks were a regular feature. The Tontine Coffee House (left) was located on the southeast corner of Wall and Water Streets. The New York Tontine, an association of investors, was formed in 1792. Each subscriber put up $200 for investment, and nominated a person – usually a child – to receive their share of the net income of the property. When the building was demolished in 1855, 51 of the original 203 nominees survived. Elegant Park Row (below) was the location of the Park Theater, built in 1798.

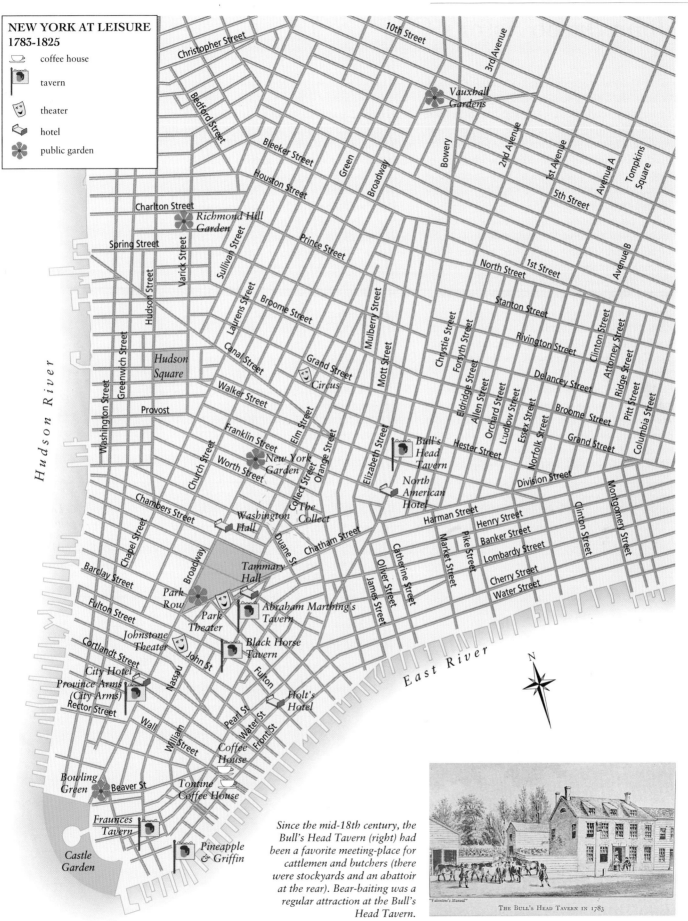

NEW YORK AT LEISURE
1783-1825

- coffee house
- tavern
- theater
- hotel
- public garden

Christopher Street

10th Street

3rd Avenue

Vauxhall Gardens

Bleeker Street

Green

Bowery

2nd Avenue

1st Avenue

Avenue A

Tompkins Square

Bedford Street

Houston Street

Broadway

5th Street

Charlton Street

Richmond Hill Garden

Prince Street

North Street

1st Street

Avenue B

Spring Street

Varick Street

Sullivan Street

Stanton Street

Hudson Street

Christie Street

Forsyth Street

Rivington Street

Clinton Street

Attorney Street

Hudson Square

Broome Street

Canal Street

Grand Street

Mulberry Street

Delancey Street

Ridge Street

Pitt Street

Greenwich Street

Walker Street

Circus

Mott Street

Eldridge Street

Allen Street

Orchard Street

Ludlow Street

Essex Street

Broome Street

Grand Street

Columbia Street

Washington Street

Provost

Franklin Street

Elm Street

Hester Street

Norfolk Street

Laurens Street

New York Garden

Orange Street

Bull's Head Tavern

Division Street

Montgomery Street

Church Street

Worth Street

Collect Street

Elizabeth Street

North American Hotel

Chambers Street

The Collect

Harman Street

Henry Street

Clinton Street

Washington Hall

Duane St.

Chatham Street

Banker Street

Pike Street

Chapel Street

Tammany Hall

Olive Street

Catherine Street

Market Street

Lombardy Street

Hudson River

Barclay Street

Park Row

Abraham Marthing's Tavern

James Street

Cherry Street

Water Street

Fulton Street

Park Theater

Johnstone Theater

John St

Black Horse Tavern

East River

Cortlandt Street

Fulton

City Hotel

Nassau

Province Arms (City Arms)

Rector Street

Holt's Hotel

N

Wall

William Street

Pearl St

Water St

Front St

Coffee House

Bowling Green

Beaver St

Tontine Coffee House

Fraunces Tavern

Castle Garden

Pineapple & Griffin

Since the mid-18th century, the Bull's Head Tavern (right) had been a favorite meeting-place for cattlemen and butchers (there were stockyards and an abattoir at the rear). Bear-baiting was a regular attraction at the Bull's Head Tavern.

"Valentine's Manual"

THE BULL'S HEAD TAVERN IN 1783

John Jacob Astor's City

In 1803 New York exported $3,100,000 worth of commodities to foreign ports. By 1807, this figure had reached $16,400,000, in large part due to John Jacob Astor, who came to New York in 1784 after working for four years in his brother's musical instrument workshop in London. Astor came to New York looking for local agents to represent their firm. By chance, he entered the fur trade.

The North American fur trade was controlled by British firms through trading companies based in Montreal. Direct exports to America were banned by British regulations and pelts had to be shipped to Montreal and London for re-export to New York. Astor began a series of annual fur-buying trips which established business connections in Albany and Montreal; he sold directly to hat and clothing manufacturers, and put large lots of furs for sale at the great fur auctions in Europe.

Astor took the profits, and invested them in speculative trading ventures to China. In 1792, the *America* and the *Washington* sailed from New York to Canton, carrying furs and other goods and currency from New York merchants. The goods were sold, and a return cargo of silks

and spices was bought for resale back in New York. Astor never engaged in retail trade: rather he provided goods to other merchants. By 1793 he had become the most important American fur merchant and a year later, the fur trade was opened to direct shipments to New York.

In 1800-1, the *Severn* departed for China, carrying furs bought by Astor in Montreal. It returned carrying cargo bought from the proceeds in Canton. Over the next two years, the cargo was disposed of in voyages to France and Germany. The proceeds of the *Severn* voyage provided Astor with the capital to begin substantial investment in New York real estate.

From 1800 to 1815 Astor invested $695,000, and sold property worth just under $200,000, fueling the rise of real estate values and becoming in turn the chief beneficiary of the growing demand for housing which accompanied the city's rise in population. He mainly bought lots outside the built-up area of the city, but seldom built housing. He leased New York lots to speculative builders, or resold property at whatever advance was possible.

Originally from the Ashdorf family of Waldorf near Heidelberg, John Jacob Astor (below) spoke with a strong German accent. He was one of the major players in New York's export growth of over 500 percent between 1803 and 1807.

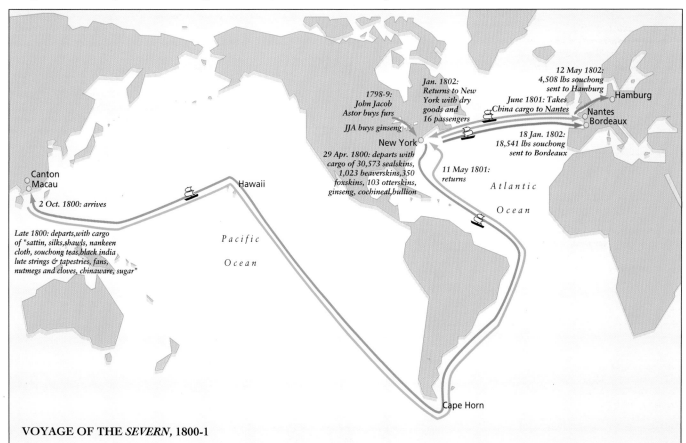

VOYAGE OF THE *SEVERN*, 1800-1

1798-9:
John Jacob
Astor buys furs

JJA buys ginseng

29 Apr. 1800: departs with cargo of 30,573 sealskins, 1,023 beaverskins, 350 foxskins, 103 otterskins, ginseng, cochineal, bullion

Jan. 1802:
Returns to New York with dry goods and 16 passengers

12 May 1802:
4,508 lbs souchong sent to Hamburg

June 1801: Takes China cargo to Nantes

18 Jan. 1802:
18,541 lbs souchong sent to Bordeaux

11 May 1801:
returns

2 Oct. 1800: arrives

Late 1800: departs, with cargo of "sattin, silks, shawls, nankeen cloth, souchong teas, black india lute strings & tapestries, fans, nutmegs and cloves, chinaware, sugar"

Canton
Macau

Hawaii

Hamburg
Nantes
Bordeaux

New York

Atlantic Ocean

Pacific Ocean

Cape Horn

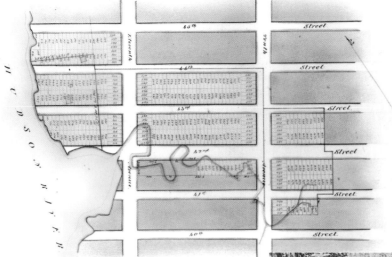

The success of the 1800-1 voyage of the *Severn* had two consequences for Astor, and for New York. It strengthened his commitment to the China trade and, with the city in a period of rapid and sustained growth in population, its profits enabled Astor to translate the fluctuating revenues from his trading voyages into the steady and rising income of the property owner. His purchases included specific locations with commercial potential (he bought the Vauxhall Gardens in 1804, and, in partnership with John Beekman, the Park Theater in 1805). He continued his heavy investments in New York real estate until his death, buying the City Hotel in 1828 for $101,000, and building the luxurious Astor House in 1836.

The records of Astor's property holdings, such as this 1834 map of real estate transactions (above), fill two stout leather-bound volumes held by the New-York Historical Society.

When the Severn *sailed from New York in 1800, it carried furs bought by Astor in Montreal over the previous winter (above right) – no fewer than 30,573 sealskins, 1,023 beaver pelts, 350 fox pelts and 103 otter pelts. Although he was only a minority shareholder in the necessary capital outlay of $100,000, the voyage of the* Severn *in 1800-1 (map, left) nevertheless provided Astor with the capital to begin his life-long passionate investment in New York real estate. The captain of the* Severn, *acting as Astor's agent, sold Astor's furs in Canton, and bought goods with the proceeds. The* Severn *returned on May 11, 1801, and in June departed for Nantes, carrying a significant proportion of the China cargo. On its return with drygoods in January, Astor shipped souchong tea to Bordeaux and to Hamburg in May; on each journey he invested the proceeds in goods that could be sold in New York or transshipped elsewhere.*

Voyages like that of the Severn *made Astor's fortune. Gentlemen across New England borrowed money for similar ventures, and when they went wrong the effects could be catastrophic. When the ship in which he had heavily invested in 1795 failed to return, Dr. Bryant of Cummington, Massachusetts (father of the poet William Cullen Bryant) was forced to flee to avoid debtors' prison, and sail as a ship's surgeon around Cape Horn. The family fortunes never recovered.*

A graph (right) of Astor's purchases of New York real estate over 15 years. The dollar scale on the left is topped by the profits from the Severn *voyage ($184,000), which were invested in 1803.*

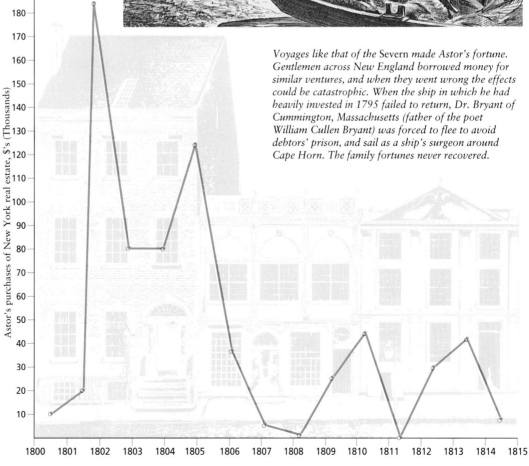

The City Transformed

By 1797, the line of the city's future growth had been established by the repeated accommodation of street line to the riverside. The DeLancey farms, which defined the land from the north of Division Street to the East River, were sold in the 1780s, and were now a grid of city blocks and small lots. The area below Division Street was laid out in a regular grid in the 1790s, and the city had expanded northwards after the war in a pattern of overlapping grids.

In the 1790s the City Surveyor, Casimir Goerck, had laid out larger parcels of civic land on a regular grid pattern. When the city requested the state legislature to appoint commissioners to lay out a plan for the development of the whole island in 1806, it was probably clear that a plan akin to Goerck's grid design would be followed. The commission took four years to complete the plan: a simple rectilinear grid was to be extended over all existing rights of way, agricultural holdings, hills, waterways, marshes, and houses. Broadway survived the plan, but little else was allowed to remain. It was an extension of a city which had grown largely without either plan or central direction. The effects of the grid took decades to be fully realized and little disruption was felt.

The rationale was economic: regular-shaped plots, right-angled intersections, valuable corner lots and straight streets would encourage the city's economic development. Other considerations were also relevant: space was allocated for a military parade ground and Hudson Square was planned. Nevertheless, the provision of park land was clearly inadequate.

The plan probably assumed that the city would retain its contemporary scale, in both height and variety. By 1811, the variety of the city's many architectural styles, richly-colored structures and diverse building materials probably needed little encouragement from town planners. There were no large-scale groups of rowhouses, and – apart from the City Hotel – few public structures of any size. Private residences were small and unostentatious. Factories were little more than artisanal workshops. Shipyards had perhaps the greatest need for space, but ships in 1811 were relatively small.

Criticism has been made that other design principles could have created focal points for sites of important buildings and uses. But at no point had the city's streets been laid out to give distinctive vistas, or heightened social prominence, to the city's leading institutions. The Commissioners had no instructions to redesign and rebuild the city; no one was ever given the power over the design of New York that Baron Haussmann exercised over Paris.

The 1811 Commissioners' plan (below) reflected an age which was not given to conspicuous consumption or lavish display. It assumed that the 20 or 25-foot frontages of the small lots bought by mechanics in the sale of former loyalist estates would be adequate for the modest and republican future then foreseen. Large, irregular lots would have created more interesting urban life, but excluded mechanics from important areas of the housing market.

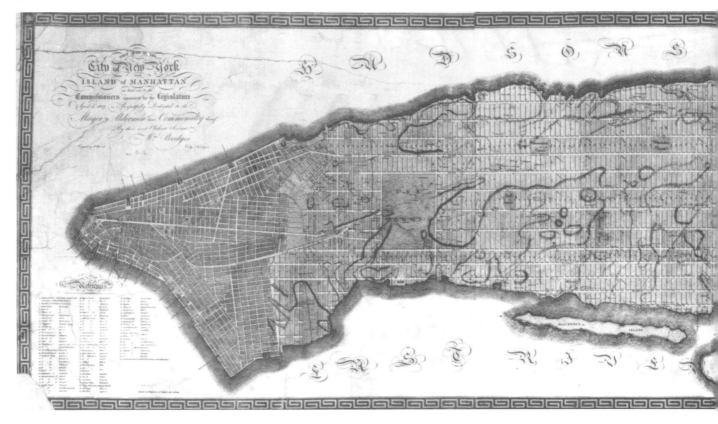

In 1797, the streets of New York followed two orientations (map, right). From the Battery to the end of the developed residential areas of the city on the East River, and from the Battery along the Hudson to the farthest reaches of Greenwich Street, the city streets reached up from the riverside. These streets mark the lines of movement from the docks and wharves to the warehouses, markets and workshops of the city's artisans. The dramatic expansion of the city northwards after the British evacuation created another orientation. At Chatham Street, the Collect Pond abruptly halted the march northwards. Orange, Mulberry and Mott Streets pick up the orientation of Roosevelt and James Streets, making a halfturn to the north. A new orientation was thus established, carrying the streets northwards, parallel to the Bowery Road.

In 1788, paving ordinances required the owners of lots facing the public slips to pay for the paving of nearby streets. Outside the commercial center, however, most city streets were unpaved. The engraving (above left) shows the laying of pavement at the corner of Broadway and White Street.

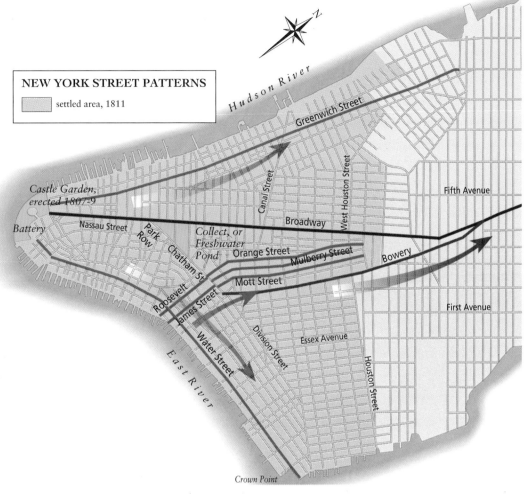

NEW YORK STREET PATTERNS

☐ settled area, 1811

Chapter 5 The Age of "Go Ahead" 1825–1860

The Croton aqueduct at the Harlem River, painted by F.B. Tower.

"There's nothing new in town, except the Croton Water which is all full of tadpoles and animalculae, and which moreover flows through an aqueduct which I hear was used as a necessary by all the Hibernian vagabonds who worked upon it ... I shall drink no Croton for some time to come. ("Jehaggar") Post has drunk some of it and is in dreadful apprehensions of breeding bullfrogs inwardly."
George Templeton Strong, August 1, 1842.

In 1828 Broadway extended as far north as 10th Street, and the Common Council ordered the opening of 14th Street from the Bowery to the North River. In 1860 commissioners were appointed to lay out streets and avenues north of 155th Street. Change, at least on the scale experienced by the city, seems to have caught everyone unawares. There was no more potent a measure of the spirit of the age than the soaring population figures: New York's population rose from 123,706 in 1820 to 813,669 in 1860, about a quarter of whom were Irish-born.

Older citizens nostalgically recalled the city in which they had grown up. "New York, as you knew it, was a mere corner of the present huge city," wrote Washington Irving to his sister in 1847, "and that corner is all changed, pulled to pieces, burnt down and rebuilt – all but our little native nest in William Street, which still retains some of its old features; though those are daily altering. I can hardly realize that within my term of life, this great crowded metropolis, so full of life[,] bustle, noise, shew and splendor, was a quiet little City of some fifty or sixty thousand inhabitants. It is really now one of the most rucketing cities in the world and reminds me of one of the great European cities (Frankfort for instance) in the time of an annual fair – Here it is a Fair almost all the year round."

As ancient landmarks such as the old Tontine Building on the corner of Wall and Water Streets disappeared (torn down in 1855), familiar reference points moved, with unnerving speed, to different locations. The Brick Church on Beekman Street was sold by the trustees (for $270,000) in 1856. By 1858 there was a new Brick Church on the northwest corner of Fifth Avenue and 37th Street and on the old site the *New York Times* building was already in operation. In 1856 the New York Institution for the Deaf and Dumb occupied a large building on Fourth Avenue between 49th and 50th Streets, and Columbia College was at the site on Church Street it had occupied since the revolution. By May of the next year the Church Street site had been demolished and sold, the college had moved uptown to Fourth Avenue, and the Institution had relocated on Washington Heights. The Broadway Theater was demolished in April 1858. By November 2, the site was occupied by a store. Streets were in constant turmoil as they were paved, torn up, realigned, widened, and paved again. Things indelibly established in the public's esteem proved astonishing ephemeral. When the Astor House was built in 1836, it was universally proclaimed to be the *ne plus ultra* of luxury and ostentation. However, by the early 1870s, it already seemed distinctly uncomfortable, old-fashioned and unappealing.

"Sunlight" and "Gaslight" New York

New York was increasingly coming to be seen as something physically alien and threatening. New Yorkers were sure that the things which made the city livable were being swallowed up by unprecedented forces of change. William Cullen Bryant argued in 1844 that parks were needed by the city because "commerce is devouring inch by inch the coast of the

Dog-fighting at Kit Burns' – one of the many popular amusements available in the city's taverns.

island, and if we would rescue any part of it for health and recreation it must be done now." Even more alarming imagery appeared in the *New York Times*: "The huge masses of masonry which are springing up in every direction seem to threaten us with a stifling atmosphere of bricks and mortar."

New Yorkers were of two minds whether to celebrate the heroic pace and scale of change, or to join the city's cultural leaders in their tone of denunciation and lament. In the end, it suited many to both admire and lament what was happening to New York, thus to establish a distinctive urban tone of enthusiastic ambivalence or rueful pride. It was a tone which filled the hundreds of guidebooks, primers of city life, sketches, and sensation-seeking reportage which from the 1840s became a journalistic cottage industry in the big city. The proliferation of this literature, such as Ned Buntline's *The Mysteries and Miseries of New York: A Story of Real Life*, 1848, and George G. Foster's *New York by Gas-light; with Here and There a Streak of Sunshine*, 1850, were signs that the pace of change had accelerated, and that even New Yorkers were struggling to understand the new forms of life which were emerging in the city.

View of Wall Street, from the corner of Broad Street, 1850

"*Commerce is devouring inch by inch the coast of the island, and if we would rescue any part of it for health and recreation it must be done now.*"
William Bryant, 1844.

An opulent city

It was not only the older generation which saw the city as remorselessly declining. The extent of the corruption of the city can be measured in the changing attitudes towards wealth and ostentation. From the 1830s the commercial streets of New York were filled with large buildings modeled on Greek and Roman temples. Did the imposing Merchants Exchange and the vast Custom House on Wall Street mark the loss of Republican virtue, and the arrival of an Imperial culture of excess and power which would threaten the survival of democracy itself? There were signs of the loss of republican simplicity when it became fashionable to use silver ornamentation upon the front doors of the most elegant New York houses. Much to the disgust of the *New York Evening Post*, granite pillars were added to brick facades; and there was "too much disposition among those who put up houses to build in a different style from their neighbors;" white marble ostentatiously faced the

Colonnade Row on Lafayette Place in 1831.

Consider descriptions of two private residences built at the end of this period, both "uptown," far from the commercial center of the city. The first, on the northwest corner of Fifth Avenue and 34th Street: "The marble work, which forms the most distinguishing characteristic of this palatial abode, receives its entire shape and finish in the basement and first floor of the building... The reception and drawing rooms, and the breakfast and dining rooms [afford] space for as splendid a promenade or ball as could be furnished probably by any private residence in Europe." The second

mansion was erected at Fifth Avenue at 52nd Street: "On the first floor are the grand hall of tessellated marble, lined with mirrors; the three immense dining-rooms, furnished in bronze and gold with yellow satin hangings, an enormous French mirror in mosaic gilding at every pane ...". The first mansion belonged to the merchant A.T. Stewart, the second was "The Palace" built by the abortionist Madame Restell. There was more of the puzzling symmetry between "sunshine" and "gaslight" in the careers of Stewart and Restell than contemporaries cared to contemplate. Stewart was born in Belfast and orphaned at an early age. He emigrated to New York in 1818. Without friends, but with a thousand pound legacy from his grandfather, Stewart opened a small shop on Broadway. From 1828 to 1837 he moved location several times and greatly expanded his shop. In 1846 he built a magnificent "marble" store on Broadway between Chambers and Reade Streets. He moved into an even bigger building on Broadway at 9th Street. Stewart's real estate

The Bay Harbor of New York, by Samuel B. Waugh, 1855, with Castle Garden on the right.

holdings, said to be second only to William B. Astor's, included the Metropolitan Hotel, the Globe Theater, and nearly all of Bleecker Street.

If Stewart heroically embodied the "immigrant" success story in Antebellum New York, so ironically did Madame Restell. She was born Caroline Ann Trow in a rural village in Gloucestershire, where she received no education. Trow worked as a maid in a butcher's home before marrying a tailor, Harry Somers. After the birth of a daughter, the Somers family emigrated to New York in 1832. Her husband soon died. Mrs Somers supported herself as a dressmaker, then as a pill-maker for various common ailments of the lung, liver, and stomach. She met Charles Lohman, a Russian of German descent, who as "Dr. A.M. Mauriceau," sold quack medicines and published "medical companions." Lohman married Mrs Somers and together they "invented" Madame Restell the celebrated female physician through advertisements in the *New York Sun* and the *Herald*. In a climate of general indifference to abortion, Restell's services, and her Preventive Powders soon brought her wealth and notoriety. She shared with Stewart a tenacity, cleverness, sensitivity to the market, and a taste for the good things in life. Her "Palace" which occupied the corner lot on 52nd Street cost $200,000 to build and was said to be one of the finest private residences in the city. It set a new standard of lavishness, but it was soon to be trumped by August Belmont, Cornelius Vanderbilt and others who built on Fifth Avenue.

City of Contrasts

The notorious Old Brewery at Five Points and A.T Stewart's Fifth Avenue mansion establish the extremes of a pervasive, simultaneous sense of opposite social, economic, and moral orders which defined the character of New York. Contrasts were legion: consider the magnificent commercial palace of Lord & Taylor on Broadway, and the cheap clothing shops on the Bowery; the elegant brownstone row houses above Washington Square which lined lower Fifth Avenue and the overcrowded, dilapidated structures on Delancey, Rivington, and Stanton Streets which housed the Irish immigrants. During the day, Broadway was the home of the fashionable and elegant, at night it was haunted by prostitutes, con-men, and criminals. As Washington Irving noted in the satirical *Salmagundi* essays

"Overturn, overturn, overturn! is the maxim of New York… The very bones of our ancestors are not permitted to lie quiet a quarter of a century, and one generation of men seem studious to remove all relics of those which preceded them. Pitt's statue no longer graces Wall Street, the old Presbyterian Church has given place to the stalls of the money-changers, and the Croton River has washed away all traces of the tea-water pump."
Phillip Hone, diary 1845.

(1808): "A man who resides in Pearl Street or Chatham Row derives no kind of dignity from his domicil; but place him in a certain part of Broadway, anywhere between the Battery and Wall Street, and he straightaway becomes entitled to figure in the *beau monde* and strut as a person of prodigious consequence!"

There seemed, in the 1840s and 1850s, little consequence if riches had been acquired respectably, or not. Wealth, opulently displayed, was the fact, the self-assertion which the age demanded. Sober Federal houses were torn down, to be replaced by Italianate mansions, French chateaux, and pseudo-gothic castles which grew like mushrooms on Fifth Avenue, only to be torn down for even larger and more fantastical establishments later in the century. The street was soon lined with ornate mansions, restaurants, fancy shops, hotels, and gambling establishments catering for the wealthy, transforming the route north from Washington Square to Central Park. Fifth Avenue was as much a complex symbol of the new spirit of the age of "go ahead" as were the notorious slums of Five Points.

View of City Hall, September 1, 1858. Lithograph by Saxony, Major & Knapp.

The Hub of the Nation

In the 1780s a journey by horse from New York to Boston, following the famous Boston Post Road to New Haven, Hartford and Worcester, took between four and six days. By the 1830s stagecoaches covered this route, with frequent changes of horses, in a day and a half. The same jouney by rail in the 1840s could be completed in little more than half a day.

New York took the lead in canal construction in 1810, when a commission recommended a route to the West via Lake Erie. The first section, from Utica to Salina, was completed by 1820. When the canal was opened by 1825, a celebration ended with the symbolic pouring of water from Lake Erie into New York harbor.

The canal was a great stimulus to the growth of New York commerce and western settlement. In 1828, investors funded a canal and railroad linking the Delaware and the Hudson, which brought Pennsylvania coal to New York City. Coal heating, far cheaper than wood, arrived in the 1840s. The first railroads in New York were built as feeders to this canal, while the lines which formed the New York Central Railroad were built alongside the route of the Erie Canal.

Travel on the canal was leisurely, averaging less than two miles per hour in the 1850s. The fastest steamboats on the Hudson could do 20 miles per hour, but when they carried freight in towed canal boats or barges the average speed was significantly lower. Rail freight in 1858 averaged less than 15 miles per hour.

As the city expanded in the 1830s, the need for improved public transportation persuaded

Common Council to license the first street railroad line, the New York and Harlem, with a branch line to the Hudson. The cars were generally drawn by two horses, and were fitted with two upholstered benches running lengthwise. On the more popular lines the cars were stagecoaches or "stages" with a seating capacity

of twelve, though overcrowding was common. The drivers, reputedly the rudest people in the city, collected fares through an opening behind the driving seat.

Changes in the city's political culture meant that licenses for lines were granted through bribery of the Common Council. Honest mayors, like Ambrose Kingsland and Jacob Westervelt, vetoed obviously corrupt franchises in the early 1850s, but the Forty Thieves (as the Common Council was known) overrode such vetoes.

The Grand Canal Celebration of the Erie Canal opening was on November 4, 1825 with people attending from all over the country. The canal was 350 miles in length, four feet deep, 40 feet wide at water level, narrowing to 28 feet at the bottom.

Although there were about 4,000 miles of improved roads in New York State by 1821, road travel remained slow and inconvenient. It cost $100 and took three weeks to transport a ton of goods by wagon from Buffalo to New York City. After the opening of the Erie Canal in 1825 it took eight days and cost $15. Travel on the canal was leisurely. The canal's route is shown below.

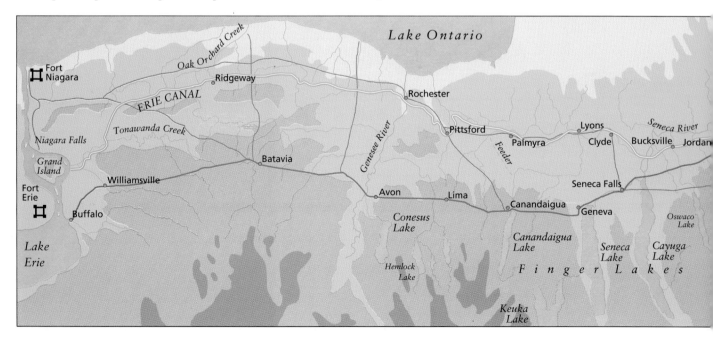

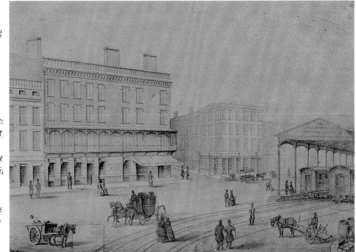

The New York and Harlem Line was first chartered in 1831, and was permitted to lay tracks along Fourth Avenue from 23rd Street to the Harlem River, with a branch line west on 125th Street to the Hudson. Permission was given to extend the line to 14th Street, and in 1832 to Prince Street. The railroad had its offices in Grand Central Terminal (right) and made the first New York railroad journey on November 26 1832. Further extensions made it highly profitable and greatly serviceable to the city (map below). The upholstered interiors of New York's street railroad cars (left) allowed the passengers to travel in some comfort.

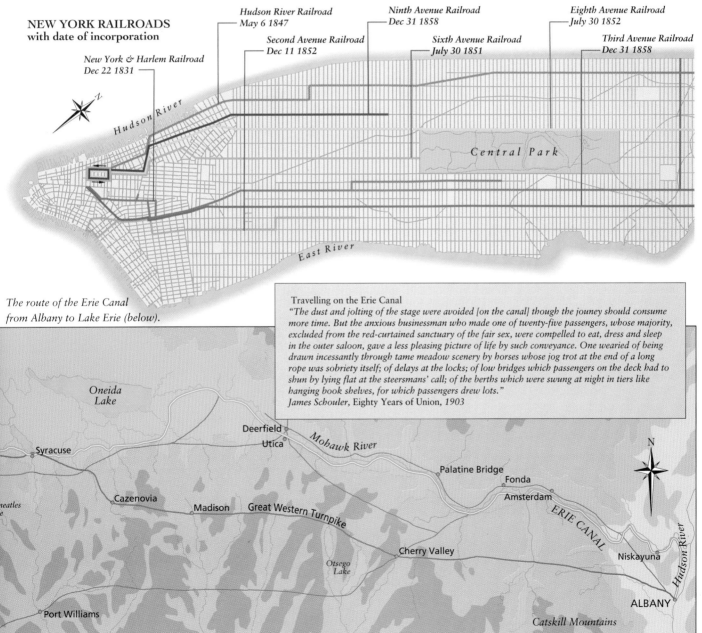

NEW YORK RAILROADS
with date of incorporation

New York & Harlem Railroad
Dec 22 1831

Hudson River Railroad
May 6 1847

Second Avenue Railroad
Dec 11 1852

Ninth Avenue Railroad
Dec 31 1858

Sixth Avenue Railroad
July 30 1851

Eighth Avenue Railroad
July 30 1852

Third Avenue Railroad
Dec 31 1858

Central Park

Hudson River

East River

The route of the Erie Canal from Albany to Lake Erie (below).

Travelling on the Erie Canal
"The dust and jolting of the stage were avoided [on the canal] though the journey should consume more time. But the anxious businessman who made one of twenty-five passengers, whose majority, excluded from the red-curtained sanctuary of the fair sex, were compelled to eat, dress and sleep in the outer saloon, gave a less pleasing picture of life by such conveyance. One wearied of being drawn incessantly through tame meadow scenery by horses whose jog trot at the end of a long rope was sobriety itself; of delays at the locks; of low bridges which passengers on the deck had to shun by lying flat at the steersmans' call; of the berths which were swung at night in tiers like hanging book shelves, for which passengers drew lots."
James Schouler, Eighty Years of Union, 1903

Oneida Lake

Syracuse

Deerfield

Utica

Mohawk River

Palatine Bridge

Fonda

Amsterdam

ERIE CANAL

Cazenovia

Madison

Great Western Turnpike

Cherry Valley

Niskayuna

Hudson River

Otsego Lake

Port Williams

ALBANY

Catskill Mountains

The New Facade

Real estate prices soared as the city was rebuilt after a disastrous fire in 1835. "Everything in New York is at an exorbitant price," Phillip Hone wrote a year later. "Rents have risen 50 per cent for the next year."

The fire of 1835 accelerated the march uptown. The old residential areas on lower Broadway, Bowling Green, and Greenwich Street were rebuilt as stores, warehouses, and offices. In 1828 half of the city's wealthiest 50 families lived in the first three wards. By 1835 only 25 percent of the wealthiest remained downtown. Lower Fifth Avenue, Union Square, and Gramercy Place were the newly fashionable addresses in the 1840s.

As workshops had grown in size, the old pattern of household labor had declined, forcing workers who received wages to enter the market for living space. Rented property became increasingly the norm by the 1830s. By 1860, only one family in ten occupied a whole house. Leases of undeveloped land were acquired as a capital investment, and houses were built specifically to let to tenants.

Older single-family homes were "packed" with sub-tenants – immigrants looking for cheap accommodation – and within a brief period a Federal merchant's home could be turned into a slum property housing dozens of people.

During this period the city became a living history lesson, an eclectic jumble of inspirations, allusions and visual quotations from the history of architecture. After the construction on Lafayette Place in 1832 of the spectacular "Colonnade Row" of nine houses in the Greek Revival style, status was expressed through a "Greek mania." "Grecian doorways" appeared; buildings boldly pronounced a neo-classical pedigree.

In 1831 Samuel Ruggles, a heavy investor in building lots north of Fourteenth Street, set aside

The disastrous fire of 1835 (above) encouraged the move 'uptown' in the 1840s. Italianate mansions transformed Fifth Avenue, (seen below), into an elegant residential thoroughfare. Republican simplicity gave way to lavish display, inside and out. Private residences boasted Corinthian columns and splendid reception rooms, decorated with statuettes, bronzes, clocks and candelabras.

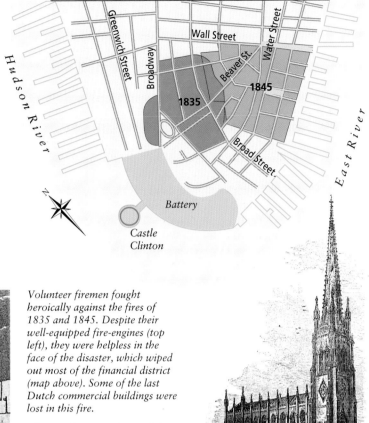

Gramercy Farm as a park and laid out 66 lots for houses. The park was fenced, planted, and deeded to the owners of its houses. Gramercy Park was a well-tended oasis where some of the city's most eminent figures resided, and remained an elegant hint of a gracious urban life which was bustled aside by the pressure of commercial life.

Volunteer firemen fought heroically against the fires of 1835 and 1845. Despite their well-equipped fire-engines (top left), they were helpless in the face of the disaster, which wiped out most of the financial district (map above). Some of the last Dutch commercial buildings were lost in this fire.

The Merchant's Exchange (left) stands in desolate ruins after the 1835 fire, but it was soon rebuilt. Trinity Church (right), was rebuilt in 1839, with a brownstone facade.

Two Nations in the 1830s

Disturbing changes were taking place in New York in the 1830s. Sickness and ill-health, crime, poverty, intemperance and social disorder aroused fears that the moral fiber of the republic had been eroded. The poor lived in overcrowded homes which lacked light and ventilation, and where sanitary facilities were unknown. Their streets were awash with filth. As the victims were the poor, however, there was little inclination to confront the causes of so much misery. During the depression following the war with Britain in 1812, over 16,000 individuals received public relief, and even larger numbers were on relief during the depression of 1837.

Religious and humanitarian leaders feared the effects of over-generous relief, calling for the moral reformation of the poor. The link between poverty, ignorance, and intemperance led humanitarians to call for expanded provision of public schools, and restricted provision of liquor licenses. A savings bank was created to encourage the poor to develop habits of thrift.

New York merchants and lawyers took the lead in the national mobilization for benevolence. The Bible Society, the Home Missionary Society, and the Sunday School Union were sustained by gentlemanly patrons. But in the 1830s, less than half of the city's aldermen could be classed as "rich." The new politics turned increasingly upon the votes of the large, amorphous wards in which the mechanic and not the gentleman was dominant.

An elegant private house at the corner of University Place and Twelfth Street.

The 1834 mayoral election was the first to be decided by a genuinely popular vote (map below). Gulian Verplanck, political satirist, former Democratic congressman and genial bon viveur, received the Whig nomination. His opponent was the Tammany candidate and supporter of Jackson, Cornelius Lawrence. The three days of balloting were marred by riots and mob violence, especially in closely-contested wards such as the Sixth, where Irish Democrats attacked Whig committee rooms. The mayor summoned mounted troops to quell the disturbances. The Whigs elected a majority on the Boards of Aldermen and Assistant Aldermen, but Lawrence narrowly defeated Verplanck.

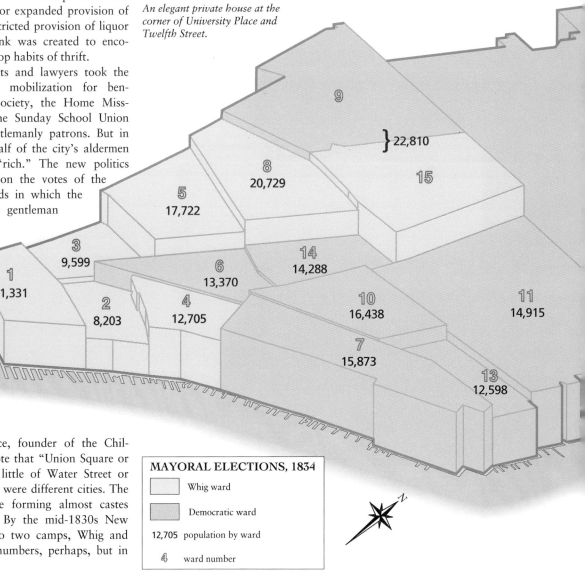

MAYORAL ELECTIONS, 1834
Whig ward
Democratic ward
12,705 population by ward
4 ward number

Charles Loring Brace, founder of the Children's Aid Society, wrote that "Union Square or the Avenues know as little of Water Street or Cherry Street as if they were different cities. The poor and the rich are forming almost castes toward one another." By the mid-1830s New York was dividing into two camps, Whig and Democratic, equal in numbers, perhaps, but in little else.

The rich in the 1830s lived in attractive Italianate row houses, were attended by the best society physicians, and carefully instructed their servants to keep the street in front of their houses swept clean. Wealthy New Yorkers supported the Whigs. Engravings like "The Poor in Winter" (below right) not only represented the plight of the poor, but through the child watching from the window, suggested the role of Christian concern to unite rich and poor.

MANHATTAN'S WARDS

By the 1830s the chasm between New York's rich and the elegant life of Fifth Avenue, and the city's poor, living in slums such as Five Points, was deepening. This is reflected in the widely contrasting assessments of wealth by ward in 1833 (below).

12
11,808

$22,531,600

$10,173,050 $8,690,000 $6,918,676 $4,762,200

$10,956,120 $7,165,035 $7,685,805

$5,613,250 $4,452,400

$6,851,551

$6,489,080 $4,047,300

$2,351,300 $5,497,200

REAL ESTATE ASSESSMENT, 1833

$2,351,300

assessment by ward

Croton Water

By the 1830s, the city faced a crisis. Water for cooking and consumption could no longer safely be drawn from wells within the city boundary. Water was brought by the hogshead to private homes, but the poor were forced to rely on well-water made palatable by adding spirits. The Temperance campaigners soon vigorously called for a municipal provision of water.

New York experienced recurrent outbreaks of yellow fever and the deadly cholera. A polluted aquifer, overcrowded housing, the lack of sewers, public ignorance of basic sanitary precautions, and the existence of foul and polluting industries near wells and residential areas contributed to an unprecedented mortality rate. In 1830 there was one death per 39 inhabitants.

In 1837 the construction began of the dam, aqueducts, tunnels, piping, and reservoirs which would provide the city's water. The Croton River in upper Westchester county was dammed near its mouth on the Hudson. Water was carried by 150 miles of pipes throughout the city. By 1871, there were 340 miles of pipes in place.

By the end of 1844, just 6,175 houses had been connected to the system. But Croton water had a dramatic impact upon domestic hygiene and interior design. By the middle of the decade, baths and running water were being built in the best private homes. For most New Yorkers, it

would be more than half a century before private baths were generally available. Public bathing facilities, which charged 3¢ general admission, became one of the many rituals of urban life.

Croton water had another, inadvertent beneficial consequence. The decline in the amount of water drawn from the city's wells resulted in a rise in the water table which flooded many cellars. Addressing this problem (only the larger houses had cellars), the city built sewers in many residential streets. By 1852, 148 miles of sewers had been constructed.

The Manhattan Company, founded in 1799, created New York's first water supply system, with a reservoir at Chambers Street (depicted above in 1825). The plan (below) shows the route of the Croton Water Aqueduct into the city, which was completed in 1842. This epic undertaking was largely built by immigrant workers, mostly Irish, who manfully rioted in 1840 when the contractors tried to reduce laborers' wages from $1 to 75¢ a day.

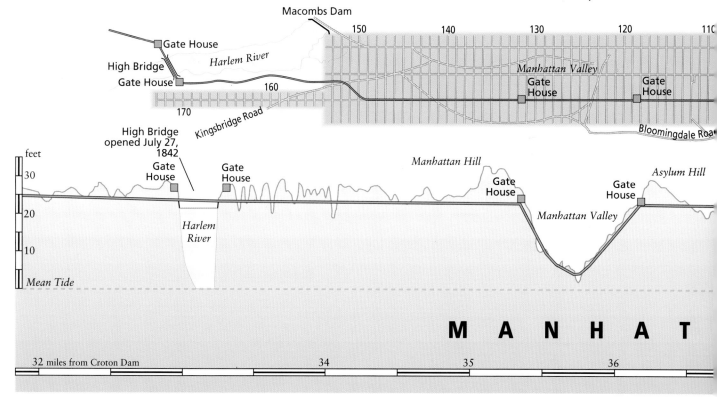

The Croton water aqueduct was a continuous underground canal of stone and brick masonry, which ran 32 miles to the Harlem River Valley. It crossed the river in two iron pipes along the High Bridge, which was 1,450 feet long and built of hewn granite. Additional pipes were added in 1864 (right). Water then ran by conduit and pipes to a receiving reservoir (35 acres in what later became Central Park at 86th Street) holding 150 million gallons. The magnificent Egyptian-style distributing reservoir (capacity 20 million gallons, below) stood on Fifth Avenue at 42nd Street, on the present site of the New York Public Library.

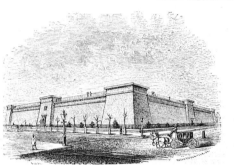

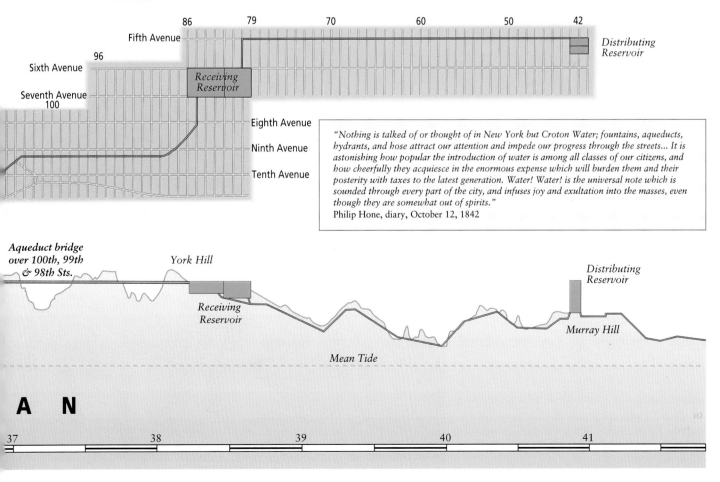

"Nothing is talked of or thought of in New York but Croton Water; fountains, aqueducts, hydrants, and hose attract our attention and impede our progress through the streets... It is astonishing how popular the introduction of water is among all classes of our citizens, and how cheerfully they acquiesce in the enormous expense which will burden them and their posterity with taxes to the latest generation. Water! Water! is the universal note which is sounded through every part of the city, and infuses joy and exultation into the masses, even though they are somewhat out of spirits."
Philip Hone, diary, October 12, 1842

Fernando Wood's New York

Fernando Wood was the dominant presence in the complex political battles of the 1840s and 1850s. He led an undistinguished life before being elected to Congress in 1840, where he was an unyielding supporter of slavery and the South. Wood mastered the Bowery, the heartland of Tammany Democracy, while keeping in line the brothel-keepers, toughs of the dock wards, and the Five Points saloon element who became the illegal voters, ballot-box stuffers and "hitters" who assured Democratic victories. To respectable New Yorkers, Wood was a creature of everything that seemed threatening in the city. His political skills and corruption marked Wood as a demagogue. In personal life he was personable, even fastidious, and remained far removed from the "gaslight" political forces he led.

Wood was unscrupulous, dishonest and a rather attractive man. The corruption synonymous with his name began in earnest with his second term, which coincided with the financial panic of 1857. Major public works, like the construction of Central Park, bolstered Wood's support, but an alliance of citizen's groups, alarmed at the growth of the city's taxes, united behind a Democratic paint merchant, Daniel F. Tiemann, who won the mayoral race by a majority of 43,216 to Wood's 40,889.

The city's Irish supporters remained loyal to Wood, and re-elected him for a third term in a tightly-fought election in December 1859. The champion of the Southern cause, Wood was mayor of New York City when the Civil War broke out in 1861.

Between the Bowery and Broadway lay two places which stood for Fernando Wood's New York: on Centre Street, three blocks east of Broadway, was the Tombs, the city's prison; two blocks further to the east was the notorious Five Points, the worst slum, it was said, in the world. The whole area, on land reclaimed from the site of the Collect Pond, was rough and dangerous. "From Canal to Chatham Street", one guide book noted, "there is not the slightest sign of cleanliness or comfort."

Finished in 1838, the Tombs was built in the style of Ancient Egyptian architecture. Within the Tombs there were two prisons. The outer building held a women's prison, enclosing a courtyard used for hangings, and a male prison which contained 150 cells in four tiers. Half of the male prisoners were illiterate and uneducated. Those convicted of the most serious crimes were housed on the damp ground floor, while the least serious were on the upper tiers.

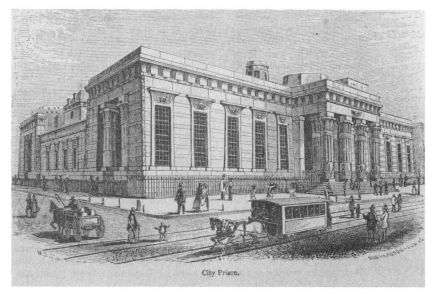

City Prison.

The role of the Tombs was to regulate the world of Five Points.

Five Points, around the intersection of Park Street and Worth, was a warren of narrow streets and decayed, foul-smelling buildings with a nationwide reputation for murder and vice. At its heart was the Old Brewery, a tenement in which rooms cost $2 to $10 per month and which housed uncounted hundreds in the greatest squalor. It was the most densely occupied building in the city, containing at one time 1,200 persons. In the eyes of the city, those who lived there were poor, verminous, uneducated, and degraded by poverty, intemperance and vice. They were largely of foreign origin.

The city's response to poverty, destitution and lawlessness was the building in the l830s of "The Tombs" (above), a sombre fortress prison on the site of the old Collect Pond. The severe depression of 1837, recorded in Edward W. Clay's " The Times" (below), brought European social problems disturbingly close to the national celebration of American independence. A mob stands before a bank which has suspended specie payments; begging and drunkenness dominate the scene. Memories of the 1837 depression came flooding back with the 1857 economic collapse.

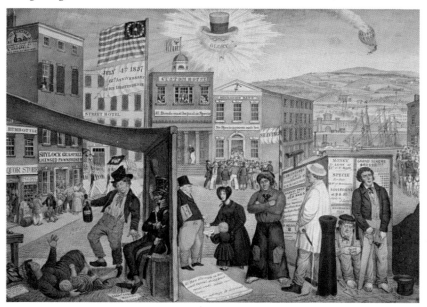

Slum life: Wood's New York was a city of saloons and overcrowded tenements. The rum shop (below) and the many brothels (map, right) brought degradation and vice into the very homes of the poor. The connections between vice and politics remained one of the city's most enduring social problems.

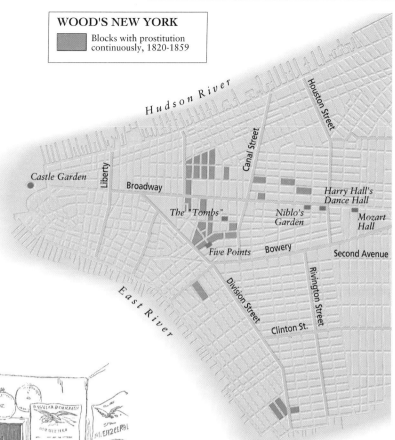

WOOD'S NEW YORK

Blocks with prostitution continuously, 1820-1859

Hudson River

Castle Garden

Liberty

Broadway

Canal Street

Houston Street

The "Tombs"

Niblo's Garden

Harry Hall's Dance Hall

Mozart Hall

Five Points   Bowery

Second Avenue

East River

Division Street

Rivington Street

Clinton St.

John Clancy, editor of the New York Leader, *and John Kelly were Tammany "sachems" or leading "braves." Republican political opponents, led by Harpers Weekly, sought to blacken them with political cartoons (left) portraying them as candidates of the liquor groceries, porter houses and "the infamous dens of Gambling and Lewdness."*

The three-cornered mayoral elections in 1859 were tightly fought (map, right). By this time, Wood had broken with Tammany Hall, and set up his own political machine (Mozart Hall). He competed vigorously with his old allies for dominance of the city's Democratic electorate. He was re-elected, with the help of his Irish supporters. The electoral rate also shows the continued loss of residential areas in the lower wards.

1363 923 1178
22

982 861 583
12

2091 2008 1974
20

1609 1609 1771
16

1411 826 835
19

1441 2112 2348
9

1576 1574 1472
21

1411 1496 957
8

733 1461 1257
15

2064 1825 1421
18

665
5

884

1011

243 221 175
3

1638 1013 365
14

2576 2231 1799
17

1110 1340 153
6

820 548 273
1

155 156 163
2

1464 513 262
4

913 1189 773
10

2207 1767 1087
11

1849 1275 1034
7

1272
13

1081

873

MAYORAL ELECTIONS, 1859

	Wood, Mozart Hall
	Havemayer, Tammany Democrat
	Opdyke, Republican
665	Number of votes cast
5	Ward number

New York and its Benevolent Culture

The cultural life of 19th century New York City was clearly divided along class lines, with a thriving popular world of entertainments, theaters, circuses, and exhibitions centered on the Bowery. The popular audiences flocked to the Broadway Theater where a vast Stars and Stripes was on patriotic display, a rebuke to other theaters which catered to foreign tastes.

The New York upper class preferred its culture to be well-combed and benevolent. Wealthy New Yorkers were fascinated by Italian opera at the Park Theater. The Grand Opera House and the Academy of Music also catered to the new taste for serious music.

At the end of this period the merchant Peter Cooper donated a large Institute on Astor Place for self-improvement and education, which became the location of many large political meetings. The Astor Library and the Mercantile Library also on Astor Place reflected the belief in self-improvement and the secular benevolence of the city's wealthy.

The city was changing so rapidly in the 19th century that writers seldom seem to have tried to write about the common life of the city. The representative figure was Washington Irving, who wrote entertaining satires and pious biographies of national figures. William Cullen Bryant, after Irving the preeminent man of letters in the United States, was editor of the *New York Evening Post*, and author of romantic nature poems. Edgar Allen Poe, who lived in New York in the 1830s was the restless and brilliant author

of *The Mystery of Marie Rogêt*, 1842 (based upon the celebrated New York murder case of Mary Rogers) and other horror stories.

Writers of the younger generation in New York, like Herman Melville and Walt Whitman, lacked the patronage of wealthy merchants to assure their path. They found the writer's life in New York blighted by unfair copyright laws, a conservative literary establishment, and a public uninterested in disturbing images of American life. Books fashionable in London found a ready audience, to the great regret of American writers. Original literary geniuses like Poe, Melville, and Whitman were not to the taste of New York.

The sympathy felt between New York writers and artists in this period was based upon a web of social and cultural associations, from the "Bread and Cheese Club" founded in 1824 to the artistic and literary Century Club of 1847. The "Hudson River School," preeminently Thomas Cole and Asher B. Durand, celebrated the love of nature they shared with the writers.

Urban tensions which remained submerged in New York culture occasionally were caught up in contemporary political issues. In 1849 the Astor Place Opera where the English tragedian William Macready was playing, was the focus for resentment on the Bowery at the sycophancy of the city's elites before all things English. On the night of May 10, a throng flowed up the Bowery and tried to force their way into the theater. To disperse them the militia fired into the crowd, killing 22 people.

The elegant structure of the Astor Place Opera House (left, seen looking west along Astor Place) dominated a refined residential neighborhood, home of John Jacob Astor, Philip Hone, and important civic institutions such as the Astor Library (1854, enlarged 1859, 1881), and the Cooper Union (1859). After the 1849 riot, the Opera House was purchased by the Mercantile Library Association, and housed a library of 120,000 volumes by the 1870s. Walt Whitman (top) and Herman Melville (above) regularly attended the Astor Place Opera House (Donizetti's Lucia di Lammermoor was a particular favorite). Melville, but not Whitman, joined the men of "good sense and respect for order" who petitioned Macready to perform again at the Opera House after the 1849 riot.

BENEVOLENT NEW YORK

🏛 museum / cultural institution

🎭 theatre / Opera House

♪ popular entertainment

🏠 residence of New York authors

✒ author's birthplace, with date

📖 journals / publishers:
  1 New York Aurora
  2 New York Tribune
  3 The Broadway Journal
  4 Knickerbocker Magazine
  5 The Democratic Review
  6 The Literary World
  7 The New World
  8 The Evening Mirror

Restell's Palace
Columbia College   50th Street

Fifth Avenue
Fourth Avenue
Third Avenue

Crystal Palace   40th Street

Second Avenue

Broadway
30th Street

First Avenue

Fifth Avenue Theatre
Madison Square
Gramercy Park

Grand Opera House
Sixth Avenue
20th Street

Eleventh Avenue
Tenth Avenue
Ninth Avenue
Eighth Avenue
Seventh Avenue

Herman Melville
1847-50

Union Square

Nilson Hall
Academy of Music

American Bible Society

Astor Place Opera   10th Street

E.A.Poe 1837
Clinton Hall
Astor Library

J.F.Cooper 1833-6
Cooper Institute

E.A.Poe 1844
Tivoli Theater
Vauxhall Garden Theater

E.A.Poe 1837
J.F.Cooper 1833

Pfaff's Café
African Grove
Niblio's Garden & Theater

Houston Street

Richmond Hill Theatre

Harry Hill's Dance Hall

Mulberry Street
Bowery

Niblo's Garden

Greenwich Street

Canal Street

Broadway
Olympic Theatre

Division Street

Broadway Theater
American Theatre

National Theater
Italian Opera House
Theater in Mt. Vernon Gardens

Bowery Theater

Anthony St. Theater
Lyceum Theater
City Theater

American Art Union

Franklin Theater

Water Street

Park Theatre
Peale's Museum

Chatham Garden Theater

Barnum"s American Museum

Fulton

East River

Herman Melville 1820's

E. A. Poe 1844

E. A. Poe 1844

Washington Irving 1784

Luman Reed 1832

Custom House

Castle Garden
(used for concerts and popular entertainment).

Herman Melville 1819

Hudson River

N

New York provided a thriving world of entertainment – from Harry Hill's Dance Hall on Houston Street to the elite Park Theater – as well as many cultural and educational institutions which owed their existence to enlightened benevolence (map above). The city also provided a home and inspiration to many of America's foremost writers and men of letters and the celebrated artists of the "Hudson River School."

Benjamin Baker's A Glance at New York, *first performed in 1848, introduced the immensely popular New York fire boy Mose (below) and his girlfriend Lize. Mose was an attempt to represent the slang, customs and dodges of New York street life in the 1840s. The city's newspapers lined Printing House Square (seen from the Park in this engraving from 1868). The New York Times had been located here since 1858.*

The Crystal Palace exhibition of 1853, located to the west of the Croton distributing Reservoir on Fifth Avenue, is illustrated below; it was an important expression of the optimism of the age.

Central Park

Central Park, built between 1857 and 1860, was the first urban park in America, for many years the largest, and one of the handsomest examples of 19th-century romantic landscape architecture.

The first proposals for a park came from highminded and idealistic men, but the project was taken up by New York's politicians in 1851 when the healthful and civilizing mission of a public park became wedded to the practical notion that it would be a good investment. The park would trigger off growth in property values in the sparsely-settled region far above the Croton reservoir on Fifth Avenue at 42nd Street.

Frederick Law Olmsted, co-designer with Calvert Vaux of the winning design, was appointed Superintendent of the park in 1857. He accepted no kickbacks from the Park workforce, and kept local politicians at arm's length. In an age of rampant corruption and blatant stock market fraud, New Yorkers were awestruck at public works on this scale being conducted with integrity. It restored faith that the city could function for the public betterment.

New York in 1850 was divided by class, religion and race, as well as by politics. The respectable classes feared rowdiness and violence in the streets. Olmsted saw the Park as a way to educate the tenement-dwellers, and to enhance the sense of community connecting rich and poor, Irish immigrant and Episcopalian Yankee. A nattily-uniformed police force, and a widely publicized set of regulations governing behavior in the park, were successful in maintaining order. There were 7,839,373 visits to the Park in 1866, but only 110 arrests were made.

The Park today is no longer quite the terrain designed and constructed by Olmsted. The profusion of large trees, railings, macadamized roadways, specialized play areas and games-fields affords little of what Olmsted hoped visitors would experience: the unfolding of vistas, the contemplative delights of varied landscapes and perspectives.

Frederick Law Olmsted and Calvert Vaux were joint-winners of the competition to design Central Park in 1857, with their "Greensward" design (below). The park was intended to please both poor and rich alike, enhancing a sense of urban community.

The site of what was to become Central Park was probably the ugliest on the island, with two shantytowns inhabited by rag-pickers (below) whose pigs and goats roamed freely. Walls to keep out wandering pigs were built to protect new plantings.

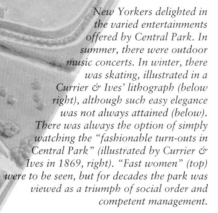

New Yorkers delighted in the varied entertainments offered by Central Park. In summer, there were outdoor music concerts. In winter, there was skating, illustrated in a Currier & Ives' lithograph (below right), although such easy elegance was not always attained (below). There was always the option of simply watching the "fashionable turn-outs in Central Park" (illustrated by Currier & Ives in 1869, right). "Fast women" (top) were to be seen, but for decades the park was viewed as a triumph of social order and competent management.

The map (right) is a facsimile of a survey showing the land incorporated into Central Park, made in 1856. The tract of land, running two and a half miles north from 59th Street, between Fifth and Eighth Avenues, was rocky, swampy and pestiferous.

Chapter 6 "New York will be alive ..." 1860–1898

An aerial perspective (looking northwards) of New York in the 1860s. Castle Garden can be seen at the foot of the Battery. A ship passes between the Battery and Governor's Island. The striking semicircular building is Castle Williams, erected by the U.S. Army in 1811 and converted to a military prison in 1912.

"This is a wonderful city ... There is a special fitness in the first syllable of its name, for it is essentially New, and seems likely always to remain so... The only old things here are yesterday's newspapers... A few years hence and Boston will be a place of the past, with a good history no doubt, but New York will be alive." (Charles Eliot Norton, in a letter to James Russell Lowell, 1861).

"The New Yorkers have got Aladdin's lamp, and build palaces in a night. The city is gay, entertaining, full of costly things,– but its lavish spending does not result in magnificence, it is showy rather than fine, and its houses and churches and shops and carriages are expensive rather than beautiful. Architecture is not practised as a fine art, it is known here only as a name for the building trade." Charles E. Norton.

As the commercial center of New York moved north after the Civil War, the city was turned upon its head. The street life and commercial life of Federal New York centered around the area above City Hall. By the 1870s, Union Square was beginning to seem a little "downtown." Fashionable life was concentrated on the narrow strip of land between Fourth and Sixth Avenues, from 8th Street in the south up to 40th Street. Central Park still lay a pleasing carriage ride further north, but even along its eastern and western perimeters new, elegant houses were being constructed. The solid brick and brownstone homes which lined the streets adjacent to this fashionable district of restaurants, saloons and stores housed the city's bourgeoisie. The story of the great move uptown is suggested by the experience of Dr. Sloper in Henry James's *Washington Square* (1881) who had lived "... in an edifice of red brick, with granite copings and an enormous fan-light over the door, standing in a street within five minutes' walk of the City Hall." As "the tide of fashion began to set steadily northward ... and when most of his neighbors' dwellings (also ornamented with granite copings and large fan-lights) had been converted into offices, warehouses, and shipping agencies

... he determined to look out for a quieter home. The ideal of quiet and of genteel retirement in 1835 was found in Washington Square ..."

The Gilded Age?

The formerly bustling streets off lower Broadway below Canal Street were now lined with commercial buildings, deserted and gloomy at night. As the commercial districts were drained of their after-hours life, the new offices and commercial structures became increasingly monumental. The sharp edge of the Fuller Building jutted assertively uptown. New Yorkers called it the "Flatiron building," a homely metaphor for a richly-decorated masterpiece of commercial over-statement designed by Daniel Burnham & Co. Artists loved it; photographers, whose romance with the city was in full swing by the 1890s, saw the Flatiron as an icon, like the Statue of Liberty and the Brooklyn Bridge, which defined the spirit of the age. It was soon surpassed by

A postcard depicts the bustling entrance to the Brooklyn Bridge.

other, taller "cathedrals of commerce," but Burnham's building, with its implausible wedge shape, retained a place in the city's affections never achieved by grander and more implacable structures. New York was not a city, nor the Gilded Age a period, given to excess modesty. It was no longer enough simply to be in business and to make money, like Rowland H. Macy with his huddle of brick buildings on 14th Street. It was the department store-owner A.T. Stewart, with his cast-iron palaces, who correctly predicted the commercial aspirations of the city.

By the time of the Civil War, only five wood-frame buildings survived on Pearl Street to remind the commercial world of the modest origins of its new prosperity. Eighty-nine such structures still lined Allen Street, which proceded northwards, parallel to the Bowery, but four blocks to the east. The prosperity of a street could be measured by the proportion of wooden to brick and stone buildings. Prosperity moved through the city selectively, and somewhat mysteriously, leapfrogging certain streets or whole districts. This was, indeed, Adam Smith's "invisible hand" at work. Commercial calculation, and perhaps the "tide of fashion", seemed to determine the city's growth. What was left behind in the veritable Klondike atmosphere of real estate speculation were the poor. The Irish tenements on the west side, the German ones in "Kleindeutschland," and the overcrowded Jewish and Italian slums to the east of the Bowery, worried the respectable and alarmed sanitary reformers. Although the world of the tenements was not without its own social order and values, from the outside it was a terrifying site of illness, vice, and degradation.

Who was to blame for such inhuman conditions? The conventional view placed responsibility upon the residents, whose personal habits, ignorance and habitual drunkenness caused the deterioration of housing. Poverty and ignorance were to blame; but the lack of vigorously enforced housing laws, and a political culture in which the owners of the city's limited real estate saw their properties merely as sources of income, allowed a fatal indifference to prevail.

By the 1870s the city could boast of two substantial tall buildings, the Tribune Building (260 feet) and the Western Union Building (230 feet); an elevated railroad which spread soot, ash and noise as it carried passengers along Greenwich Street from the Battery to Cortlandt Street; elegant restaurants, like Delmonico's on Fifth Avenue; and hotels to rival the most luxurious in Europe. The mansions of the rich attracted gaping crowds along Fifth Avenue. At night the city's lavish entertainments set new standards in a country never quite comfortable with pleasures of the flesh and the vine.

The "Tide of Fashion"

It was no easier after the Civil War, than it had been a generation earlier, to see beneath the bustle, to penetrate to the meaning of such a place. After all, the nation's largest city was not a bystander as the future of the nation unfolded. The days of rivalry with Boston and Philadelphia were now over. Other cities, such as St. Louis and Chicago, were growing faster than New York after the Civil War, but the supremacy of the city in size, as well as its economic, commercial and cultural predominance was unchallenged. New York was intensely scrutinized.

A view of Wall Street in the 1870s. Compare the earlier view of this scene on page 47.

Visitors trailed the long, interesting route from the Battery to Central Park, from the Five Points to Fifth Avenue, in search of the truth about this intimidating city. They did not always like what they saw, and indeed there was much to dislike about New York. Why would the city boast so about every building? Why insist that Central Park was the finest, handsomest, most picturesque place on the planet? After his visit to New York Anthony Trollope wrote: "The first question asked of you is whether you have seen the Central Park, and the second as to what you think of it. It does not do to say that it is fine, grand, beautiful, and miraculous. You must swear by cook and pie that it is more fine, more grand, more beautiful, more miraculous, than anything else of the kind anywhere."

"...Long lines of incomplete macadamization, "lakes" without water, mounds of compost, piles of blasted stone, acres of what may be greensward hereafter but is now mere brown earth; groves of slender young transplanted maples and locusts, undecided between life and death, with here and there an arboricultural experiment that has failed utterly and is a mere broomstick with ramifications. Celts, caravans of dirt carts, derricks, steam engines, are the elements out of which our future Pleasaunce is rapidly developing." George Templeton Strong describing the chaotic scenes in Central Park, 1859.

Harlem High Bridge in 1868.

Rapidly enhancing real estate values meant that even the most impressive residence, the most imposing commercial edifice, could not withstand the "tide of fashion." At the same time, rapid growth ensured that the city was never complete, never without scaffolds, plaster dust, and piles of rubble. The city carried its past lightly – so much so that to outsiders, who knew little of the city's history, it seemed to be scarcely a community at all. New York seemed a place without roots, or reverence for the past. It would be possible to point to the formation of the New-York Historical Society, the many "Knickerbocker" societies devoted to localities or family groups with historical associations, with the inevitable after-dinner addessses on "The Old Taverns of New York," to suggest that some groups within the city actively cultivated versions of the past. But it is with the actions of people, and not their sentimental attachments, that New York revealed its willingness to reinvent itself, generation after generation. This process was possible because the majority of New Yorkers in fact had slight roots in the city. Edith Wharton's family and Theodore Roosevelt's could proudly point

"Broadway is an eminently cheerful street. On every hand one sees evidences of prosperity and wealth. No unsuccessful man can remain in the street. Poverty and failure have no place there. Every sin shows its most attractive guise in Broadway."
James Dabney McCabe, *Lights and Shadows of New York Life; or, The Sights and Sensations of the Great City,* 1872.

to the presence of ancestors in the city in the early 18th century. Their friends, class-mates at school, and social acquaintances were equally likely to be drawn from a select group of old families whose names were familiar to New Yorkers over many years. For all the social leadership such people provided (or failed to provide: there was much complaint about an "absent" leadership from the city's old families and richest inhabitants), and for all their unassailable position on Mrs. Astor's "400," her list of those who might be invited to one's home, there was a swirling, bustling city around them, inhabited by the recent immigrants from Germany, who had settled in "Kleindeutschland" (the 10th, 11th, 13th and 17th wards on the East Side); or the Irish who made up the majority of the city's laborers and had pioneered the experience of living in tenements since they had begun to emigrate in the 1840s.

Two Nations
By the 1880s, small communities of Italians and East European Jews looked as though they were soon to become extremely large communities. Everywhere the city was filled with people who had come from elsewhere to New York, usually for the express purpose of making their way in the city's many industries or its commerce. Without sustained historical roots in the community, they were untroubled by the passing of quaint Dutch customs, or the demolition of inconveniently small colonial-era buildings. They were no less determined than the oldest families in the city to create a life which accorded with their own sense of communal loyalty, family values and personal ambition. They too applauded furiously at performances of plays which reflected their lives, read newspapers in their mother-tongues, and most decidedly told and retold family stories.

They were not less truly New Yorkers for going directly about their business single-mindedly, amidst a profusion of confessional, regional and voluntary associations, lodges, fellowships and clubs which they summoned into existence. Gentlemen from old New York families had their Union Club on Fifth Avenue; a contemporary directory in 1892 records the existence of 136 religious societies on the lower East Side (93 were Russian-Polish, with the rest classified as Austro-Hungarian); by 1914 there were 534 benevolent societies in the same district, embracing virtually every immigrant family. These communities – the embodiment of the Two Nations which made up New York – brought their histories, their stories, to the city.

For many years the earlier arrivals cared little for the cultural luggage of the newcomers, and it was made easy to discard the past with little more than a shrug of relief. "Once I live in America," asserted Jake, the hero of Abraham Cahan's novella

An immigrant arrives, 1870
"So as properly to make my own place in the procession ... as I conceived the custom of the country to be, I made it my first business to buy a navy revolver of the largest size, investing in the purchase exactly one-half of my capital. I strapped the weapon on the outside of my coat and strode up Broadway, conscious that I was following the fashion of the country. I knew it upon the authority of a man who had been there before me and had returned, a gold digger in the early days of California ..."
Jacob Riis, The Making of an American, (1901).

Yekl (1896) "I want to know that I live in America. *Dot'sh a' kin' a man I am*! One must not be a *greenhorn*. Here a Jew is as good as a Gentile." Cahan, who had emigrated to the lower East Side in the early 1880s, was perhaps the first immigrant of his generation to become a widely-read novelist. (He was also an influential editor of the Yiddish-language *Forverts*, and an active figure within the Socialist Party.) *Yekl* told the story of an immigrant who welcomed the escape from being a "greenie," and who embraced American life in all its gaudy vulgarity. For Cahan, Jake's fate was not essentially tragic: it was a "whimsical transformation," affecting hundreds of thousand of immigrants. The old world, with its pieties, had to be discarded to make one's way in the new. Assimilation and a vociferous American-ization" movement demanded nothing less.

Nonetheless, it was the collective memories of the assimilated, or those halfway along that road, which created the strongly ethnic neighborhoods of the city and which gave a particular fervor to the celebration of traditional saints' days in Little Italy, and shaped the patriotic joy in "Kleindeutschland" when the Prussian army defeated the French at the battle of Sedan in 1870.

A view looking south from a new station on the Metropolitan "el", at the intersection of 9th Avenue and 81st St.

Civil Wars

News of the attack on Fort Sumter reached New York in time for late editions of newspapers on April 12, 1861. The city's Democratic politicians wanted to avoid secession at all costs, and had repeatedly called for compromise with the South; they knew that many jobs depended upon the cotton trade. The attack on Fort Sumter was greeted with public indignation, and when the Sixth Massachusetts Regiment marched through the city on the 17th (on its way to defend the capital), they were greeted with cheers. On the 19th the proud Seventh New York Regiment marched down Broadway. To the delight of Unionists, the hotels and stores competed to display the largest flags, banners and pennants and the street was lined by patriotic crowds.

But the mood of unity did not long survive the military disasters at Bull Run in the summer of 1861, and the bumbling and inconclusive conduct of the war. New York had become a center for opposition to the war. Price-gouging, insider trading, and the provision of inferior material to the army did much to deepen cynicism.

In March 1863, Congress passed a national conscription law, which was deeply disliked in New York where the wealthy made no pretence at personally serving in the army. When General Robert E. Lee invaded Pennsylvania in early July 1863, the Governor of New York, Horatio Seymour, sent 20,000 troops to block Lee at Gettysburg, thus denuding the city's garrison.

The draft lottery began in New York on July 11,1863. On Monday the 13th a riot began when firemen from Fire Engine Company

Number 33 (the 'Black Joke' Company), who thought they should be exempt from the draft, broke up the lottery at the Ninth District Provost Marshal's office at Third Avenue and 47th Street and set the building on fire. When the fire's smoke was seen, riots broke out. Across the city on July 14, a hunt for all African-Americans began. Those caught were beaten, murdered,

Volunteer firemen (above, in a Currier & Ives engraving) were the initiators of the riots, which left many wounded on both sides (map, below). The total recorded deaths were 119, with damage to property of $1.5 million.

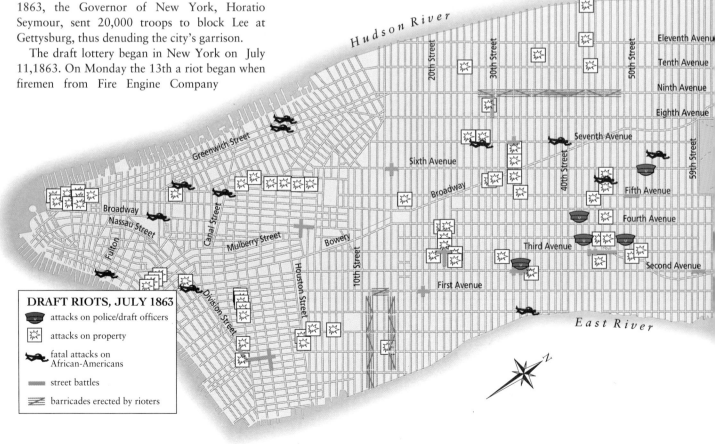

DRAFT RIOTS, JULY 1863

- attacks on police/draft officers
- attacks on property
- fatal attacks on African-Americans
- street battles
- barricades erected by rioters

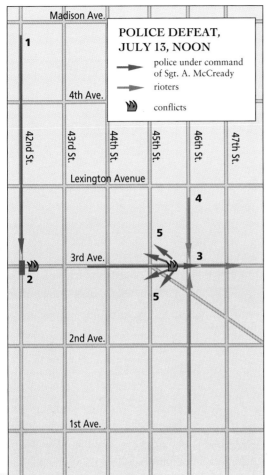

POLICE DEFEAT, JULY 13, NOON

→ police under command of Sgt. A. McCready
→ rioters
🔥 conflicts

Madison Ave.
4th Ave.
42nd St. 43rd St. 44th St. 45th St. 46th St. 47th St.
Lexington Avenue
3rd Ave.
2nd Ave.
1st Ave.

1 14 police move east along 42nd St., picking up reinforcements of 30 men
2 Police form line across 3rd Ave., blocking rioters
3 Rioters are driven north to 46th St. and 3rd Ave.
4 Rioters' reinforcements arrive, blocking police retreat
5 Police force breaks up. Individuals attempt to escape through nearby houses. Many beaten up and left for dead

On July 13, a detachment of the Provost Marshal's guard, heading south on Third Avenue, was halted at 42nd Street by an angry mob. Soldiers fired on the crowd, and were chased away by the unimpressed rioters. A howitzer was used in a vain attempt to clear Second Avenue. On Lexington Avenue the homes of prominent Republicans were robbed and torched. Later that afternoon, the police fended off attackers at Mulberry St. But it was too late for Colonel O'Brien of the Eleventh Regiment, New York State Volunteers, who had ordered the use of the howitzer on Second Avenue – he was identified by a mob and brutally murdered. Looters attacked the Colored Orphan Asylum and wanted to lynch the terrified inhabitants.

and sometimes even mutilated. There were many examples of ordinary citizens hiding the victims, and when practicable intervening to halt the worst abuses. Soldiers and police did their best to protect the African–Americans and undoubtedly saved hundreds of lives.

The draft riots caused a fierce revulsion against New York, and especially against the immigrant Irish, who were prominent in the violence. Court records reveal the rioters to be "respectable people with jobs and settled homes, a fair cross-section of New York's younger male working class." The attacks on police and on African-Americans soon expanded to opportunistic and arbitrary targets: the homes of the rich and shops which sold to the poor were looted. Saloons and brothels were attacked; much liquor was stolen. Bullion stored in the Sub-Treasury building on Wall Street was secreted by officials to Governor's Island.

Disorder ceased at the end of the week when regular army troops reached the city, relieving the exhausted police. Among the troops sent to the city from Gettysburg was the all-Irish Sixty-ninth Regiment, which tore through the ragged barricades of the Irish rioters. Within the draft riot there was a murderous race riot, as well as a civil war among the New York Irish. At the height of the rioting there were over 700 African-Americans taking shelter at the New York Police Department on Mulberry Street.

70th Street 80th Street 90th Street
ral Park

POLICE VICTORY, JULY 13, 4.45 pm

→ police → rioters 🔥 conflicts

1 Large mob, moving south, threatens police H.Q.
2 200 police head west to Broadway to block mob
3 50 police flank mob from west
4 50 police sent north to flank the mob from east at 4th St.
5 Mob surprised, dispersed, beaten and chased by police

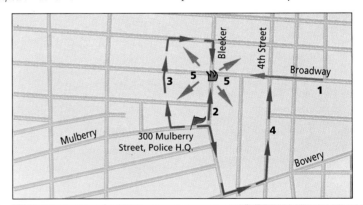

Bleeker
4th Street
Broadway
Mulberry
300 Mulberry Street, Police H.Q.
Bowery

Shops (such as the drug store, right) became targets for looting rioters. New York became a transit camp for troops during the war. Tents were set up on the Battery (far right).

"Kleindeutschland"

From the 1840s, newly-arrived Germans settled into a 400-block area east of the Bowery, north of Division Street, and south of 14th Street along the East River. They called it "Kleindeutschland" (little Germany). They were not the largest immigrant group in New York (the Irish came earlier, and in greater numbers) but German New York was to be found in a distinct geographical area, while the Irish lived in tenements widely dispersed across the city. It gave German life an extraordinary vitality.

Avenue B (known as "German Broadway") was the main commercial street of Kleindeutschland, lined with small shops and basement factories. Everywhere there were goods piled on the canopied sidewalks. Nearby Avenue A was lined with lager beer halls, oyster saloons and grocery stores. On the Bowery, there was an abundance of people strolling, enjoying the bustle and the "gartens" where families drank beer (the Atlantic Garden, a great hall lined with bars and lunch counters, was always crowded).

Americans admired the industriousness, moral values and character of the Germans, who replaced the long-vanished New York Dutch as custodians of these solid values. The common American stereotypes of the Irish emphasized the opposite qualities. The German-Irish comparison was irresistible, for there was an ethnic division of labor between the two communities. The Germans were mainly engaged in manufacturing, the Irish were employed in general labor or domestic service. There were "German" trades in New York in the 19th century (tailors, boot and shoemakers, cabinet and piano-makers, cigarmakers, and upholsterers), and Germans played a major role in creating the trades union movement of the city.

There were three waves of German emigration to America: approximately 1.3 million Germans came before the Civil War. The second great wave followed the Civil War, 1865-1879, and the third began in 1880, and included nearly 1.8 million. The German immigrant population of the United States was significantly more urbanized than the population of either Germany or the United States as a whole.

In New York, Germans originally settled in the 11th ward along the East River, where small artisan workshops, shipyards, slaughterhouses,

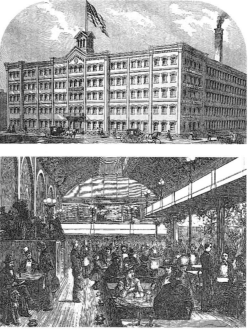

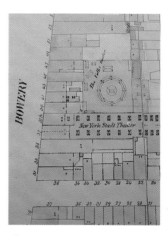

The Bowery Amphitheatre was bought in 1854 and reopened as the Stadttheater, catering to mass audiences for German-language melodrama, farce, and popular entertainments (map above).
The Steinway & Son piano factory (left) relied heavily on German skilled labor. Vast beer halls, such as the one depicted on the Bowery in 1877 (below left), were the focus of German social life in Kleindeutschland.

"On every side [at the Atlantic Garden] are family groups, father, mother, and children, all merry, all sociable, all well-behaved and quiet. There is not the remotest danger of insult or disturbance, or need of the presence of any policeman"
Harper's Monthly, 1871.

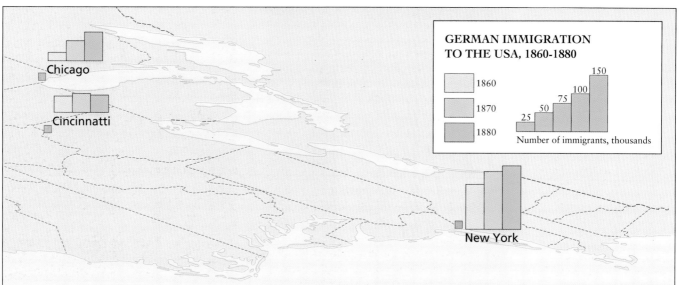

GERMAN IMMIGRATION
TO THE USA, 1860-1880

	1860
	1870
	1880

25 50 75 100 150
Number of immigrants, thousands

Chicago

Cincinnatti

New York

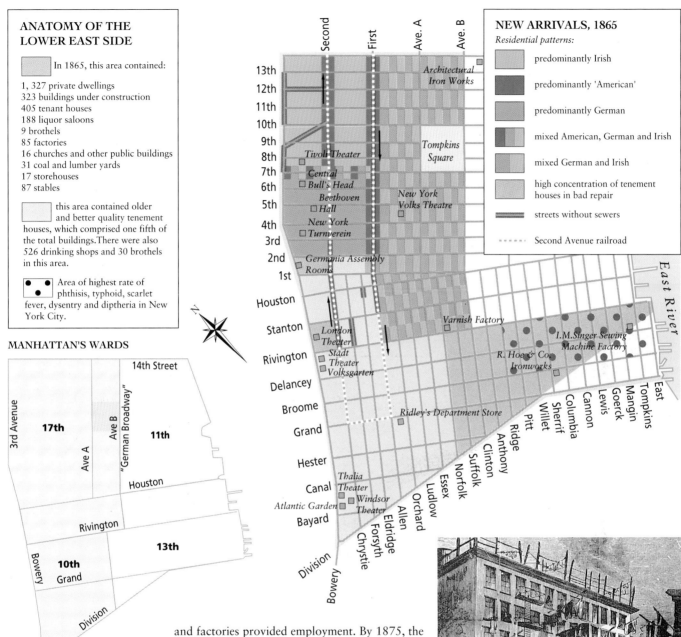

ANATOMY OF THE LOWER EAST SIDE

In 1865, this area contained:

1, 327 private dwellings
323 buildings under construction
405 tenant houses
188 liquor saloons
9 brothels
85 factories
16 churches and other public buildings
31 coal and lumber yards
17 storehouses
87 stables

this area contained older and better quality tenement houses, which comprised one fifth of the total buildings. There were also 526 drinking shops and 30 brothels in this area.

Area of highest rate of phthisis, typhoid, scarlet fever, dysentry and diptheria in New York City.

MANHATTAN'S WARDS

14th Street

3rd Avenue

"German Broadway"

Ave B

Ave A

17th

11th

Houston

Rivington

Bowery

10th

13th

Grand

Division

NEW ARRIVALS, 1865
Residential patterns:

predominantly Irish

predominantly 'American'

predominantly German

mixed American, German and Irish

mixed German and Irish

high concentration of tenement houses in bad repair

streets without sewers

Second Avenue railroad

Second

First

Ave. A

Ave. B

13th
12th
11th
10th
9th
8th
7th
6th
5th
4th
3rd
2nd
1st

Architectural Iron Works

Tompkins Square

Tivoli Theater

Central

Bull's Head

Beethoven

Hall

New York Volks Theatre

New York

Turnverein

Germania Assembly Rooms

Houston

Stanton

London Theater

Varnish Factory

Rivington

Stadt Theater

Volksgarten

I.M. Singer Sewing Machine Factory

R. Hoe & Co. Ironworks

Delancey

Broome

Grand

Ridley's Department Store

Hester

Canal

Thalia Theater

Windsor Theater

Atlantic Garden

Bayard

Division

Bowery

Chrystie

Forsyth

Eldridge

Allen

Orchard

Ludlow

Essex

Norfolk

Suffolk

Clinton

Attorney

Ridge

Pitt

Willet

Sherrif

Columbia

Cannon

Lewis

Goerck

Mangin

Tompkins

East

East River

East of Avenue A, below 22nd Street, lay some of the largest industrial works in New York. The Gas Light Co. occupied two whole city blocks below East 22nd Street. Nearby were chemical works, iron foundries, gasometers, and brick factories (map, above right). The tenements on the lower East Side were industrialized. The archetypal tenement (far right), with brawling residents and dilapidated conditions, encouraged the German immigrants to seek better housing in Yorkville and Harlem.

and factories provided employment. By 1875, the 10th, 11th, 13th and 17th wards were over 64 percent German. These wards were strongly differentiated between Protestants and Catholics. The largest German community in New York were the Bavarians, who settled where the Prussians were fewest. By 1875 German-Americans made up one-third of the city's population.

Nonetheless, by the 1870s the process was well underway of emptying Kleindeutschland of its "upper" levels of society. Immigrants from East Europe, the *Ost Juden*, were beginning to settle in 10th and 13th wards. A building boom in Yorkville (83rd to 89th Street on East Side) led to a northwards shift of German-American population. Kleindeutschland long remained a center of German-American cultural life, but by the turn of the century only a small percentage of the city's German-born residents remained.

Fifth Avenue

Running north from Washington Square to the Harlem River, Fifth Avenue first appears on the Commissioners' 1811 plan. Until the 1840s it was one of many unpaved dirt avenues which stretched to the north of the built-up city. An assortment of cottages, farms, inns, cattle markets, and horticultural nurseries lined the avenue, much as they had done since the days of the early Dutch settlers.

New Yorkers invented Fifth Avenue inadvertently in 1834 when the socially-prominent Brevoort family decided to build a Georgian mansion on the northwest corner of Fifth and 9th Street. The Brevoort house was followed in 1854 by the Brevoort Hotel, an elegant hostelry with an upper-class clientele. To wise-cracking New Yorkers, the residents of the street were *Fifth Avenoodles*. The churches with prosperous memberships, like the First Presbyterian, Fifth Avenue Presbyterian, and the Church of the Ascension, were built near the new homes of their parishioners, mostly doctors, merchants, auctioneers, manufacturers, architects, and bankers. Two mayors lived on Fifth Avenue in its early years (the sperm-oil merchant Ambrose Kingsland, and George Opdyke, whose home was attacked during the Draft Riots in 1863). A "Fifth Avenue" address has since been one of the most distinguished in the nation, signifying social position, prosperity, and respectability.

The Fifth Avenue Hotel (above) at Madison Square, was opened in 1858, and was a favorite meeting place of New York's Republican leaders. The white marble-faced mansion of A.T. Stewart (left), the department-store owner, was located at 34th Street. It was built in 1864 on the site of Samuel P. Townsend's mansion, and was then the most costly private residence on the continent, costing over $2,000,000.

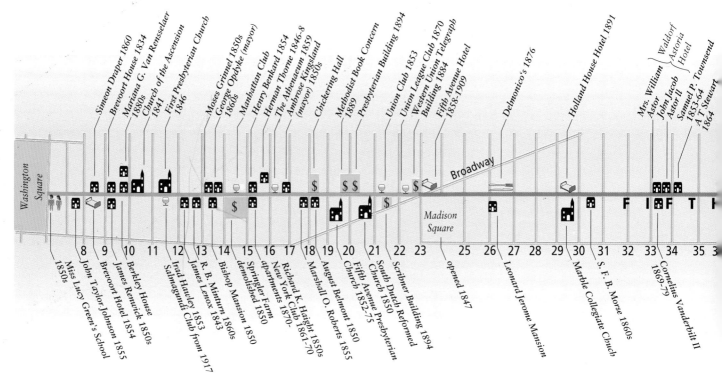

When the Vanderbilts spent $15 million on four mansions on Fifth Avenue (right), they succeeded in making even the neighboring 'palace' of Madame Restell, the abortionist, look modest. The house of August Belmont (center) was considered the last word in luxury and magnificent ostentation. The Waldorf Astoria Hotel (below) was a monument to the rivalry and ultimately, the business acumen, of two of New York's great families, the Waldorfs and Astors. Delmonico's Restaurant (below right) opened at 26th Street in 1876, and was a haunt of fashionable New Yorkers. In 1898, the restaurant moved to grander quarters on 44th Street.

In the 1840s and 50s, Fifth Avenue was lined with comfortable brownstones, and exuded an atmosphere at once placid and self-approving – an atmosphere of "established repose", as Henry James described it in *Washington Square* (1881). By the end of the century, Fifth Avenue was dominated by the ostentatious mansions of the super-rich of the Gilded Age. After the Civil War the simple Greek revival row houses went out of fashion. The windows and doorways of Manhattan residences became more ornate. New Yorkers were more prosperous, and the wealthy adorned their homes accordingly. The finest residences in the city were soon outpaced by even larger piles, erected by railroad magnates, industrialists and other Gilded Age notables. Fashions in hotels changed: the Brevoort was dwarfed by the Fifth Avenue Hotel, which was in turn overtaken by the Waldorf-Astoria.

The homes of the wealthiest men in the city vied for new levels of ostentation and magnificence. Both August Belmont and Leonard Jerome, stellar presences in the city's fast set, had private ball-rooms, theaters, and art galleries in their homes. Madame Restell, the notorius abortionist, kept a coach and a magnificent pair of grays for her afternoon rides in Central Park. The architect Richard Morris Hunt's mansion for William H. Vanderbilt (at 52nd Street, 1879-81) introduced a dizzying world of fantasy chateaux, Romanesque towers, and other architectural extravaganzas, reflecting the yearning for ever greater levels of majesty and conspicuousness.

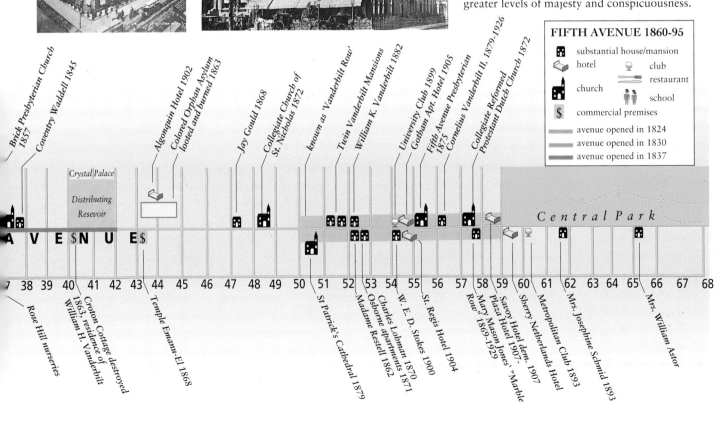

FIFTH AVENUE 1860-95

substantial house/mansion
hotel
club
church
restaurant
school
$ commercial premises
avenue opened in 1824
avenue opened in 1830
avenue opened in 1837

A City of Stores

Before the Civil War, the principal shopping area of New York was located along Broadway, from City Hall to Houston Street. The greatest showcase of New York fashion was the A.T. Stewart dry goods store on Broadway between 9th and 10th Streets, a building with a cast-iron facade painted white, universally known as Stewart's "marble palace." The increasing specialization of retail trade was reflected in the rapid growth of stores which carried a wide assortment of "dry goods" which included silks, fabrics for dresses, calicos, muslins, velvets, as well as a range of manufactured items such as shawls, suits, ladies' underwear, gloves, cloaks, and bonnets.

Rowland H. Macy opened a small fancy dry goods store in 1858 at 204-6 Sixth Avenue. Small retailers, especially those located far from the main area of retail shopping, had to find ways to compete with much larger operations. They learned to specialize, and Macy took the lead in underselling the competition and in aggressive advertising. Year by year Macy increased the variety of goods sold. He opened departments selling furnishings, furs, household goods, kitchen utensils, and books, and added a soda fountain in 1870. Macy led the way with annual clearance sales (1863), and the prominent seasonal display in the shop windows of dolls and mechanical toys (1874). The motto "We will not be undersold" appeared in 1875. The term "department store" did not come into widespread use until the 1890s, but by the time of Macy's death in 1877 his store was New York's first fully-fledged department store. Lord & Taylor, in their fine store on Broadway, kept

Macy's "dry goods" store opened in 1858

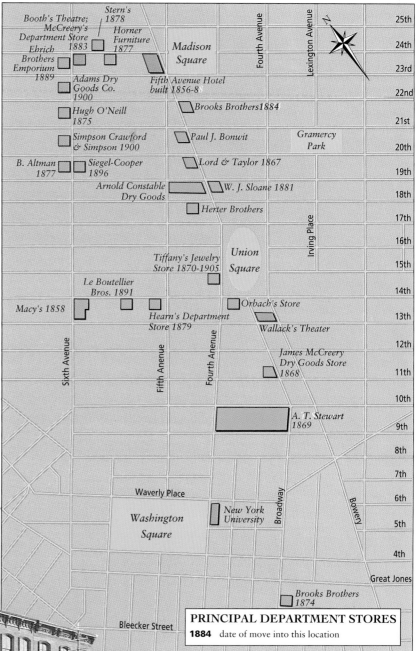

PRINCIPAL DEPARTMENT STORES

1884 date of move into this location

pace with Macy's, sometimes adding a line before their rivals, sometimes following.

By the 1890s, location had become central to success in retailing. The 10th Street location once occupied by A.T. Stewart was by the 1870s distinctly unfashionable. Step-by-step, the clubs, fashionable hotels, elegant restaurants, theaters, and houses of worship joined the move north, leaving behind them a spectacular, somewhat rundown legacy of buildings to be put to other uses. In 1902 Macy's moved 20 blocks north to Herald Square, after 43 years on Sixth Avenue.

Stewart dominated retail dry goods trade in New York, and was the largest importer in the nation. On average, 15,000 customers a day entered his 10th Street store (right), with average daily receipts of $60,000. Customers entered a large, bustling building (Stewart employed 320 clerks and 200 cash-boys) and were directed by a polite usher to the desired counter.

The central rotunda extended through all above-street floors

A.T. Stewart's "dry goods" store: Floor Guide

Sub-cellar:
boiler room, steam pumps, parcel desk, cellarage

Basement:
carpet assembly

First floor:
salesroom, haberdashery, silks, bonnets, cloaks

Second Floor/Third Floor
Carpets, ladies suits, shawls

Fourth Floor:
ladies wear manufactory

Fifth Floor:
furs and upholstery manufactory

Sixth Floor:
laundry, storeroom

From the Iron Age to the Skyscraper

Throughout much of the 19th century, the streets of New York City were lined by five-story buildings. The larger commercial structures reached the imposing height of eight stories. Until 1892, the tallest building in the city was the graceful 284-foot spire of Trinity Church. The growing demand for limited amounts of good commercial real estate put a premium on height and speed of construction. In addition, the owners demanded an imposing quality of design which asserted the cultural significance of the enterprise.

The age of "cast-iron" building was introduced to New York in 1848 by James Bogardus, who built a factory for himself at Duane and Center Streets described as "the first complete

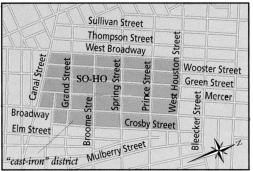

Cast-iron was widely used in New York until the 1870s, and the "cast-iron" district in SoHo (left) contains the largest number of surviving examples of this technique. At the close of the 19th century, many more cast-iron buildings stood in the streets of lower Manhattan. Today, 250-300 still stand, mainly because threats of demolition in the 1960s were fiercely contested by preservationists.

cast-iron edifice ever erected in America, or the world." Bogardus's factory was made of pre-cast uniform materials, bolted together. Cast-iron buildings were produced at Daniel Badger's Architectural Iron Works at Avenue C and 14th Street, and at the Novelty Iron Works at the foot of 12th Street and the East River, for shipping in prefabricated form to destinations across the country. Cast-iron buildings could rapidly be erected by semi-skilled workers, circumventing the traditional control exercised by artisans over the process of construction. Behind cast-iron fronts, brick would normally be used. Beams and floors were normally made of wood.

The only limitation on cast-iron buildings was the number of stories people were willing to walk up stairs. Otis's steam-powered "safety hoister" demonstrated at the Latting Observatory, adjacent to the Crystal Palace in 1853, carried viewers to a 225-foot platform overlooking the street. Within four years the first cast-iron building to incorporate an elevator, the Haughwout Building, was erected on Broadway.

With each successive story of a masonry building, the additional weight required ever-thicker walls to support the structure. The most valuable commercial space on the ground floor was thus

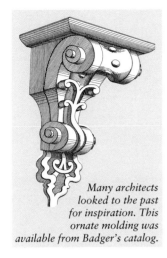

Many architects looked to the past for inspiration. This ornate molding was available from Badger's catalog.

lost in the attempt to build additional stories which obtained lower rents. With the completion of William LeBaron Jenney's Home Insurance Building (1883-4) in Chicago, the skyscraper revolution began in earnest (the term "skyscraper" was first applied to tall buildings in 1891). Jenney switched in mid-construction to a metal cage of iron which supported the weight of the structure. Of all the early New York skyscrapers, the 20-story-high Flatiron, built by Daniel H. Burnham & Co. in 1902, was the first skyscraper to become a major cultural icon. New York artists and photographers were enthralled by the jutting, wedge-shaped building which seemed to express the new assertiveness of technology and the modern urban spirit.

D.H. Burnham's richly decorated Flatiron (below), opened 1902, created a bridge between the picturesque world of gaslight New York and the skyscrapers of the aggressive 20th century commercial market. Stieglitz, Steichen, and Alvin Langdon Cobura took photographs of the Flatiron from Madison Square Park.

287 Broadway (left) was built in 1871, and designed by John B. Snook, better known for his design of the first Grand Central Station. It was commissioned as an office building housing lawyers' chambers and a bank. The mansard roof with dormer windows derives from the French Second Empire, and was added some time after the original building was completed. Its six floors were accessible by Otis elevator.

Daniel Badger's Architectural Iron Works issued a catalog of prefabricated iron parts which could be shipped all over the country by railroad or boat. Virtually every architectural style (right and above) was available – no decoration was too delicate to be cast in iron. Patterns were carved, and pressed into damp sand to form moulds into which molten metal could flow.

Mass Transit

Traffic in 19th-century New York moved at the ambling speed of horse-drawn cart, wagon and omnibus. City roads were churned up by traffic, inadequately paved, and poorly drained. The first regular public transports in the city were the omnibuses running along Broadway in the early 1830s, large lumbering stagecoaches like the vehicles which travelled between New York, Boston and Philadelphia. They carried twelve passengers (for a 10¢ fare) and were notoriously slow and overcrowded. The horse railway, introduced in 1832, ran over smooth metal rails laid in the middle of the street. The horse railways were faster than the omnibuses and, with a fare of 5¢, they deservedly won popular support.

Broadway remained "a Babel scene of confusion." By 1860, the 14 horse-railroad companies carried more than 38,000,000 riders annually. It was increasingly obvious that surface transportation could never solve the city's congestion. Traffic would have to be carried below the streets, in tunnels, or above, in the form of elevated railways. Proposals for "underground railroads" and elevated "cable railroads" soon followed. The trial of the first "el," along Greenwich Street, took place on July 3, 1868. But the cable propulsion system was too noisy and the supporting iron stanchions were frail and dangerous.

In 1871, the Ninth Avenue "el", operated by the New York Elevated Co., opened as far as 30th Street, and was extended northwards in 1878. The Rapid Transit Commission, empowered by the State Legislature to lay out routes and assign franchises to private

The Beach Pneumatic railway (left) opened in 1870. Two small tunnels under Broadway ran for 312 feet. A Roots Patent Force Blast Blower pushed the car, which was lavishly decorated and carried 22 passengers, down the tunnel, and then sucked it back. But the Beach line failed and was soon forgotten. In 1869 construction began on the Grand Central Depot (below), which served three of the city's main railroad lines. Rail commuting was now becoming practical.

THE ELEVATED RAILROADS OF NEW YORK

—— original 9th Avenue line
● 9th Avenue line stations (with date of construction)
—— line of elevated railway
● "El" stations
▬ main railroad stations

operators, was formed on July 1, 1875. Routes were awarded on Second, Third, and Sixth Avenues, and by 1880 the "el" had reached the Harlem River.

By 1890, the city possessed a mass transit system with greater total mileage than London. The city had become unthinkable without the overcrowded "el", but by the 1890s it was clear that a second great round of building was required to enable the mass transit system to keep pace with the growing city.

The first trial of the "el" (above right), ran in 1868. By 1875, the "el" was reaching northwards (above) and stations (above left), trestles, girders, and black smoke all contributed to a fall in property values along "el" routes. The growing volume of rail transport created a need for larger city depots. The New York and Harlem Railroad station (right, in 1860) was replaced by Grand Central Terminal.

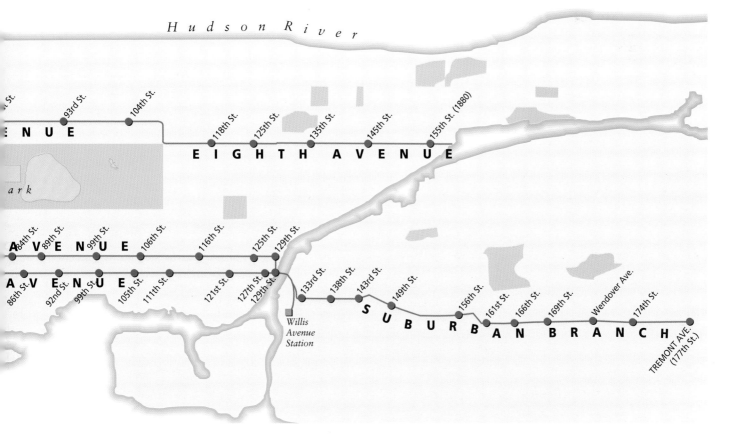

Icons and Engineers

The city of New York has 2,098 bridges, but just one, crossing from City Hall Park in lower Manhattan to Brooklyn Heights, is 'the Great Bridge,' the famous Brooklyn Bridge. No other structure has been so often painted, etched, lithographed, photographed and written about.

Until the completion of the Golden Gate in San Francisco, no bridge in America so completely effected the marriage of form and function as the Brooklyn Bridge. Until 1903, with a length of 6,106 feet, it was the longest suspension bridge in the world. Its solid granite towers rise 272 feet above the mean water line. When opened in 1883, it encouraged many Americans to rethink the role of engineers and designers. They were the invisible heroes of urban life, the ones who made things which worked day in and day out. In an era when the most spectacular buildings could be demolished when it no longer served an economic purpose, or be left stranded as commercial life moved uptown, bridges and tunnels were permanent. They connected the city to the surrounding communities, and made possible the city's growth. The quality of their design and the civic optimism of the capital investment they represent, remain.

The designers of the Brooklyn Bridge, John A. Roebling (a German immigrant who settled in Pittsburgh in 1831) and his son Washington Roebling, were the first of these largely invisible men, civil engineers who had mastered the

techniques of designing and building bridges. They were followed by C.F. Holland, builder of the Holland Tunnel, and O.H. Ammann who built the George Washington bridge. The solution of complex design problems inherent in such large structures (if the bridge itself hung on flexible steel cables how could it be stable?) was only the beginning of the process which led to the construction of the bridge: the Roeblings had to promote the idea of a bridge, and deal with politicians as well. Characteristically, it was a private sector enterprise, funded by bonds issued by the cities of Brooklyn and New York. Toll for pedestrians was one cent.

A photograph by William Henry Jackson taken in 1890 (above) looks south along the Harlem River to Washington Bridge in the foreground (built in 1888) and High Bridge. The oldest remaining bridge connecting the city to the mainland, High Bridge was built between 1837 and 1848 as part of the Croton Aqueduct system, carrying about 24 million gallons of water a day into the city. It was designed on Roman architectural principles, with massive stone arches over both land and water. By 1939, few of the old arches remained.

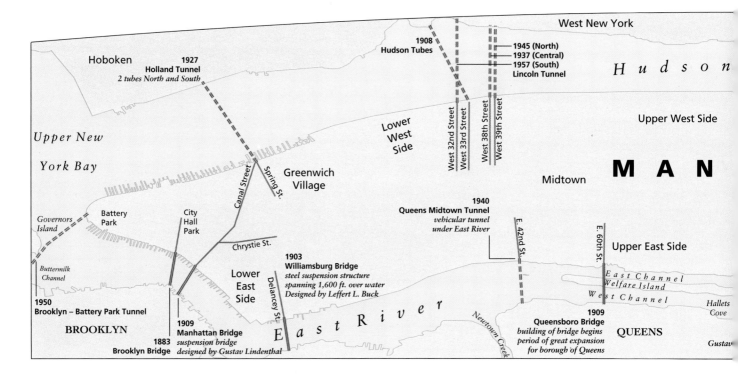

"Seen even from afar, this bridge astounds you...walk across it, feel the quivering of the monstrous trellis of iron and steel... and you will feel that the engineer is the great artist of our epoch...", Paul Bourget, Autre-mer; impressions of America, 1895
The views (above) of the Brooklyn Bridge, still under construction in 1877, and the completed bridge (right) both appeared in Harper's Weekly. *On May 19, 1885, Robert E. Odlum jumped off the bridge for a bet (top right). He died 45 minutes later from internal hemorrhaging.*

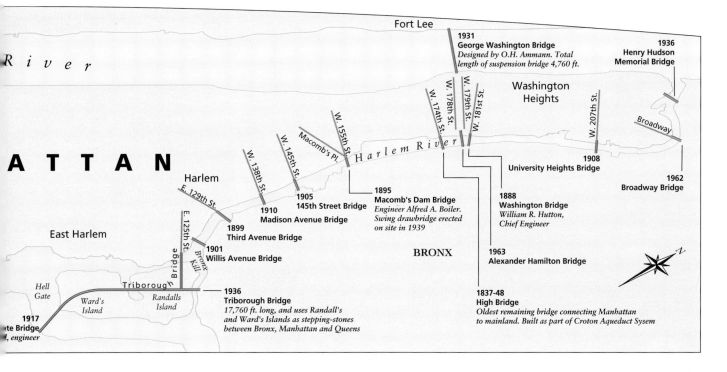

River

ATTAN

Fort Lee

Washington Heights

Harlem

East Harlem

BRONX

Hell Gate

Ward's Island

Randalls Island

Triborough Bridge

Bronx Kill

E. 125th St.

E. 129th St.

W. 138th St.

W. 145th St.

Macomb's Pl.

W. 155th St.

Harlem River

W. 174th St.

W. 178th St.

W. 179th St.

W. 181st St.

W. 207th St.

Broadway

**1931
George Washington Bridge**
Designed by O.H. Ammann. Total length of suspension bridge 4,760 ft.

**1936
Henry Hudson
Memorial Bridge**

**1908
University Heights Bridge**

**1962
Broadway Bridge**

**1888
Washington Bridge**
*William R. Hutton,
Chief Engineer*

**1895
Macomb's Dam Bridge**
*Engineer Alfred A. Boiler.
Swing drawbridge erected
on site in 1939*

**1905
145th Street Bridge**

**1910
Madison Avenue Bridge**

**1899
Third Avenue Bridge**

**1901
Willis Avenue Bridge**

**1936
Triborough Bridge**
*17,760 ft. long, and uses Randall's
and Ward's Islands as stepping-stones
between Bronx, Manhattan and Queens*

**1963
Alexander Hamilton Bridge**

**1837-48
High Bridge**
*Oldest remaining bridge connecting Manhattan
to mainland. Built as part of Croton Aqueduct Sysem*

**1917
te Bridge**
, engineer

Tenements

Tenant-houses – later called tenements – were a solution to the housing crisis of 19th-century New York. The custom of converting three- or four-story one-family houses into use by two families per floor was already far advanced by 1850. Additional tenement buildings, usually of wood, were often erected on the back portion of city lots, increasing the density of population without greatly altering the city's appearance.

The first large blocks of apartments erected for artisans, such as Gotham Court, on Cherry Street in the 7th Ward, took the problem a half step forward. As you approached this imposing brick structure down the narrow alley which ran its length, the first thing you noticed were the clothes lines running out of virtually every window, signs of unceasing housewifely struggle against dirt, and the pungent odors of a dozen national traditions of cooking. The inadequate provision of sewerage and the difficulty of airing out mattresses, explained the building's terrible mustiness. A closer inspection revealed the overwhelming presence of vermin and lice.

It was only in 1864, when there were already 15,000 tenements in the city, that the first systematic sanitary survey of New York was completed. The physicians who visited every building in each of the 29 sanitary inspection districts, found a system of housing and industry which was unregulated, threatening to health and subject to persistent overcrowding. Legislation followed to establish the Metropolitan Board of Health, which was given significant powers to inspect housing and improve sanitation. The long struggle to improve housing conditions in the city had begun.

The New Tenement House Law of 1879 restricted the proportion of the lot which could be built upon, and mandated the elimination of "dark" rooms. Design competitions sought to improve the standards of design; proposals were made to widen the worst streets, thus eliminating notorious slums like Mulberry Bend and the Five Points. Legislation in 1887 and 1895 set out improved standards, and required more rigorous inspection. But the growth of population, the impact of low pay and unemployment, and the political and financial interests which insulated the largely invisible owners of the tenements from responsibility for the condition of their properties, undermined the efforts of reformers. There were 42,700 tenement houses in Manhattan in 1900, housing 1,585,000 people. Of all the problems the city confronted in this period, the tenement was the most intractable.

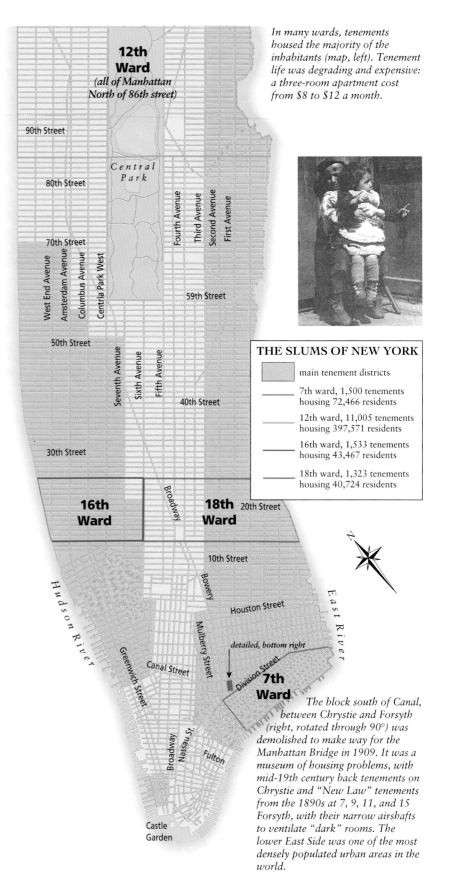

In many wards, tenements housed the majority of the inhabitants (map, left). Tenement life was degrading and expensive: a three-room apartment cost from $8 to $12 a month.

THE SLUMS OF NEW YORK

main tenement districts

7th ward, 1,500 tenements housing 72,466 residents

12th ward, 11,005 tenements housing 397,571 residents

16th ward, 1,533 tenements housing 43,467 residents

18th ward, 1,323 tenements housing 40,724 residents

12th Ward *(all of Manhattan North of 86th street)*

16th Ward

18th Ward

7th Ward

detailed, bottom right

The block south of Canal, between Chrystie and Forsyth (right, rotated through 90°) was demolished to make way for the Manhattan Bridge in 1909. It was a museum of housing problems, with mid-19th century back tenements on Chrystie and "New Law" tenements from the 1890s at 7, 9, 11, and 15 Forsyth, with their narrow airshafts to ventilate "dark" rooms. The lower East Side was one of the most densely populated urban areas in the world.

The photographs of Jacob A. Riis, taken in the slums in the 1880s, as well as his newspaper articles, lectures with lantern-slides, and a stream of books illustrated with his own photographs (beginning with How the Other Half Lives, *1890), did much to arouse public concern. Children pose for Riis on the roof of the "Barracks" in Mott Street, while lines of washing partially obscure a rear tenement in Roosevelt Street (far right). Riis' "Bandit's Roost" (right) was taken in an alley off "The Bend," a block (demolished in the 1890s) below Bayard, between Baxter and Mulberry, at the heart of the old "Bloody Sixth" ward in the lower East Side.*

The map below clearly shows how additional tenements were inserted behind city lots. Back tenements had some of the most foul and decrepit conditions in the city.

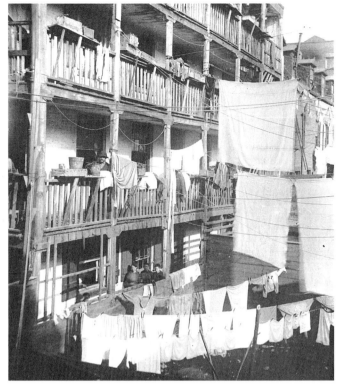

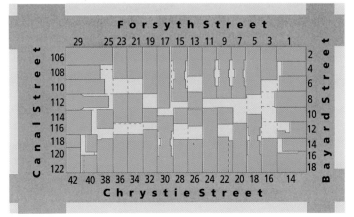

PART 3

"*The New York of today is the projection into space, the product in layout, in architecture, and above all, in its way if life, of "big business." It is a state of mind. Nothing done there is motivated by historic traditions. So far as impinging on its life goes, Hendrick Hudson might as well have landed in Bermuda, and Peter Stuyvesant been governor of Pensacola. It belongs to no region ... It has accepted "finance capitalism, line, hook and sinker ... Great impersonal corporations are of its essence.*"
Christian Gauss, *Park Avenoo and Main Street*, 1938

Elevated railroad tracks, New York City,
late 19th century
New York Transit Museum Archives, Brooklyn

Chapter 7 Greater New York 1898–1945

The 1900 census – the first after the legal consolidation of Greater New York – revealed that there were nearly three and a half million people in the city. The Irish formed a substantial proportion of New York's population, but one which was widely dispersed throughout the five boroughs. "Kleindeutschland" in 1900 had 23 percent of the city's German population, and Germans were even more concentrated in Williamsburg and Bushwick in Brooklyn, where they formed 35 percent of the total population. Half of the city's Italian population lived in the wards adjacent to Canal Street. The residential segregation by province of origin, characteristic of Italian residential patterns in New York, continued after the turn of the century.

The campaign to restrict immigration had its first great success in the 1920s. The National Origins Quota Act of 1921, followed by the Johnson-Reed Act three years later, preserved the national racial and religious mix as it had been before the peak years of the "new immigration." The number of immigrants from Italy, Poland and Russia sharply declined in the 1920s. Immigration from the principal sources of the "old" immigration (Germany, Great Britain, and Ireland) actually rose. This legislation precipi-

The Bowery at night, watercolor, by W. Louis Sontag, Jr.

Riding the "el"...
"*From the vantage point of a window seat, one surveys the slums of Harlem, Ninth Avenue, and the East Side; middle-class Tudor city, Chinatown, and the Bowery; the German and Bohemian quarters of Yorkville; the Wall Street district; the flat suburban reaches of Brooklyn; the hilly jumble of the Bronx; and the quiet tree-shaded streets of Queens. Dingy sweatshops, flophouses, dramatic family groups pass in succession. So, too, do scenes of great beauty: skyscrapers at dusk, glittering rivers, dwindling streets.*" WPA *New York City Guide,* 1939.

tated a remarkable and sustained decline in the number of New Yorkers of foreign parentage and of mixed foreign and American parentage. Immigrant enclaves began to wither away, and the city became less "foreign."

A self-confident city

From the accession of Theodore Roosevelt to the Presidency on September 14, 1901, to the death of Franklin Delano Roosevelt in 1945, New York was at the apogee of its self-confidence. New York during this period was a community with a large manufacturing base. People made things in the city, things which could be weighed, measured, packed, and exported. It was also a period in which

the city grew rapidly, survived the depression, and projected a strong sense of its identity upon the nation. For this task of self-projection New York had an unchallenged supremacy in popular culture, a supremacy which only Los Angeles, and the film industry, seriously challenged.

Trains and tracks looking north from the Grand Central Terminal.

When Americans were entertained, when they sang at home, when they went to vaudeville or the music hall, they were enjoying the fruits of composers, lyricists, and authors who lived and worked in New York. The popular songs were chosen, published, and distributed by New York firms; the simplified sheet music of popular songs, issued for amateur accompanists, were arranged in New York. The music hall as established by Tony Pastor (on 14th Street near Third Avenue), and Weber and Fields (at the corner of 29th Street and Broadway) effectively determined the popular entertainment of Cincinnati and San Francisco. The triumph of Isadora Duncan's appearance at the Metropolitan Opera House in 1908, dancing barefoot on an empty stage, led to a successful national tour and an

New York "the wonder city of the world", New York Central System poster, 1926

appearance before President Roosevelt. The most enduring dance craze of the interwar years, the Charleston, may have been popular in South Carolina as early as 1903, but it became a national enthusiasm when it was first performed in a Broadway play, *Runnin' Wild*, in 1923. The plays which were performed at theaters across the nation were those which had enjoyed success in New York. The decision by booking agencies to form a road company or to send performers across the country was taken by men behind desks in New York. The books which became best-sellers were increasingly likely to have been published by other men, behind other desks, in New York City. There were more people employed in printing and publishing in New York in 1900 than in Chicago, Philadelphia, and Boston combined.

In 1907, when Scott Joplin set up his office at 128 W. 29th Street to compose and arrange ragtime, and in 1917, when W.C. Handy brought his partnership with Harry Pace to New York, it must have seemed that New York was sucking dry the cultural life of the nation. Writers, painters, and musicians were increasingly drawn to the city. In each case there were solid professional reasons. The critical mass of New York culture had no rivals. It was also the most effectively exploited, distributed, and amplified across the nation. The city had (and has) a "plugger" culture, in which money, public relations, and creativity were harnessed together.

Equally, the city's own ethnic diversity – untypical of the nation as a whole – was effectively turned in the 1870s and 1880s into a long-lived popular enthusiasm for Irish sentimental ballads, the "coon songs" (a commercial category: the singers were known as "coon shouters") of the 1890s, the Italian songs popular after 1905, and the vogue for Yiddish songs (like Irving Berlin's "*Yiddle on Your Fiddle Play Some Ragtime*") after 1909. Racial, religious and ethnic stereotypes formed the core of the city's notably sardonic sense of humor. But racism did not always play well in New York, or at least there are hints that other values than dislike of Jews, African-Americans, Chinese, Italians, Catholics, Irish, etcetera, mattered. The world premiere of D.W. Griffith's *The Birth of a Nation* took place at the Liberty Theater in New York on March 3, 1915. A journalist present noted that the audience hissed and booed at the moments when the film made its most blatant appeal to race hatred.

The city was awash with other kinds of self-representations, mixing European realism and immigrant sentiment. *The East Side Ghetto*, Leon Kobrin's Yiddish melodrama

"The Lindy Hop made its first official appearance in Harlem at a Negro Dance Marathon staged at Manhattan Casino some time in 1928... [It] consists in a certain dislocation of the rhythm of the fox-trot, followed by leaps and quivers, hops and jumps, eccentric flinging about of arms and legs, and contortions of the torso only fittingly to be described by the word epileptic... To observe the Lindy Hop being performed at first induces gooseflesh, and second, intense excitement, akin to religious mania..." Carl Van Vechten, *Parties: A Novel of Contemporary New York Life*, 1930.

The Chrysler, Daily News, Chanin, Lincoln, and Lefcourt Buildings, New York City. From a late-1930s postcard.

played before full houses at the Thalia Theater on the Bowery in the 1899–1900 season. The villain, Lefkowitz, a rich lower East Side cloak manufacturer, seduces one of his employees, Anny, the daughter of a traditional Jew with simple and provincial notions. As weeks pass, Anny grows suspicious of the good faith of Lefkowitz, who spurns the idea of marrying her. When her naive, grief-stricken parents go to lawyers and drag the shame of their daughter into a Police Court, they are stunned to hear witnesses who have been bribed, testify that they carnally knew Anny. A young cloakmaker, Liebermann sees the forces of corruption arrayed to destroy Anny and rushes to her side, exclaiming: "To me, Anny! Do not appeal for justice to them. They have no justice for you, for me. I need no witness to your innocence – I see it in your eyes."

Touched by Anny's fate, the audience rose in cheers at the success of a cloakmaker's strike against Lefkowitz. No less than in the Bowery melodramas of the 1840s, New York was the battlefield where justice and injustice did battle. New York was awash in 1900 with cries for justice. Yiddish-language plays about Jewish proletarians did not penetrate deeply into the national conscience, but such stories appeared in English-language fiction (such as Abraham Cahan's novel *The Rise of David Levinsky* in 1917), plays and non-fictional writing, in photography and polemical

"In the century that is dawning Manhattan Island will become little more than an immense clearing house of trade... Within little more than a decade, the region from Washington Square to Central Park has been appropriated for business purposes, and in time the island itself will become a mountainous pile of sky-scraping buildings devoted to banking, business, wholesale establishments, offices, public purposes, hotels, clubs, and theaters."
Frederic C. Howe, *The City: The Hope of Democracy*, 1905.

prose. The struggle of the city's "proletarians" became a major note in the political and economic discontent of this period.

The immigrant impact

Immigrants, and especially the children of immigrants, played a crucial role in establishing the supremacy of New York. Jimmy Durante began his long career as a pianist ("Ragtime Jimmy") in Coney Island. Irving Berlin's career began as a song plugger for the Harry von Tilzer Music Co. Berlin was deft in all facets of the shifting music market. After one year of high school, George Gershwin left school at the age of 15 to become a pianist for a publisher of popular music, accompanying song pluggers on trips to other cities. He was soon working as a rehearsal pianist, piano-roll recording artist (under a variety of pseudonyms as well as his own name), and then, in 1918, as a composer for T.B. Harms & Co., the dominant force in the industry. When these immigrant *wunderkind* came together, the nation reeled. Gershwin's song "*Swanee,*" written in his parents' apartment, was recorded by Al Jolson in 1920 and became one of Jolson's greatest successes, selling 2,250,000 copies. (Four years later Gershwin wrote "Rhapsody in Blue" in that same apartment at Amsterdam Avenue at 110th Street.)

As the leading port of entry for immigrants, and as the destination of choice of so many new arrivals, New York figures largely in the "America letters" sent to family left behind in the old world. From the invention of the *carte de visite* in the 1850s, mass-produced, inexpensive photographs had accompanied hundreds of thousands of such letters, each proudly revealing the new man created by the New World. New York transformed *schlemiels* from the Pale of Settlement and the *shtetl* into gentlemen, princes in the new aristocracy of the dollar. Alas, appearances were all too often deceiving. "Our Sam", writes Mike Gold in *Jews Without Money* (1930) of a Romanian immigrant to New York, "... wore a fine gentleman's suit, a white collar like a doctor, store shoes and a beautiful round fun-hat called a derby." But when Mike Gold's father arrived in

The Empire State Building, from a postcard of the late 1930s.

A Russian radical goes apartment hunting: "*We rented an apartment in a workers' district, and furnished it on the installment plan. That apartment, at eighteen dollars a month, was equipped with all sorts of conveniences that we Europeans were quite unused to: electric lights, gas cooking-range, bath, telephone, automatic service-elevator, and even a chute for garbage.*"
Lev Trotsky, *My Life*, 1930.

New York "I came to understand it was not a land of fun. It was a Land of Hurry-Up. There was no gold to be dug in the streets here. Derbies were not fun-hats for holidays. They were work-hats. *Nu*, so I worked! With my hands, my liver and sides! I worked!"

The Land of "Hurry Up"

With the arrival of electricity, Broadway became the "Great White Way." Light and illumination offered ready meta-

A "sky boy" signals to his mates during the construction of the Empire State Building, 1931. Photograph by Lewis W. Hine. Men at Work (1932).

phors for changes that were taking place in the city. The large, brightly-lit windows of department stores provided a dramatic showcase for goods from all over the world. The city's role as pace-setter in conspicuous consumption was unchallenged. The use of steel frame construction for sky-scrapers meant that windows in the new buildings could be larger. More natural light would enable office workers to be more efficient, to work harder. A strip of lights around the Times Building in Times Square brought the world's news to the city. The new year was greeted by the fall of a ball of light. Photographers carried flashbulbs into the city's notorious tenement "dark" rooms without access to light or ventilation. The pictures they brought back of dank hallways and moldy rooms gave reformers powerful images of neglect. Surveys of sanitary and hygienic conditions brought into view the deteriorating conditions of the tenements. Vice and corruption belonged to the city's "underworld."

What 19th-century reformers understood as the struggle between sunlight and gaslight, between idealism and virtue on one hand, and vice and dissipation on the other, in the 20th century was a struggle for the victory of political reform, reason, honesty, modernity, and (electric) light against the dark, hidden world of social wrongs. But light, the supreme symbol of the enlightenment dream of liberation and reason, carried with it a darker usage of surveillance, interrogation, manipulation. "There is a terrifying abundance of light in this city," wrote Maxim Gorky in 1906 of his visit to New York. "At first it seems attractive... but in this city, when one looks at light, enclosed in transparent prisons of glass, one understands that here light, like everything else, is enslaved. It serves Gold, it is for Gold and is inimically aloof from people..."

A bird's eye view of lower Manhattan, with the East River and Brooklyn in the background. The British erected a fort here in 1693, on the site of the original Dutch Fort Amsterdam, and the military name – the Battery – remained. The circular structure facing the Bay is the West Battery, erected in 1807, and renamed Castle Clinton after the War of 1812. It was ceded to the city for use as a public arena, then remodeled as Castle Garden (1855–1890), the depot where 7,690,606 immigrants were landed. It was converted into an aquarium (1896–1941) and is presently a national monument.

"But Jesus the alcohol. Prohibition will send the entire population of New York into D.T.s if it continues. You go into a restaurant and innocently order clam bouillon and before you know it you are guzzling vitriolic cocktails out of a soup tureen. You order coffee and find yourself drinking red ink. You order tea and find it's gin. There's no escaping drinks." John Dos Passos to John Howard Lawson, November 2, 1920.

Consolidation: Brooklyn and Queens

With a population of just over 1,500 persons at the time of the evacuation of the British army in 1783, the old Dutch agricultural village of Brooklyn (formerly Breuckelen, Broken Land) was a sleepy community. Brooklyn's population expanded more than threefold between 1800 and 1820, and doubled again in the 1820s and in the 1830s. With the annexation of Bushwick and Williamsburgh in the 1840s Brooklyn went from being a good-sized community of 36,236 to an imposing 96,838.

The first regular steam ferry service connecting Brooklyn to Manhattan was opened in 1814

To Charles Dickens, Brooklyn seemed "a kind of sleeping-place for New York" (1867). The opening of the Brooklyn Bridge on May 24, 1883, accelerated the process of integration (map, below). In Francis Guy's painting "Winter Scene in Brooklyn" (below, 1817-20), with its wood houses, pigs, cattle, and free-range chickens, the city had a more humdrum aspect. Leading art world figures in New York judged Guy's style to be "crude and harsh."

(discontinued 1924), and the development of the city became ever more closely tied to that of New York. Parts of Brooklyn – such as the elegant brownstone houses on the Heights – were colonized by real-estate developers as a dormitory community for New York merchants. This development was strengthened by the opening of the Brooklyn Bridge in 1883.

The proud Greek Revival Brooklyn City Hall, 1846-51, was a symbol of surging civic self-confidence. The Union ironclad, the *Monitor*, was built at a shipyard at Greenpoint. The U.S. Navy Yard on the shore of Wallabout Bay, purchased 1801 (abandoned 1966), was a major employer of the German and Irish immigrants from the 1840s.

The census of 1880 revealed that Brooklyn, with a population of almost 600,000, was the third largest city in the nation. It was also a major manufacturing community. Commercial and real estate interests in Brooklyn warmed to the idea of consolidation into a Greater New York, although the referendum of 1894 was carried in Brooklyn by only 300 votes.

BROOKLYN & QUEENS
Modern Brooklyn and Queens:
- parkways
- highways
- streets
- parks
- cemeteries

Historic Brooklyn and Queens:
- city developed 1625-1782
- 1783-1812
- 1813-1867
- 1868-1898

Map labels: NEW JERSEY, MANHATTAN, Hudson River, East River, NEW, Greenpoint, QUEENS, Williamsburg, Governors Island, Brooklyn Heights, Fort Greene, Bushwick, South Brooklyn, Bedford Stuyvesant, Upper New York Bay, Park Slope, Crown Heights, New Lots, East New York, Prospect Park, Greenwood Cemetery, Bush Terminal, BROOKLYN, Canarsie, Borough Park, Flatbush, Bay Ridge, Bensonhurst, Jamaica Bay, Flatlands, Gravesend, FLOYD BENNETT FIELD, Lower New York Bay, Sheepshead Bay, Sea Gate, Coney Island, Brighton Beach, Rockaway Inlet, Rockaway, QUEENS, ATLANTIC OCEAN, N

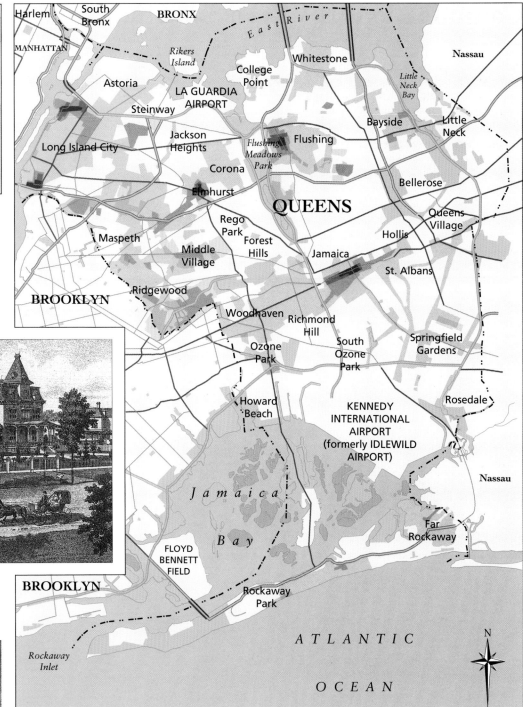

Queens (map, right) has been the site of some of the city's leading events. Flushing Meadows Corona Park has twice been the site of World's Fairs (1939-40 and 1964-5). Shea Stadium was home of the Mets and Jets. Both La Guardia and John F. Kennedy Airports are located in the borough.

The Van Wickel Residence on Clinton Avenue, Jamaica (above) suggests the prosperity and elegance of Queens.

Queens, occupying the land between the East River and Atlantic Ocean, was first settled in the 1630s, and English immigrants soon arrived on the western end of Long Island. Queens County was established in 1683, when it was named after Catherine of Braganza, queen consort of King Charles II. Horse racing (at Salisbury Plains) was organized here as early as 1665.

Throughout the 19th century it remained an agricultural district. Queens entered Greater New York in 1898 and, with the opening of the Queensborough bridge in 1909, the Long Island Rail Road Tunnel, 1910, and the Hell Gate Bridge between Bronx and Astoria in 1917, communication with Manhattan and the Bronx was greatly improved, and Queens was opened for extensive residential development. In 1920 Queens had 469,042 inhabitants. Ten years later it had a population of 1,079,129. In 1990, the population of Queens was 1,951,598 representing just over a quarter of the population of the city as a whole.

Consolidation: The Bronx and Staten Island

Jonas Bronck, the first recorded European settler of the Bronx, arrived in New Amsterdam from Denmark or Sweden in 1639. He leased land from the Dutch West India Company on the neck of the mainland immediately north of the Dutch settlement at Harlem, and bought further tracts from the local tribes. Bronck prospered mightily in the new world. At his death he owned six linen shirts and the largest library in New Netherland.

The development of the Bronx is intimately connected to its strategic place in communications between New York and New England. Control over the bridges across the Harlem River plagued the period of British colonial rule. Kingsbridge, built in 1693 where Broadway reached the Spuyten Duyvil Creek, was a possession of the manor-lords of Philipse Manor. The tolls they charged, like all taxes in colonial New York, were indignantly resented by Bronx

farmers, with crops and cattle to sell in New York. It was angry farmers who built a "free bridge" across the Harlem River which led to the abandonment of the tolls altogether.

The consolidation of the Bronx into New York proceeded in two stages: in 1874 Kingsbridge, West Farms and Morrisania were annexed to New York by the state legislature. Three years before the referendum on consolidation in 1898, the whole of the territory west of the Bronx River was also annexed. In 1890, the population of the Bronx was 88,908. After the IRT subway was extended into the borough in 1904, it rapidly expanded. Life in the Bronx became a haven for upwardly-mobile immigrants seeking a better life than the lower East Side allowed. Within the lifetime of a generation, the Bronx went from being a semi-rural backwater to its status between the wars as an elegant, densely-populated commuter zone.

The development of the Bronx depended upon the communication links which carried employees to and from Manhattan. The electric street trolley (1880s), the bridges of 1885-1905, the construction of the Second and Third Avenue els, and the IRT subway (1908), were each stages in the expanding borough's growth (below left). Life in the Bronx before consolidation was comfortable, even aristocratic, as the substantial Lorillard Mansion in Bronx Park (below) suggests. In the 1840s the Lorillard family built a mill to grind snuff which has been restored (New York Botanical Garden).

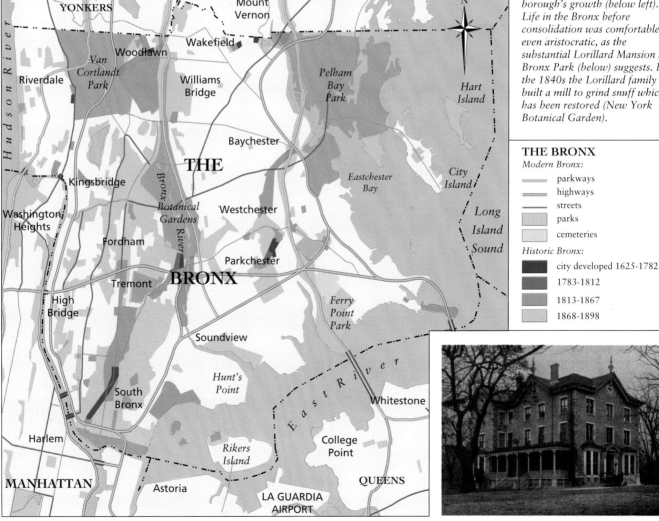

THE BRONX

Modern Bronx:

- parkways
- highways
- streets
- parks
- cemeteries

Historic Bronx:

- city developed 1625-1782
- 1783-1812
- 1813-1867
- 1868-1898

STATEN ISLAND

Modern Staten Island:

- parkways
- highways
- streets
- parks
- cemeteries

Historic Staten Island:

- city developed 1625-1782
- 1783-1812
- 1813-1867
- 1868-1898

The British called Staten Island (map, above) "Richmond" after the Duke of Richmond, Charles II's illegitimate son. The island's inhabitants were sympathetic to the British army of occupation in 1776, supported the South in 1861, and missed the frantic development of New York. For 30 years after the consolidation, the only way to reach Staten Island was by ferry. Staten Island had much to offer painters. Jasper Francis Cropsey's "Grimes Graves, Staten Island" (1866) depicts a country estate, woodlands, and substantial barn – a good place for an afternoon walk.

At first a province of New Jersey under British rule in 1664, Staten Island became part of New York, where it remained after the revolution, as Richmond County of New York State, and Richmond borough of New York City after 1898.

It is the most remote of all the boroughs, and the least urban. In 1900, Staten Island with 67,021 inhabitants had the smallest population among the five boroughs. In 1990, with a population of 378,977, it remains the smallest, and the most rural. A recent portrait remarked that it had more bait-and-tackle shops than parking garages. Ever an anomaly, Staten Island has supported the Republicans in an otherwise largely Democratic city; and voted enthusiastically for secession from the city in 1993.

Subways

The subway was an answer to the inadequacies of the "el" system. This in its turn had rescued the city from near-total gridlock with a horse-drawn streetcar system which no matter how improved (rails were laid on the streets, donkeys replaced horses, electrified trolleys replaced the donkeys) seemed too slow for the urgent pace of the city. Real estate developers wanted something faster than the "el", something that would make new housing in the two boroughs more attractive financially. The Progressives had their own agenda, arguing that improved mass transit would decentralize the city, and reduce population densities. Improved transportation would raise the city's income from real estate taxes, and help unify the diverse boroughs.

The owners of the "el" system (Jay Gould, Russell Sage and J.P. Morgan) did not want competition from a subway system, and the city's economic elite regarded any city involvement in such a project as an invitation to thievery and political patronage. This political impasse shaped the resulting compromise, which was a hybrid of public ownership, private operation, and weak public supervision.

The first line, opened in 1904 by August Belmont's Interborough Rapid Transit Co. (IRT), ran for 22 miles, and immediately secured strong public support. It was soon carrying 600,000 passengers daily, and making substantial profits. The IRT trains ran at 40 miles per hour, and triggered rapid urbanization of the western part of the Bronx. The subway was a remarkable instrument of city growth.

In the 1920s, the Brooklyn Rapid Transit Co., which ran "els", surface railroads, and electric street cars in Brooklyn, proposed joining with the IRT into the Brooklyn-Manhattan Transit Co. (BMT), a "dual system" preponderantly funded by the city, but with substantial private capital. This system created seven new crossings of the East River, and greatly extended total mileage. The IND opened in 1932. It was a municipally-owned and run system, which added 190 miles of track to the city's subways. In 1939 the entire system was amalgamated, and run by the city. In 1953 the city lost control of the loss-making system to an independent body, the Transit Authority, in a measure designed to remove mass transit from the political realm.

In 1989 the Transit Authority subways carried one out of every nine mass transit passengers in the United States. Despite the decline of the system, 46 percent of the city's workers still use the subway to reach their workplace.

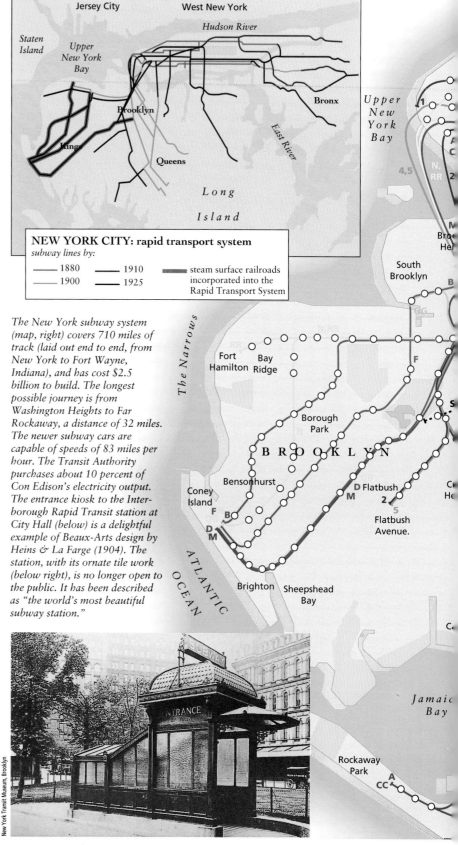

NEW YORK CITY: rapid transport system
subway lines by:

——— 1880   ——— 1910   steam surface railroads incorporated into the Rapid Transport System
——— 1900   ——— 1925

The New York subway system (map, right) covers 710 miles of track (laid out end to end, from New York to Fort Wayne, Indiana), and has cost $2.5 billion to build. The longest possible journey is from Washington Heights to Far Rockaway, a distance of 32 miles. The newer subway cars are capable of speeds of 83 miles per hour. The Transit Authority purchases about 10 percent of Con Edison's electricity output. The entrance kiosk to the Interborough Rapid Transit station at City Hall (below) is a delightful example of Beaux-Arts design by Heins & La Farge (1904). The station, with its ornate tile work (below right), is no longer open to the public. It has been described as "the world's most beautiful subway station."

New York Transit Museum, Brooklyn

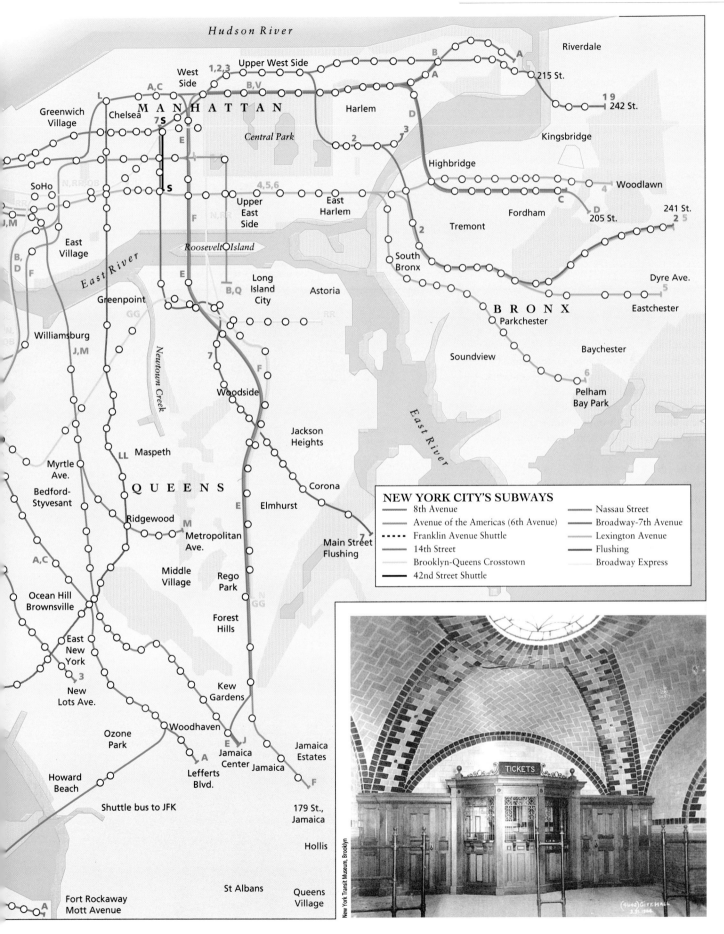

Hudson River

Riverdale

215 St.

West Side

Upper West Side

1,2,3

B,V

B

A

A

242 St.

1 9

A,C

L

MANHATTAN

Greenwich Village

Chelsea

7 S

Harlem

D

Kingsbridge

Central Park

E

2

3

Highbridge

Woodlawn

4

SoHo

N,RR

4,5,6

East Harlem

C

D

205 St.

241 St.

2 5

N,RR

E

Upper East Side

F

Fordham

Tremont

B,D

F

S

Roosevelt Island

F

2

South Bronx

East Village

J,M

East River

E

B,Q

Long Island City

Astoria

Dyre Ave.

5

Greenpoint

GG

RR

BRONX

Eastchester

N,D

Williamsburg

J,M

Newtown Creek

7

Parkchester

East River

Soundview

Baychester

Myrtle Ave.

LL

Maspeth

F

Woodside

Pelham Bay Park

6

Bedford-Styvesant

Jackson Heights

QUEENS

Ridgewood

Corona

M

Elmhurst

E

A,C

Metropolitan Ave.

Middle Village

Rego Park

Ocean Hill Brownsville

GG N

Forest Hills

East New York

3

Kew Gardens

New Lots Ave.

Ozone Park

Woodhaven

Jamaica Estates

E J

A

Jamaica Center

Howard Beach

Lefferts Blvd.

Jamaica

F

Shuttle bus to JFK

179 St., Jamaica

Hollis

Fort Rockaway Mott Avenue

A

St Albans

Queens Village

NEW YORK CITY'S SUBWAYS

8th Avenue	Nassau Street
Avenue of the Americas (6th Avenue)	Broadway-7th Avenue
Franklin Avenue Shuttle	Lexington Avenue
14th Street	Flushing
Brooklyn-Queens Crosstown	Broadway Express
42nd Street Shuttle	

Main Street Flushing 7

TICKETS

Coney Island

Throughout the 19th century, Coney Island – located on the Atlantic shore of Brooklyn – was a small, middle-class seaside resort. Although the first hotel was opened in 1829, Coney Island was hard to reach for most New Yorkers – a scheduled steamboat from the Battery took about two hours, for a fare of 50¢. Communication links improved in the 1870s, after the railroad across Brooklyn was opened in 1869, and the workers of Brooklyn and Manhattan made the resort a favorite target for group excursions.

At the far eastern end of the island, elegant watering places lined the shore of Manhattan Beach; in the middle of the island stood the Brighton Beach Hotel (which survived into the early 1920s), as well as the Public Bathing Pavilion and Iron Pier. The western end, known as Norton's Point, was a haven for gamblers and prostitutes. West Brighton offered dancing pavilions, popular amusement parks, saloons, seafood restaurants, and amusement piers.

The great era of Coney Island began in 1895, with the construction of large amusement parks. Captain Paul Boyton's Sea Lion Park opened in 1895, and began the process of raising the tone of the resort. In the 1890s, vaudeville houses in New York City were offering family shows far removed from the risqué "girly" shows and the lewdness of the concert saloons of the Tenderloin and Sixth Avenue. Coney Island, long seen as a seaside extension of New York's vice districts, followed suit. Sea Lion Park was bought and renamed Luna Park in 1903. For two decades, with a low general admission charge of 10 or 15 cents, it offered family entertainments, vaudeville, rides, and exhibitions, and was the epitome of Coney Island pleasures.

George Tilyou's Steeplechase Park was opened in 1897. Steeplechase Park aimed at a lower-class clientele who were entertained by jokes and heavy-handed humor. Performers at the Steeplechase vaudeville were instructed: "Our audiences are mostly ladies and children, and what we want is only *Polite Vaudeville.*"

By the time the subway reached Coney Island and the opening of the boardwalk in the early 1920s, the era of mass popular entertainments had begun. There were 16 million summer visitors to Coney Island in the 1930s. But the resort was incapable of upgrading its attractions, and television, the movies, and the automobile were to transform leisure time. Little now remains of the heyday of Coney Island. Residential districts have replaced the tawdry, haunted entertainments of a bygone era.

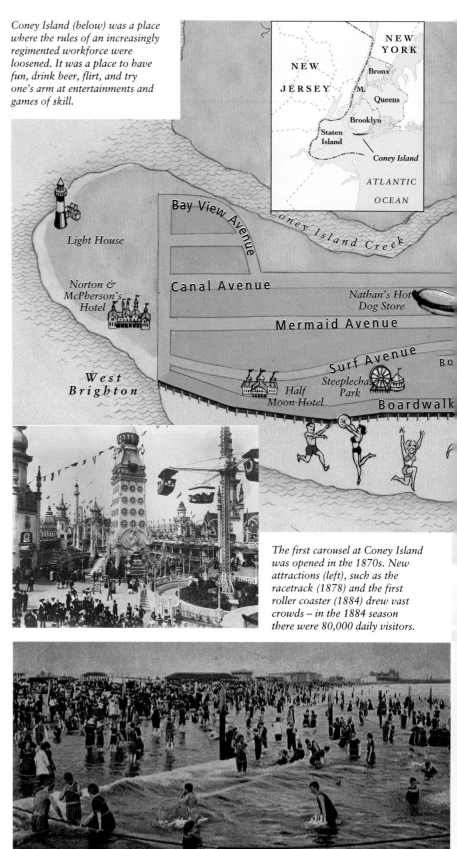

Coney Island (below) was a place where the rules of an increasingly regimented workforce were loosened. It was a place to have fun, drink beer, flirt, and try one's arm at entertainments and games of skill.

The first carousel at Coney Island was opened in the 1870s. New attractions (left), such as the racetrack (1878) and the first roller coaster (1884) drew vast crowds – in the 1884 season there were 80,000 daily visitors.

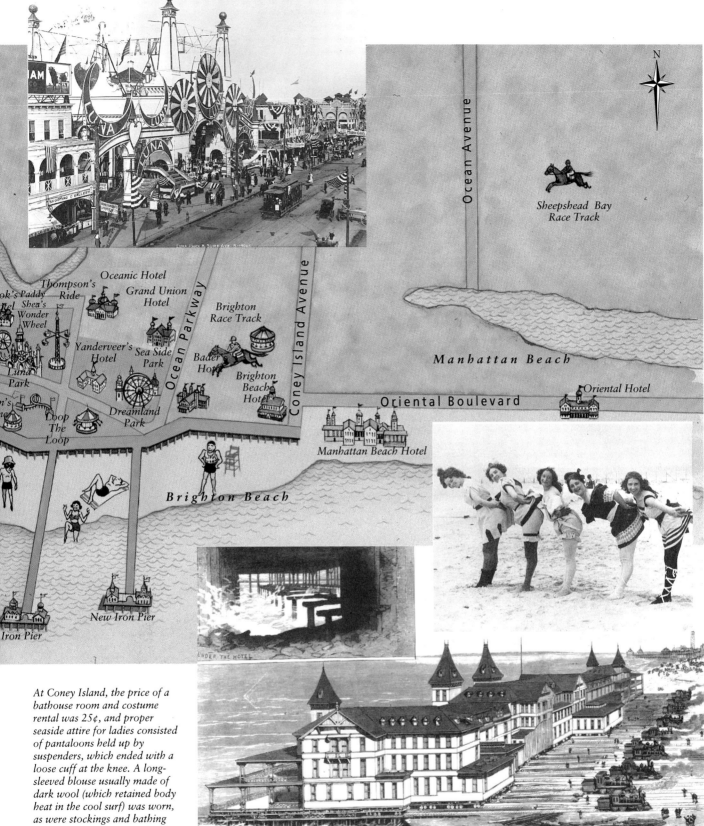

At Coney Island, the price of a bathouse room and costume rental was 25¢, and proper seaside attire for ladies consisted of pantaloons held up by suspenders, which ended with a loose cuff at the knee. A long-sleeved blouse usually made of dark wool (which retained body heat in the cool surf) was worn, as were stockings and bathing shoes (above right and left). In 1890, the Brighton Beach Hotel (right) was moved back 1,500 feet from the Coney Island waterfront.

Gangland New York

The links between gambling, vice, and political corruption were firmly established at some distant period in the history of New York. No one could say precisely when the city lost its virtue, when the honest Dutch burghers were supplanted by crooked politicians, bought judges, police on the take, and by gamblers and pimps more than willing to do business with either "law" or "enforcement."

In the 19th century, crime and street gangs were intensely local. The Gophers and their allies the Hudson Dusters (so named for their use of cocaine) ruled wide swathes of westside territory; their deadly rivals were the Five Pointers, from the most consistently gang-ridden district in the city; and the Eastmans, who ruled the east side slums between the Bowery and the East River. But these local gangs, often recruited from local tenements, were inherently unstable, and new forms of criminal activity, linked with gambling and horse-track betting, required new institutional structures.

Consider the case of Herman Rosenthal, petty bookmaker and gambler, who opened a little gambling house in Far Rockaway. Rival proprietors of gambling houses arranged for Rosenthal's place to be raided, and a move elsewhere was made. A succession of his gambling houses all fell prey to attacks by territorial rivals and police raids. So, Rosenthal went directly to the source of his troubles, Lt. Charles Becker, head of the city police Gambling Squad, and entered into a partnership agreement. For a time everyone was happy, the police were paid off, and Rosenthal made money. In March 1912 Becker demanded a $500 contribution to the defence fund of his press agent, charged with killing a man in a raid on a dice game. Rosenthal balked, and Becker ordered a raid on Rosenthal's club. Rosenthal threatened to talk to the District Attorney about the protection racket run by Becker. It was decided to shut Rosenthal's mouth, permanently, and the reliable Black Jack Zelig was given $2,000 to set up the hit. Orders were given, and Gyp the Blood, Lefty Louie, Dago Frank and Whitey Lewis were given the contract. They failed to kill Rosenthal in early July, and the gambler made a deposition, published in *The World*, that the police were dirty. On July 16, 1912, Rosenthal was shot dead on 43rd Street, east of Broadway. The shooters were caught, and Zelig agreed to turn state's evidence. But he, too, was killed on a Second Avenue trolley car at 13th Street. The four gunmen and Becker were convicted and executed.

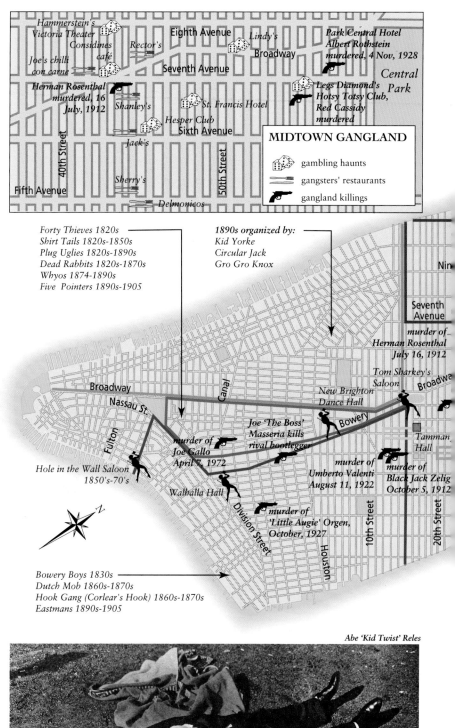

MIDTOWN GANGLAND

- gambling haunts
- gangsters' restaurants
- gangland killings

Forty Thieves 1820s
Shirt Tails 1820s-1850s
Plug Uglies 1820s-1890s
Dead Rabbits 1820s-1870s
Whyos 1874-1890s
Five Pointers 1890s-1905

1890s organized by:
Kid Yorke
Circular Jack
Gro Gro Knox

Bowery Boys 1830s
Dutch Mob 1860s-1870s
Hook Gang (Corlear's Hook) 1860s-1870s
Eastmans 1890s-1905

Abe 'Kid Twist' Reles

With the death of Becker, the role of corruption in New York changed. During Prohibition crime in New York was "organized," becoming a full-time business which required high levels of capital investment, accountants and proper business organization. Gangsterism penetrated deeply into the city's manufacturing, commercial and political life. It remained a violently competitive kind of enterprise. For all their internecine murderousness, the Mafia "families" of New York were basically business corporations with customer-unfriendly management styles.

Wiseguys... Abe Reles was a lieutenant in Murder, Inc., the nationwide syndicate enforcers created after the murders of Giuseppi Massaria, Joe Maranzano, and the "Mustache Petes" of the old Sicilian mafia in New York. There were an estimated 200-250 Murder Inc. hits in New York. The victim (right) is Albert "Plug" Schuman, killed by Irving "Knadles" Nitzberg, a friend of Schuman who got the contract in 1937.

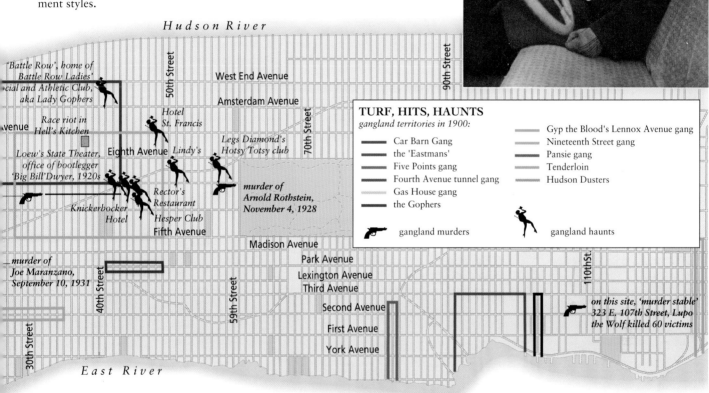

Meyer Lansky

Benjamin 'Bugs' Siegal

Charles 'Lucky' Luciano

Albert Anastasia

Luciano and Lansky, his consigliere, dominated the syndicate in the 1930s and 1940s. When Reles turned "canary" in 1940, he sent the Brooklyn core of Murder, Inc. to the chair. Held in protective custody in a Coney Island hotel, he was pitched out of his hotel room to his death in 1941. (Frank Costello was said to have bribed the police guard). Lansky expanded syndicate operations into Havana. He bribed the Cuban dictator Batista to allow mob-controlled gambling. Siegel was sent to Los Angeles to run the rackets. A psychopath with vision, Siegel dreamed up the idea of legalized gambling in Las Vegas, and built the Flamingo Hotel. He was killed by the syndicate in 1947 for skimming money from the hotel.

Hester Street

Between 1880 and 1920 most of the two million Jews from Russia, Poland, Austria-Hungary and the Balkans who arrived in the United States settled in New York and made their homes on the lower East Side. They lived in the thousands of tenements thrown up cheaply and quickly by small builders. They were usually five stories tall, with four tiny apartments on each floor. Large families and their borders were squeezed into the ill-lit and crowded rooms. With little fresh air and minimal plumbing, sanitation was inadequate and health inevitably suffered. High infant mortality rates and widespread tuberculosis testified to the shocking conditions.

Nonetheless, Jewish culture and religion flourished. Hundreds of synagogues and religious schools were established, ritual baths built, and religious goods manufactured. There were Yiddish theater companies and literary societies, Yiddish and Hebrew publishers, and Yiddish newspapers: the most famous was *The Jewish Daily Forward* (1898) located in its own building at 175 East Broadway. Jews who had emigrated from the same village or town or city in Europe set up *landsmenschaften*, social and mutual aid groups which provided insurance, burial benefits and even cemeteries. New arrivals in the lower East Side settled into their new lives with the assistance of the Hebrew Immigrant Aid Society.

Jewish immigrants earned their living in a variety of ways. They sold goods from pushcarts, operated restaurants, cafeterias, and small retail shops and a great number worked in the garment industry. Children and adults often labored from dawn to dusk in their small apartments doing piecework, paid by the number of items they had completed on a given assignment. They also worked in sweatshops – workshops that were squeezed into tenement apartments or loft buildings – and were crowded, poorly-lit, stifling in summer and cold in winter. Wages were low and hours long. The sweatshops were fertile ground for union organizing – the ILGWU (International Ladies

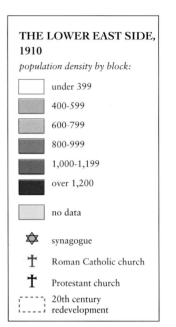

THE LOWER EAST SIDE, 1910

population density by block:

- under 399
- 400-599
- 600-799
- 800-999
- 1,000-1,199
- over 1,200
- no data

✡ synagogue
✝ Roman Catholic church
✝ Protestant church
⌐‒‒‒ 20th century redevelopment

Twentieth-century slum clearance has substantially altered the street pattern east of Pitt Street and south of Grand Street

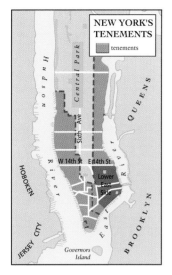

The lower East Side was a bustling area of street markets and pedlars as portrayed in George B. Luks' "Hester Street" (1905, right), and the photograph (below), taken from a tenement balcony on Hester Street in 1900.

Garment Workers Union) was established in 1900 – but real progress was not made until the tragedy of the Triangle Shirtwaist Company factory fire on March 25, 1911, when 146 immigrants, many who were Jews, died. Their deaths eventually led to many reforms in both building and fire-code safety regulations.

Jewish immigrants were eager to be assimilated into American life, and they attended night schools for citizenship classes and English. These were offered in the public schools and also at neighborhood settlement houses which served all ethnic groups. Between 1890 and 1910, more than two dozen were opened on the lower East Side alone. Among the first were the University Settlement (1886), the College Settlement (1889), and the Nurses' Settlement (1893, later the Henry St. Settlement). Here college-educated men and women who wanted to help improve conditions in the lower East Side worked for housing reform, public health services, and improved recreational and educational facilities. Children benefitted from kindergartens, summer camps and playgrounds as well as the Visiting Nurse Service on Henry Street.

The Danish photographer and journalist, Jacob Riis led campaigns to reform conditions in the lower East Side. The need for open space was particularly acute, for play areas were to be found only on rooftops, in the streets, and down insalubrious alleys. As a result of campaigns, some of the worst tenements were cleared in the 1890s to build Seward and Mulberry Bend parks, and playgrounds were inserted throughout the area on vacant lots.

Greenwich Village

In the 18th century Greenwich Village was indeed a village of small wood-frame houses, tree-lined mud streets, and one grand country estate, Richmond Hill, built by Major Abraham Mortier, Paymaster-General of the British army, on land leased in 1767 from Trinity Church. Richmond Hill was Washington's headquarters in the fruitless attempt to defend New York in 1776, and when the Federal Government was briefly in New York after the revolution it was the home of the Vice-President, John Adams.

Richmond Hill was afterwards bought by Aaron Burr. In one of his seasonal financial panics, Burr sold much of the surrounding estate to John Jacob Astor, who filled the swamps, cut down most of the 100-foot hill upon which the mansion was located, and leased the estate as 456 lots for building. In 1804 Burr's creditors forced the sale of the mansion, which was moved to a location at the intersection of Varick and Charlton Streets. It housed a tavern, circus, theater, and then, before demolition, a combination bar and library.

The streets of the Village were laid out before the Commissioners' 1811 grid plan. Bypassed by the main north-south traffic until the subway forced the cutting-through of Sixth and Seventh Avenues in the 1920s, it remained at an oblique angle to the rest of the city. The yellow fever epidemics of the 1820s drove thousands of residents out of the city, and turned Greenwich Village into a fashionable residential district. Brick houses replaced wood-frame structures. The opening of Washington Square as a park in 1827, enhanced the appeal of the area.

In the aftermath of the Draft Riots of 1863, the southeastern edge of the Village became "Little Africa," the principal residential area in New York for African-Americans. Immigrant Italians moving from the lower East Side soon followed. The Italians imparted much of the distinctive flavor of small restaurants and cafes which the Village still retains. Tenements were constructed to house the newcomers, and there was an influx of factories. At the turn of the century the Village was on the verge of becoming an industrial slum.

This trend was reversed from about 1912. The coming of the subway, and the popularity of the automobile, drove many of the small livery stables out of business, creating vacant space which artists were able to rent cheaply. In 1916 parts of the central Village were zoned for residential use. For the next decade the Village was the nation's testing-ground for cultural experiment and every kind of social and sexual liberation. The "New Woman" was invented in the Village, as was the "New Poetry." In art, theater, literature, and painting the Village was synonymous with rebellion. There had been a semi-Bohemia in New York in the 19th century, but with the emergence of the Village, cultural experiment created a self-conscious avant-garde, scornful of bourgeois taste.

Even after the cutting through of Seventh Avenue, the Village is among the areas of Manhattan which have had little post-1945 building (map, below). It remains an enclave of architecture on a human scale.

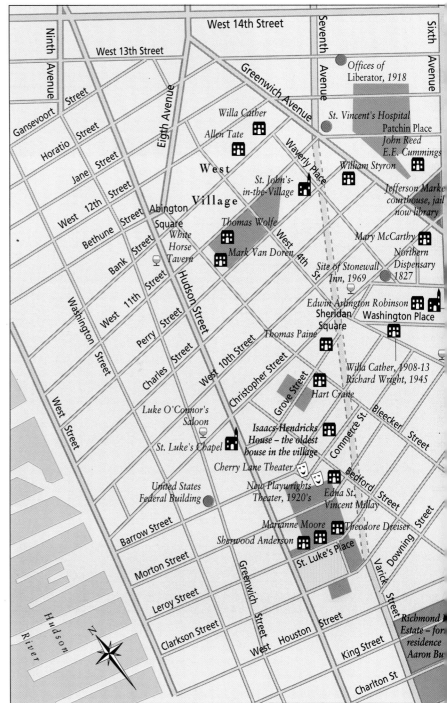

MANHATTAN
ISLAND

*main map
coverage*

'AN AMERICAN LATIN QUARTER'

🍷 bars, clubs and
restaurants

🎭 theatres

🏛 homes of writers
and artists

⛪ churches

▨ zoned residential
districts

⬤ other sites

┄ Seventh Avenue,
cut through 1919

▨ New York
University

Church of the Ascension
10th Street

art Crane

Webster Hall

🏛 Mark Twain
Marianne Moore
9th Street

Elinor Wylie
Sara Teasdale
Eighth Street

Offices of Broom,
1923

🍷 Brevoort Hotel

Fifth Ave.

Edith Wharton
Club A

Waverly Place

St. Joseph's
Church

Washington Square North

Golden Swan
Saloon "Hell Hole"

vincetown
Theater

Washington Square South

John Reed,
Lincoln
Steffens

Willa Cather
1906-8

ington
Square
okstore

W. 3rd Street

Liberal Club &
Polly's Restaurant
Minetta Tavern

E. A. Poe,
1845

netta La
St

J. F. Cooper,
1833

San Remo Bar
Bleecker   Street

McDougal Street

James
Agee

Street

'Little Africa' – one
fourth of the city's
African-American
population lived here
after the Civil War

La Guardia Place

Sullivan

East Houston Street

James Agee

Church of St.
Anthony of Padua
Prince   Street

Thompson St

West Broadway

John Sloan *Backyards, Greenwich Village* 1914

When the photo (above) was
taken in 1933, Eugene O'Neill
was no longer the shy, alcoholic
young playwright discovered by
the Provincetown Players in
1915. The alcoholism remained,
but he became America's greatest
playwright, winning the Nobel
Prize for Literature in 1936. The
Eight or the Ashcan school of
painters brought to American art
a fascination with the street life
(and backyard entertainments) of
New York. John Sloan (1871-
1951) painted "Backyards,
Greenwich Village" (top) in
1914. The view of Bleecker
Street (right) was photographed
in March, 1927.

The Ethnic City

More than six out of ten adolescents in New York at the turn of the century had at least one parent of foreign origin. New York was a city made up of endless difference, of Prussians and Bavarians, Neapolitans and Sicilians. A street such as Mulberry Street was even divided between immigrants who came from different parts of Italy.

In the midst of this difference there was an enduring tribalism which we politely call ethnicity. But the unifying sinews of language, kinship, of distinctive food and national celebrations, of custom, religion and tradition, held together the groups which, according to the turn-of-the-century theories of Americanization, should have come to resemble the majority. Anglo-conformity, this loss of distinctiveness,

was offered as a positive gain in personal freedom and social mobility. The subjective meaning of Anglo-conformity was an extinction of the immigrant's identity, in return for a promise of social mobility which was often impossible to realize, and which was blocked on every side by racial bigotry and stereotyping.

Nevertheless, New York City survived its difference. Perhaps a key to the survival lay in the fluid character of the ethnic settlements, and to the role they played in easing the process of encountering the larger society and adjusting to its norms. There was throughout the entire period of mass immigration a substantial movement of immigrants and their families in

subsequent generations to other parts of the city, to outlying suburban communities, and to other locations in the country. Distinct regional differences have persisted, and are likely to do so. But the ebb and flow of new arrivals, and the impact of social mobility, meant that the ethnic identity of an area was a provisional one, likely to be held for barely a generation or two (like the Jews in the lower East Side).

Ethnic and racial boundaries were flash points, traditional battlefields. The unexpected thing is that the city's diverse populations managed to live together as well as they have.

> "In New York alone there are more persons of German descent than persons of native descent, and the German element is larger than in any city of Germany except Berlin. There are nearly twice as many Irish as in Dublin, about as many Jews as in Warsaw, and more Italians than in Naples or Venice."
> Robert Hunter, 1912.

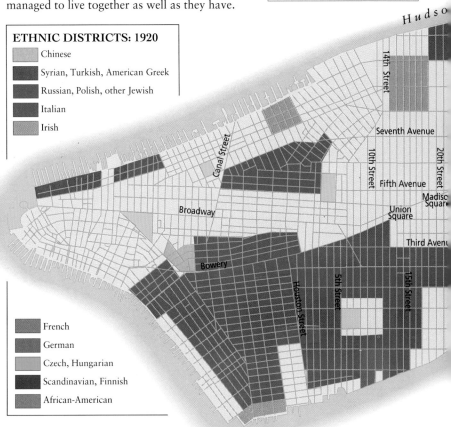

ETHNIC DISTRICTS: 1920

- Chinese
- Syrian, Turkish, American Greek
- Russian, Polish, other Jewish
- Italian
- Irish

- French
- German
- Czech, Hungarian
- Scandinavian, Finnish
- African-American

The most dreaded moment for newly-arrived immigrants at Ellis Island was the medical examination. Diseases (and especially those which indicated a depraved nature) could be grounds for refusing admission. On the left, an immigrant's eyes are examined. Height and weight were recorded. A first glimpse of the Statue of Liberty in New York harbor (above left) was the most frequently represented image of the "huddled masses" of the new immigration, 1880-1920.

"The time has come when every American citizen... must regard with grave misgiving the mighty tide of immigration that, unless something is done, will soon poison or at least pollute the very fountainhead of American life and progress. Big as we are... we cannot safely swallow such an endless-course dinner... without getting indigestion and perhaps national appendicitis."
Frank P. Sargent, Commissioner General of Immigration, at Ellis Island, January 1905.
Part of the "mighty tide" at Ellis Island, 1910 (right).

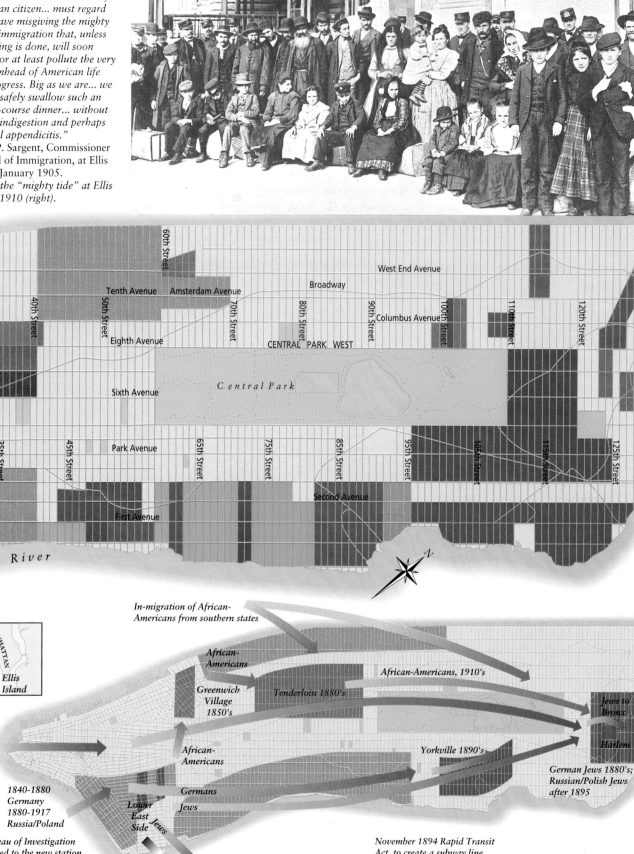

MANHATTAN
Ellis Island

In-migration of African-Americans from southern states

African-Americans

Greenwich Village 1850's

Tenderloin 1880's

African-Americans, 1910's

Jews to Bronx

Italy Sicily

African-Americans

Yorkville 1890's

Harlem

1840-1880 Germany
1880-1917 Russia/Poland

Germans

Lower East Side

Jews

German Jews 1880's; Russian/Polish Jews after 1895

The Bureau of Investigation transferred to the new station on Ellis Island on December 15, 1900. Restored and reopened as a National monument in 1991.

relocation of factories to Brooklyn

Williamsburg Brownsville

1887 Small Parks Act - builds parks in tenement districts

November 1894 Rapid Transit Act, to create a subway line on the eastside. Triggers off speculative building of residential property

THE WANDERING OF THE PEOPLES

Harlem

The African-American population in New York has moved repeatedly over three centuries of life in the city. At each stage the movement was accelerated by racism and violent attacks by white New Yorkers. After numerous attacks and dozens of murders of the small African-American population in the July 1863 draft riots, there was a substantial movement uptown, to the section of midtown on the western side of the Tenderloin that became known as "Black Bohemia." On West 53rd Street the Marshall and Maceo Hotels, the cabarets and sporting houses, became glittering centres of African-American musical talent and show-business success.

The repeated clashes between the West side Irish and the African-Americans reflected an unyielding antagonism. The Tenderloin race riot of August 1900, which led to police beatings and mob assaults, triggered another movement northwards to Harlem, eight miles from City Hall, which had been a choice residential area for aristocratic New Yorkers.

African-Americans experienced little of the upward social mobility of other immigrant groups who had been arriving in the city at the same time. The growth of the African-American population after the Civil War (from 9,943 in 1865 to 23,601 in 1890) was largely caused by migration from Virginia, and North and South Carolina. Black "immigrants" were fleeing Jim Crow laws, and hoped for a better chance in life in New York than they had in the rural South; in these motives they were sharing the experience of every other immigrant group in the city.

It was a working-class population of laborers, waiters, servants and laundresses. In 1900 there were only 42 African-American physicians and 26 lawyers out of a population of 60,666. Institutional racism declined: African-Americans were able to vote without impediment after the passage of the Civil Rights Act of 1873; the first African-American jurymen in New York were impaneled in the 1880s; the all-African-American public schools were ended in New York in 1884.

The first African-Americans to move to Harlem alarmed some white residents, and an organized effort was made to deny the newcomers access to mortgages. Real estate interests trying to expel African-Americans from Harlem received support from city newspapers. But the tide was turned when the site of one of the city's oldest African-American congregations was bought by the Pennsylvania Railroad Company, and with over $500,000 in hand, thirteen large apartment houses on 135th Street near Lenox

Avenue were purchased for rental to African-Americans. The familiar pattern of white flight followed, with elegant brick houses designed by Stanford White being sold off at an average price of $8,000 dollars apiece. The main growth of the black population in Harlem came after 1910, and hundreds of millions of dollars of property were owned by African-Americans by the 1920s.

With the growth in population and the deepening of the material base of the community, there came an extension of political organization (the National Association for the Advancement of Colored People was created in 1909); and, with the appearance of Marcus Garvey on Lenox Avenue in 1917, a black nationalist "Back to Africa" movement gained many adherents.

Harlem despised the "coon" songs which were popular on Broadway in 1900. The old minstrels, with blackface acts and an interlocutor, no less confirmed racial stereotypes. The revue *Shuffle Along* in 1921 did much to alert "downtown" about the younger black performers. Jazz was invented in New Orleans, Chicago and Kansas City, but clubs in Harlem like the Cotton Club could offer white audiences a taste of the culturally exotic – jungle decor, new dance talents like "Bojangles" Robinson and singers like Billie Holiday. Whites flooded into the night clubs of Harlem. In the late 1920s even a few blacks were allowed to join the audience.

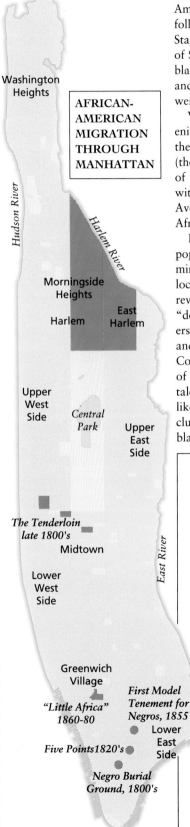

AFRICAN-
AMERICAN
MIGRATION
THROUGH
MANHATTAN

Washington Heights

Hudson River

Harlem River

Morningside Heights

Harlem

East Harlem

Upper West Side

Central Park

Upper East Side

The Tenderloin late 1800's

Midtown

East River

Lower West Side

Greenwich Village

"Little Africa" 1860-80

First Model Tenement for Negros, 1855

Lower East Side

Five Points 1820's

Negro Burial Ground, 1800's

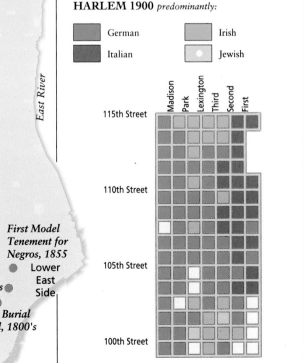

HARLEM 1900 *predominantly:*

German	Irish
Italian	Jewish

Madison Park Lexington Third Second First

115th Street

110th Street

105th Street

100th Street

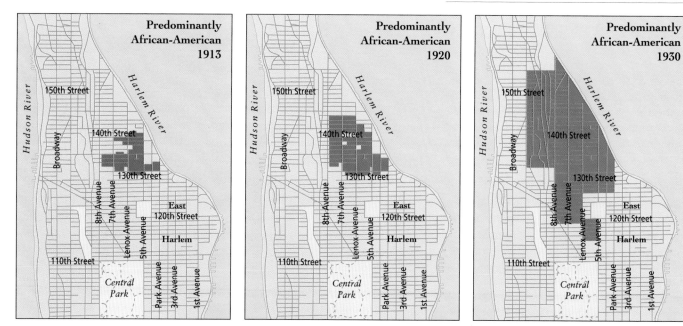

Predominantly
African-American
1913

Predominantly
African-American
1920

Predominantly
African-American
1930

Billie Holiday (right) moved to New York from Baltimore in 1927. Her singing career began in 1930 at a one-room speakeasy, Pod's and Jerry's, at 168 West 133rd St. in Harlem, where she earned $18 a week. Her big break came in 1935 when she appeared at the Apollo Theater on 125th St. Holiday's autobiography (Lady Sings the Blues, with William Duffy, 1956) begins: "Mom and Pop were just a couple of kids when they got married. He was eighteen, she was sixteen, and I was three."

The intersection of 13th St. and Lenox Avenue in 1927 (below).

Jack Oliver (1885-1938) taught Louis Armstrong to play the cornet and brought his disciple to Chicago to join the Creole Jazz Band (above, in 1920, with Armstrong playing the trumpet in the rear row). Oliver's Dixie Syncopators played the Savoy Ballroom in New York in 1927, but turned down the Cotton Club – the money wasn't good enough. The lease for Jack Johnson's Club Deluxe (northeast corner of 142nd St. and Lenox Ave.) was taken over by the Prohibition-era bootlegger "Owney" Madden. Renamed the Cotton Club in 1923, the great days of the club came when Duke Ellington's band first performed there in 1927. Ellington's success caused the club's "whites only" policy to be relaxed. Virtually to the club's demise in 1940, (right) it featured big acts and the best bands.

Beaux Arts and New York

Between 1880 and 1930, the École des Beaux-Arts in Paris was the place where Americans who wanted to be architects went to be trained. The rigorous schooling they received in architectural traditions was an important step towards the professionalization of architecture, and left a remarkable heritage of public and private buildings in New York.

Beaux-Arts architecture lost favor in the 20th century as the ideals of the Bauhaus and the International Style swept all before them. So completely did it vanish as an architectural ideal that the Beaux-Arts advocacy of tradition, of the study and eclectic use of the great structures of the past, and the vocabularies of composition, plan and form, is a lost language of public symbolism. Beaux-Arts eclecticism is embodied in the French Gothic chateaux which were built for the Vanderbilts, and the elegant Italian Renaissance residences designed by McKim, Mead and White.

Beaux-Arts training involved systematic competitions in the design of public buildings, schools, monuments of all kinds, and (from the 1840s) railroad stations. Industrial architecture was not on the syllabus, and little attention was paid to commercial buildings. The ideals of harmoniousness, elegance, balance, and cosmopolitanism strongly favored a monumentality of design, and a treatment that was disciplined and "correct" in matters of detail and treatment. Beaux-Arts buildings were assertive, powerful, and confident, while aspiring to a massive sense of stasis and balance. The Beaux-Arts ideal was above all an international taste, uniting the upper-class in a celebration not of national distinctiveness, but of a universalism and elegance which transcended local traditions or taste. A Beaux-Arts mansion in Chicago or Omaha employed the same language as one in France or Italy. The winning design for the New York Public Library by the Beaux-Arts trained firm of Carrère & Hastings, is a masterpiece of the Modern French style, a monument to the Beaux-Arts traditions of urban design and civic dignity.

For architects like Louis Sullivan in Chicago, who sought an organic form for the tall building, and one which was not copied from an archeology of European styles, the very name Beaux-Arts reeked of dead academicism. New York enthusiastically welcomed the tall building, but long adhered to the Beaux-Arts values. It was a language which was well-understood on Fifth Avenue.

Beaux-Arts architecture expressed a vision of life that is embodied in individual structures dotted across Manhattan (map, right). Park Avenue – an elegant, though lifeless, Parisian boulevard – was the only street in the city where Beaux-Arts ideals were expressed on such a massive scale.

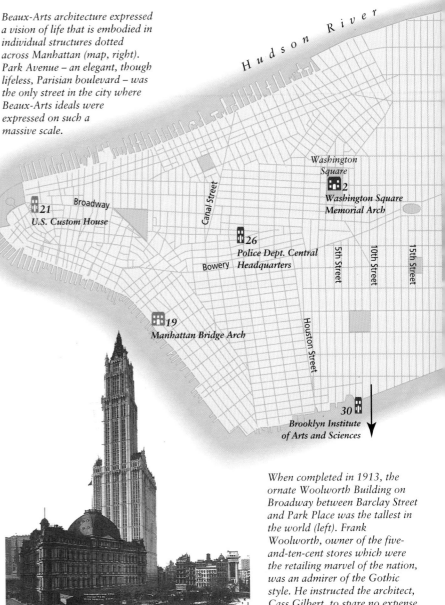

When completed in 1913, the ornate Woolworth Building on Broadway between Barclay Street and Park Place was the tallest in the world (left). Frank Woolworth, owner of the five-and-ten-cent stores which were the retailing marvel of the nation, was an admirer of the Gothic style. He instructed the architect, Cass Gilbert, to spare no expense in scale or adornment, and he paid cash, $13.5m.

In 1908 it was proposed to replace the old rail terminal at 42nd St. and Park Avenue with a new structure with the train lines running beneath the city. The new terminal (designed by Reed & Stem and Warren & Wetmore), completed in 1913 (below left), is a spectacular space, and an ingenious and efficient mechanism for public transportation.

Low Library,
Columbia University
7

West End Avenue

Amsterdam Avenue

Columbus Avenue

Central Park West

Central Park

Eighth Avenue

Seventh Avenue

Sixth Avenue

Fifth Avenue

50th Street
45th Street
40th Street
35th Street
30th Street

60th Street
65th Street
70th Street
75th Street
80th Street
85th Street
90th Street
95th Street
100th Street
105th Street
110th Street
115th Street

Pennsylvania
Station

27 13
New York Yacht Club
New York Public Library

Park Avenue 22
Pierpont Morgan Library 28
Grand Central Terminal

Third Avenue

Second Avenue

First Avenue

15

14 24
now Jewish Museum

See Inset

60th Street
65th Street
70th Street
75th Street
80th Street

Fifth Avenue
5
20 12 25 16 18 29 9 10 11 23
1 6 17 Madison Avenue
3 8

Park Avenue

East River

BEAUX ARTS NEW YORK

private house   club   institution   other building   building since demolished

dates of construction: 1892-5   1896-9   1900-3   1904-7   1908-11   1912-5

Map number	Building	Architect	Date of Construction
1	House of Richard M. Hoe	Carrère & Hastings	1892
2	Washington Square Memorial Arch	McKim, Mead & White	1892
3	House of Dr. Christian A. Herter	Carrère & Hastings	1892
4	House of Mrs William Astor on this site Temple Emanu-El, 1929	Richard Morris Hunt	1895
5	House of Mrs Josephine Schmid (demolished)	Richard Morris Hunt	1895
6	House of Harry T. Sloane now Lycée Français	Carrère & Hastings	1896
7	How Library, Columbia University	McKim, Mead & White	1897
8	House of Gertrude Rhinelander Waldo now Ralph Lauren	Kimball & Thompson	1898
9	House of Oliver Gould Jennings now Lycée Français	Ernest Flagg & Walter B. Chambers	1899
10	House of Mary E.W. Terrel	C.P.H. Gilbert	1899
11	House of John W. Simpson	C.P.H. Gilbert	1899
12	House of Mr & Mrs Ernesto Fabbri now Johnson O'Connor Research Foundation	Haydel & Shepard	1900
13	New York Yacht Club	Warren & Wetmore	1901
14	House of Andrew Carnegie now Cooper-Hewitt Museum	Babb, Cook & Willard	1901
15	Metropolitan Museum of Art	R. H. Hunt & R. H. Hunt; George P. Post, consulting architect	1902
16	House of Mrs William H. Bliss	Hiss & Weeks	1902
17	House of Joseph Pulitzer	McKim, Mead & White	1903
18	House of Henry T. Sloane	C.P.H. Gilbert	1905
19	Manhattan Bridge Arch and Colonnade	Carrère & Hastings	1905
20	The Harmonie Club	McKim, Mead & White	1906
21	United States Custom House	C.P.H. Gilbert	1907
22	J. Pierpont Morgan Library	McKim, Mead & White	1907
23	House of Senator William A. Clark (demolished)	Hewlett & Hull, Henri Deglane	1907
24	House of Felix Warburg now Jewish Museum	C.P.H. Gilbert	1908
25	House of Mrs William H. Bliss	Walter B. Chambers	1909
26	Police Department Central Headquarters from 1988 residential use	Hoppin & Koen	1909
27	New York Public Library	Carrère & Hastings	1911
28	Grand Central Terminal	Reed & Stem & Warren & Wetmore	1913
29	House of Henry Clay Frick now Frick Collection (public museum)	Carrère & Hastings	1914
30	Brooklyn Institute of Arts and Sciences	McKim, Mead & White	1915

Rockefeller Center

The need of the Metropolitan Opera for a new uptown home in the 1920s led to an approach to John D. Rockefeller, Jr. to include the opera in a midtown real estate development. What finally emerged, Rockefeller Center, is the most spectacular example of urbanism and its ideals in New York City.

Rockefeller Center was built, at the height of the Depression, without government funding. Until the sale of a majority interest to a Japanese conglomerate in 1989, it was uniquely identified with the Rockefeller family, whose philanthropy, hard-nosed entrepreneurial instincts, and passion for New York City earned them a formidable place in the city's modern history.

Although the opera was dropped from the plans by 1930 (a casualty of the depression), Rockefeller Center made provision for public space on a scale which had no precedent in New York. The Center was entered on Fifth Avenue through a narrow pedestrian corridor (Channel Garden), which gave access to a sunken square initially planned as an entrance to basement-level shops. Ice-skating, tried for the first time in 1936, was a masterly afterthought. Flanking the Channel Garden, two seven-story buildings on Fifth Avenue admitted the maximum amount of light into the entrance, and ensured there was no sense of an out-of-scale canyon effect.

The Center's larger buildings (all sheathed in pale gray Indiana limestone) were located on the symmetrical axes formed by the top of the sunken plaza. A new private street, Rockefeller Plaza, accentuated the openness of the central area. The undoubted architectural masterpiece of the Center was the RCA building (now the GE

building) at 30 Rockfeller Plaza, which rises from the Paul Manship statue of Prometheus to a dramatic height of 850 feet.

Construction of the Sixth Avenue IND subway line in 1940 enabled the Sixth Avenue "el" to be demolished. It took nearly two decades for the Center to jump the blighted path of the "el." In the 1950s the barrier of the Avenue of the Americas was crossed with a joint-venture with Time-Life. Ventures with the Hilton Hotels, Exxon and McGraw-Hill extended the size of the Center, at the cost of its original coherence. Early design proposals were denounced in the *New York Times* ("architectural aberrations and monstrosities"), but the financially troubled Center is now regarded as the finest urban complex in the United States.

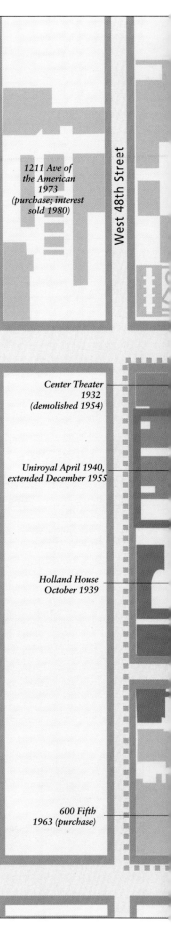

1211 Ave of the American 1973 (purchase; interest sold 1980)

West 48th Street

Center Theater 1932 (demolished 1954)

Uniroyal April 1940, extended December 1955

Holland House October 1939

600 Fifth 1963 (purchase)

The architectural masterpiece of the Center (far right) is the RCA building (now the GE building), At 70 stories, the scale of the building ought to overawe the sunken plaza, but the sharply notched set-backs give to the structure a sense of sweep and ascent which, as it narrows in the upper floors, grows more interesting to the eye, and more graceful as it rises. The aerial photos (above, mid-1950s; left, 1930s) reveal the impact of the Center over little more than two decades on the burgeoning real estate development of midtown Manhattan.

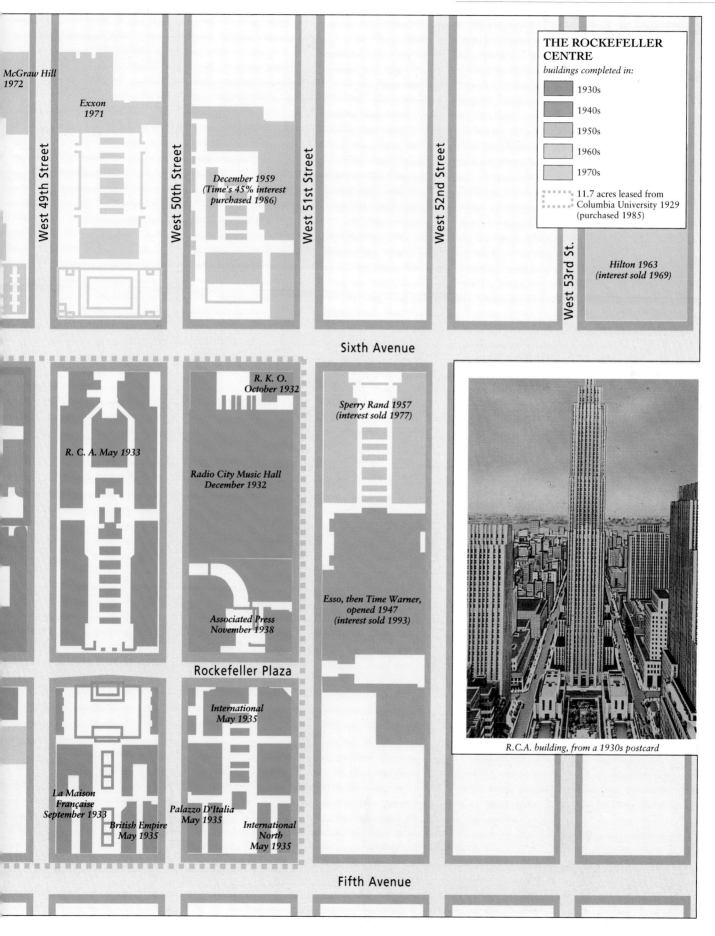

McGraw Hill 1972

Exxon 1971

West 49th Street

West 50th Street

West 51st Street

West 52nd Street

West 53rd St.

THE ROCKEFELLER CENTRE

buildings completed in:

1930s

1940s

1950s

1960s

1970s

11.7 acres leased from Columbia University 1929 (purchased 1985)

December 1959 (Time's 45% interest purchased 1986)

Hilton 1963 (interest sold 1969)

Sixth Avenue

R. K. O. October 1932

Sperry Rand 1957 (interest sold 1977)

R. C. A. May 1933

Radio City Music Hall December 1932

Associated Press November 1938

Esso, then Time Warner, opened 1947 (interest sold 1993)

Rockefeller Plaza

International May 1935

La Maison Française September 1933

Palazzo D'Italia May 1935

British Empire May 1935

International North May 1935

Fifth Avenue

R.C.A. building, from a 1930s postcard

Organizing the City

It was not until the 1920s that the first of the great Authorities were created to build and maintain much of the city's infrastructure. In 1921 the states of New York and New Jersey created the Port of New York Authority, charged with developing the terminals, transportation, and other facilities within the port district, a territory extending roughly 20 miles in all directions from the Statue of Liberty.

The Port Authority soon assumed virtual responsibility for the infrastructure of the whole port area. A first bond issue was floated in 1926, but the Authority did not become financially successful until 1931 when it assumed responsibility for Holland Tunnel. The Port Authority then completed the George Washington Bridge, crossing the Hudson from 179th Street to Fort Lee, New Jersey.

Robert Moses, creating the Triborough Bridge Authority in the 1930s, dramatically expanded the impact of public authorities upon the city. Moses drafted legislation which allowed him maximum autonomy and independence, and his parks, highways, bridges, and other improvements, funded by the toll income which capitalized bonds, enhanced his reputation as a man who could get things done. The Authorities were designed to be insulated from direct political interference, though the governors of both New York and New Jersey retain the power to veto Authority actions, and each state legislature is required to authorize new projects.

The Port Authority has served road transportation with nearly the assiduity of Moses' Triborough Bridge and Transit Authority.

The Port Authority bus terminal (below) in midtown Manhattan is a transport hub. Over 6,000 coaches arrive and leave daily.

Between 1937 and 1957 it constructed the midtown Lincoln Tunnel, connecting 39th Street with Weehawkin, and the Authority's decisions about tolls and pricing have had vast influence upon public transportation in the city. But with a range of other transportation links administered by other autonomous bodies, planning transportation in New York is like imposing order upon a bowl of spaghetti.

The stunning range of activities of the Port Authority nevertheless suggests a veritable colossus amidst the ruins. Combined gross operating revenues for the year ending December 31, 1992 were nearly two billion dollars ($1,933,512,000).

Tolls from the Holland Tunnel (above) financed Port Authority projects such as the building of the George Washington Bridge (top), the longest suspension structure in the world until the completion of the Golden Gate Bridge in San Francisco.

The Port Authority controls the regional system of four airports, accounting for 71 million passenger movements in 1992. La Guardia (right) was opened in 1939. The Authority also runs New Jersey's Port Elizabeth container port (far right).

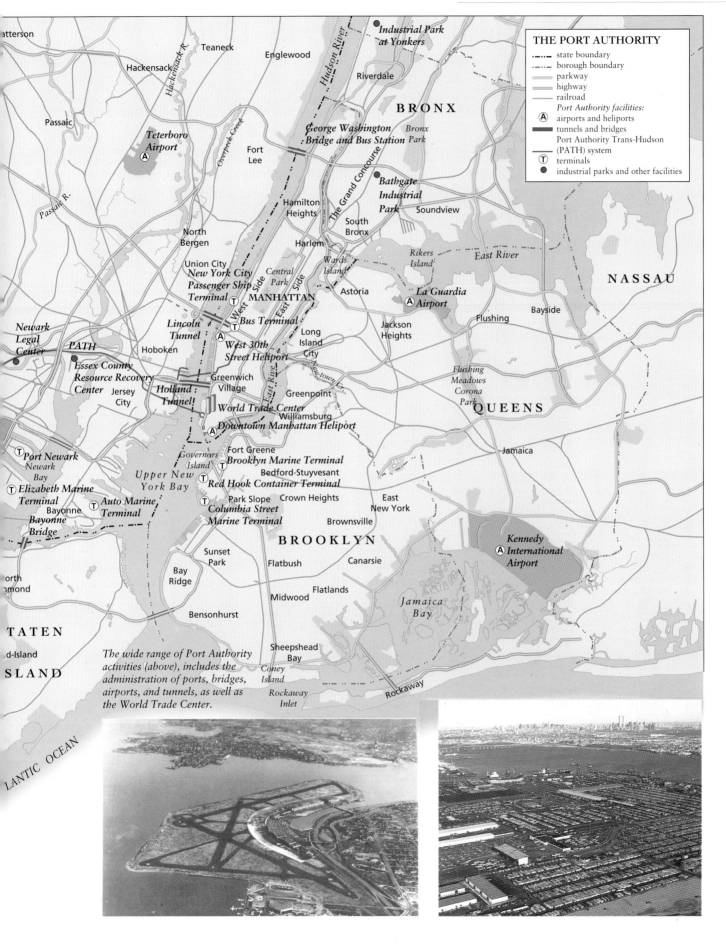

state boundary
borough boundary
parkway
highway
railroad
Port Authority facilities:
(A) airports and heliports
tunnels and bridges
Port Authority Trans-Hudson
(PATH) system
(T) terminals
● industrial parks and other facilities

Patterson

Teaneck

Englewood

Hackensack

Hudson River

● Industrial Park
at Yonkers

Riverdale

BRONX

Passaic

Hackensack R.

Overpeck Creek

Teterboro
Airport
(A)

Fort
Lee

George Washington
Bridge and Bus Station

Bronx
Park

Passaic R.

The Grand Concourse

Bathgate
Industrial
Park

Soundview

Hamilton
Heights

South
Bronx

North
Bergen

Harlem

Rikers
Island

East River

NASSAU

Union City

Wards
Island

New York City
Passenger Ship
Terminal
(T)

Central
Park

Astoria

La Guardia
Airport
(A)

Bayside

Newark
Legal
Center

PATH

Lincoln
Tunnel

Bus Terminal
(T)

West Side

East Side

MANHATTAN

Long
Island
City

Jackson
Heights

Flushing

● Essex County
Resource Recovery
Center

Hoboken

(A) West 30th
Street Heliport

Newtown Cr.

Flushing
Meadows
Corona
Park

Jersey
City

Holland
Tunnel

Greenwich
Village

East River

Greenpoint

QUEENS

World Trade Center
(A) Downtown Manhattan Heliport

Williamsburg

(T) Port Newark

Newark
Bay

Governors
Island
(T)

Fort Greene
Brooklyn Marine Terminal

Bedford-Stuyvesant

Jamaica

(T) Elizabeth Marine
Terminal

(T) Red Hook Container Terminal

(T) Auto Marine
Terminal

Park Slope
Columbia Street
Marine Terminal

Crown Heights

East
New York

Bayonne

Bayonne
Bridge

Upper New
York Bay

Brownsville

Kennedy
International
Airport
(A)

North
Diamond

Sunset
Park

Flatbush

Canarsie

BROOKLYN

Bay
Ridge

Flatlands

Midwood

Jamaica
Bay

Bensonhurst

STATEN

Sheepshead
Bay

d-Island

ISLAND

*The wide range of Port Authority
activities (above), includes the
administration of ports, bridges,
airports, and tunnels, as well as
the World Trade Center.*

Coney
Island

Rockaway
Inlet

Rockaway

ATLANTIC OCEAN

Chapter 8 Cultural Capital 1945–1996

A general view from midtown Manhattan, looking towards the World Trade Center and the financial district. Daniel H. Burnham's Flatiron Building, 1902, marks the intersection of Broadway and Fifth Avenue at 23rd St.

"The city governments must... strive to develop a more beautiful and humane city, not just a commercial city. The quality of public spaces (parks, streets, subway stations) should be preeminent in the planning and rebuilding of New York – and respect for public spaces should be preeminent in the behavior of New Yorkers. Such respect, which must become a dominant part of New York's public culture, should be the individual New Yorker's contribution to the life of the city." New York Ascendant: The Commission on the Year 2000, June 1987, Robert F. Wagner, Jr. Chair.

After 1945, New York was not so much a city but a manifestation of a new power in the world. In the emerging "Free World," triumphant victor in the war against fascism and soon to commit itself to the longer struggle against the Soviet Union and Communism, New York stood unashamedly for a metropolitan culture which had broken loose from the provincialism and regionalism of its past.

"The masterword in the critical discourse of the era," wrote Thomas Bender in *New York Intellect* (1987), "was freedom..." There were many kinds of freedom in New York in 1945, freedoms which were being discovered artistically as well as socially

An unusual restaurant facade on the corner of Walker and Church Streets.

and economically. The arts in particular seemed to open the possibility of the city seizing what the United States had never had before, a leading role in western culture. Refugee artists and intellectuals, precariously trying to sustain themselves in an alien environment, were among the most acute observers of the face of the new metropolis.

Cultural Arbiter

With the emergence of nationwide media in the interwar years (from the radio networks to *Life*), the role of the city in the worldwide communication network assured the supremacy of New York taste, images, assumptions. In the past, the city had often been provincial and avowedly hostile to the new. The provincialism and "correctness" of New York elite taste were potent inhibitions on the development of young artists. When it came to mocking modern art, the New York press led the braying pack in 1913 when the Armory Show brought the first modern paintings to public display in the city.

The city had become more receptive to the new art in the 1920s, and with the general loosening of controls during the pro-hibition era an extraordinary richness of cultural life had developed. People came to New York and found there a milieu in which the impossible could be attempted. Behind the privilege (and the accidental bonus) of its international postwar position, lay the serious music, dance, opera, the popular theater, and painting which had transformed the provincialism of the city. New York now sustained the core of American cultural adventurousness. The New York intellectuals emerged in the

Advertising hoardings decorate the walls of Manhattan's skyscrapers.

View uptown from the Battery.

postwar years as the key interpreters of the national culture. Their combative style, and perhaps also their immigrant roots and broad cultural horizons gave the city an ascendancy in the intellectual and artistic life of the nation that money and power alone cannot explain.

New York was the natural choice for the headquarters of the United Nations. Major corporations found solid reasons for their headquarters to be located in the city. New York art dominated the world art markets. The New York theater was unchallenged nationally. The World Series was effectively an interborough rivalry for a decade from 1947. It was a swaggering, optimistic city that taught the nation about good times, about being on a roll.

On the other hand, how could it possibly last? The Dodgers and the Giants left town. (Money and not sentiment were the deciding factors.) New York's problems were gargantuan. The woes of the city are altogether too familiar. Over the past two decades, a series of touchstone riots and murders have come to represent the city's failed, violent social order. For a generation and more, New York has been symbolized less by "huddled masses" staring piously at the Statue of Liberty or by pictures of the Empire State Building as a marvel of technology and modernity, than by white flight, financial crisis, racism, urban decay, corruption, and murder. Despite the city's position as home of the national television networks, and the leading role played by the *New York Times* and the *Wall Street Journal* in print journal-

The northern triangle of Times Square (right) is named for Father Francis P. Duffy, a hero of World War I, known as "the fighting chaplain" of New York's 69th Regiment.

"I found that America was the country, par excellence, of making images of everybody, everything. Everything had to have an image, the car had to have an image, a shoe had to have an image, the politician has to have an image. One day I was sitting in a kind of bar, and I saw a politician projecting his image, and I said to myself: 'Glamour, the image of our image - that is my project'." The photographer Lisette Model, an anti-fascist exile in New York.

ism, the city's collapsing reputation is as much the creation of New Yorkers' dissatisfaction with their own community as of any penetrating insight from the national media elsewhere.

A new script for the City

It is harder now than at any time in the past to see New York for what it truly is. Over-simplified portrayals, stereotypes, and clichés about the Big Apple are much easier to disseminate. Why strain for complex understanding when the old litany of disaster and self-mutilation is at hand? The nation was comfortable with the new imagery of New York, which drew politicians and commentators to the South Bronx where the lessons of the wicked city were drawn in capital letters. New York was through. New York was a Disaster. It was time to "Escape from New York."

When the first tidy subway trains (painfully and expensively cleaned of their graffiti) rolled into midtown stations, people looked around for the film crews. Clean subways were news. The local success of the BIDs (Business Improvement Districts), culminating in the reopening of Bryant Park with scarcely a wino in sight, and the increasing momentum behind plans to reconstruct Times Square and get rid of the porno movies on 42nd St., were promising signs of hope. And then the crime figures began

In midtown Manhattan, St. Patrick's Cathedral, built in 1880, rubs shoulders with modern skyscrapers. The Archbishop's Residence is on Madison Avenue, with the Cathedral rear left.

to decline. Felonies in Midtown South police precinct fell by 9.3 percent from 1991 to 1992. Total citywide burglaries were the lowest for 23 years. The number of rapes was the lowest since 1971. Murders declined 7.4 percent. The figures for 1993 and 1994 continued the trend. A British newspaper suggested "It's time to revise New York City's reputation ..." (*Independent on Sunday* 7 January 1996); time, in other words, for the city to reinvent itself – this time as a success story.

The New York of the immigrants, and of the ethnic working class of a generation or two ago, retains a certain presence in the city's collective memory. At the heart of this "historical sense" is the belief that in the past a sense of community governed relations between individuals and groups within the city. The conviction that there has been a "loss of community" has thus served to cast upon the past a sepia-tinted, sentimental varnish.

The steps of the Federal Hall Memorial Museum, formerly the Sub-Treasury Building (1833–42) serve as an informal amphitheater for watching the busy street life of Wall Street and Broad Street. The pedestal supports John Q.A. Ward's bronze statue of George Washington, to mark the site where Washington took the oath of office as president in 1789. The statue was put in place in 1883.

Buskers and street stalls enliven the streets of lower Manhattan.

The tale of the census

One begins with the idea that New York is not so much a city or a community but a vast geographical and administrative basket in which essentially autonomous social units are to be found. In the 1990 census East Harlem, Washington Heights, and the lower East Side differ in innumerable ways from the "other" Manhattan (the financial district below Canal St., Greenwich Village, Clinton, and Chelsea, midtown, the westside and upper west side, and the upper east side). Over 31 percent of the residents of the upper east side in 1990 held graduate degrees or professional qualifications; under 5 percent of the residents of East Harlem were educated to a similar level. Per capita income on the upper east side was $59,125; in East Harlem it was $8,888. 2.7 percent of upper east side families were below the poverty level in 1990, compared to 37 percent in East Harlem.

The 1990 census data remorselessly makes and re-makes the same point: that there are two communities in New York, rich and poor, as separate from each other as though someone like Robert Moses had ordered the erection of a Berlin Wall of stone, cement and barbed wire across 96th Street. It is no less a linguistic wall. Over the 1980s, the percentage of people living in New York who speak Spanish at home rose to just under 25 percent of the total. Running through the history of New York City is a tale of Two Nations, and of the consequences of that fact for many individual lives.

The World Trade Center, two 1,350-foot-tall stainless steel towers, providing ten million square feet of office space.

Center of the Art World

New York City has offered 20th-century artists a uniquely modern subject-matter, but successive "schools" or "scenes" have identified themselves with a neighborhood, or a particularly local perspective. The Ashcan School of John Sloan, Robert Henri, and George Bellows lived in Greenwich Village, finding a rich subject for their realist style in the tenements, saloons, and the crowded working-class street life of the East Side and the Village.

The Fourteenth Street School of the interwar years (Reginald Marsh, Raphael Soyer, Isabel Bishop, Kenneth Hayes Miller) continued the tradition of figurative American Scene painting, and produced a realist record of the quotidian routine of the city, and of the growing participation of women in public life.

After 1945, a profusion of ateliers, art schools, clubs, and artist's studios in the low rent area from 8th to 12th Streets on the East Side, between First and Sixth Avenues (known generally as "Tenth Street") was at the heart of the new movement called Abstract Expressionism. In the late 1950s, as rents rose in the Tenth Street area, pioneer artists began to drift into SoHo, a 43-block district south of Houston Street and north of Canal. The name "SoHo" (South of Houston) was invented in the 1960s when artists took unauthorized possession of loft space in the midst of industrial decay. Within a decade SoHo had become a district of artists' lofts and "downtown" experimental galleries.

The revolution begun in 1945 led to the triumph of abstract art in New York. Within two decades New York had ceased to be an essentially local (and provincial) art market, tagging along after the latest Parisian movement, and had become the dominant force in western art.

What brought the New York avant garde to its apotheosis was a political moment – the bustling optimism of the dawn of the "American Century" – and the postwar exhaustion of European art, as well as the presence on the scene of formidable sympathetic critics like Clement Greenberg, and Meyer Schapiro.

The Abstract Expressionists were the first generation of American artists to fully reflect the cosmopolitanism of New York City. Artists such as William de Kooning, Hans Hofmann, Arshile Gorky, Jack Tworkov, Mark Rothko, and Philip Guston came from the Netherlands, Bavaria, Armenia, Poland, Russia, and Canada respectively, while Franz Kline came from Pennsylvania, Robert Motherwell from Washington State and Jackson Pollock from Wyoming. Artists such as

"It is our function as artists to make the spectator see the world our way not his way." Adolph Gottlieb and Mark Rothko, 1943

In 1925, Georgia O'Keefe began to paint the urban landscape, including the view of Brooklyn Bridge (right). It was the first time a woman painter had succeeded with a subject traditionally urban, male, and technological.
When Frank Lloyd Wright was invited to design a museum for Solomon R. Guggenheim's collection of non-objective art, he demonstrated that there are alternatives to the glass-sheathed vertical slab (center right, completed 1959).

Adolph Gottlieb, and Barnett Newman came from New York's immigrant community.

The "second" generation, coming of age in the 1950s, was more "American" in taste. They were fascinated by popular culture, not high art. Andy Warhol's first one-man show in New York came in 1962. By then the battles had been fought, and the age of Pop Art had arrived on the world art stage. Art in New York retained its neighborhood roots, but it now had a worldwide audience.

"Empire" was a 8-hour silent film made by Andy Warhol in 1964 of the Empire State building as seen from the Time-Life building, from dusk to dawn (film still, far right). "The Empire State building is a star!" he said.

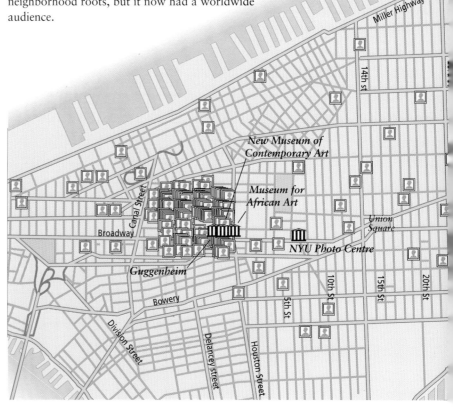

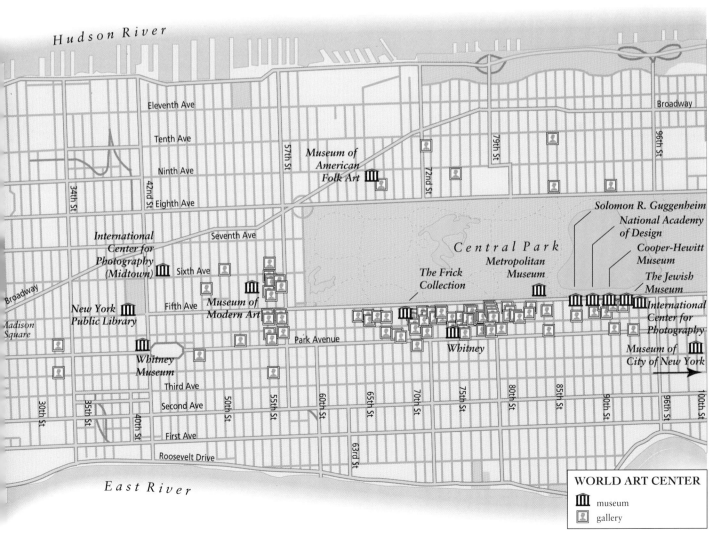

Hudson River

Eleventh Ave

Tenth Ave

Ninth Ave

Eighth Ave

Seventh Ave

Sixth Ave

Fifth Ave

Park Avenue

Third Ave

Second Ave

First Ave

Roosevelt Drive

Broadway

Madison Square

34th St

42nd St

57th St

72nd St

79th St

96th St

Broadway

30th St

35th St

40th St

50th St

55th St

60th St

63rd St

65th St

70th St

75th St

80th St

85th St

90th St

96th St

100th St

East River

Museum of American Folk Art

International Center for Photography (Midtown)

New York Public Library

Museum of Modern Art

Whitney Museum

Central Park

The Frick Collection

Metropolitan Museum

Whitney

Solomon R. Guggenheim

National Academy of Design

Cooper-Hewitt Museum

The Jewish Museum

International Center for Photography

Museum of City of New York

WORLD ART CENTER

museum

gallery

Our Team

New Yorkers were as passionate about sports as they were about politics and making money. The city's aristocrats and fashionable young bloods set the tone for a distinctly aristocratic sporting life, centered upon horse racing, yachting, and a fondness for amateur athletics. Third Avenue was a favorite venue for informal horse races and trotting. Wealthy New Yorkers, led by Leonard Jerome, set up the racetrack where the first annual Belmont Stakes was run in 1867 – the earliest of the three classic American races. In 1866 the American Jockey Club and the New York Athletic Club were formed. Under NYAC auspices the first national track and field championships were held a decade later.

Baseball, on the other hand, belonged to the city's working class. The first recorded baseball game was played by two New York teams at the Elysian Fields in Hoboken, New Jersey, in 1846. For a century no other sport remotely rivalled it in the affections of the city. Local rivalries soon drew vast crowds to baseball games. A series of all-star games in 1858 between teams from New York and Brooklyn, played at Willetts Point, Queens, began one of the nation's most enduring sports rivalries. Sport loyalties transcended class, race and ethnicity, giving identity to the huge diversity of the city's peoples.

The 1920s was the decade of professional sport in New York. Two of Jack Dempsey's greatest heavyweight bouts, against Georges Carpentier (1921) and Luis Firpo (1923), were held in New York. It was the era of Babe Ruth, and the Yankees' "Murderers' Row." New York Americans entered the National Hockey League in 1925, the Rangers joined in 1927. The Giants entered the National Football League in 1925.

The departure in 1957 of the Giants for San Francisco, and the Dodgers for Los Angeles, ended the period of New York's greatest influence upon American sport. There will be triumphs in the future, but not the dominance the city once enjoyed.

Horseracing became less of an aristocratic pursuit when the Sheepshead Bay Racetrack (below left) opened in Coney Island.

Amongst the city's many sportsgrounds (map, below), there were three great shrines to the city's passion for baseball: the Polo Grounds, home for 67 years of the New York Giants; the Yankee Stadium, where the greatest dynasty in American sport flourished, and Ebbets Field, home of the Dodgers.

OVER A CENTURY OF SPORTING NEW YORK

🏇	Race Track	🏀	Basketball
🏈	Football	🎾	Tennis
✕	Baseball	▌	Cricket
⚒	Ice Hockey		

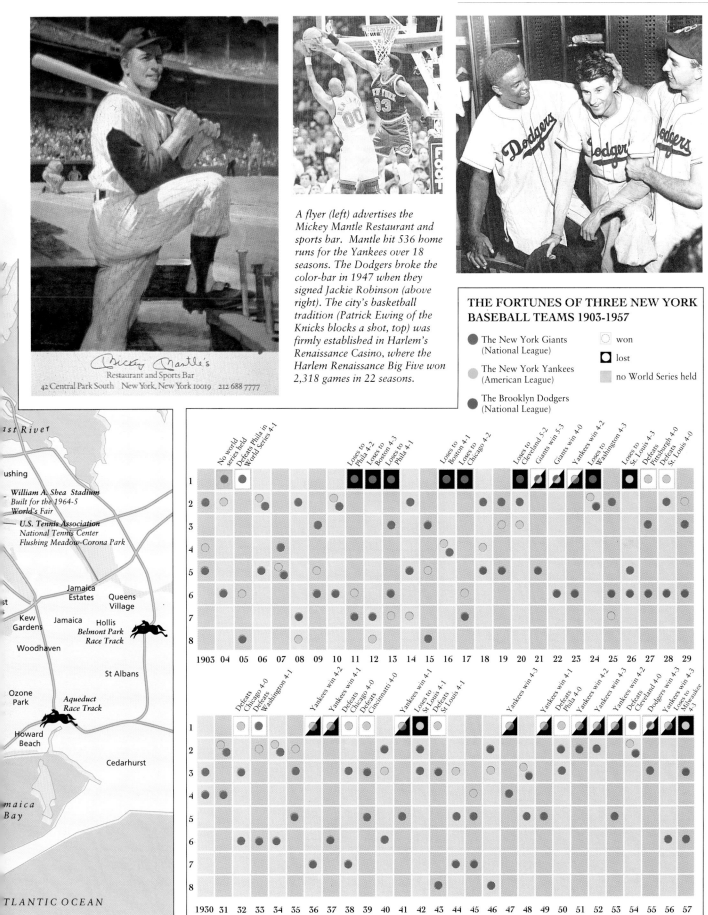

A flyer (left) advertises the Mickey Mantle Restaurant and sports bar. Mantle hit 536 home runs for the Yankees over 18 seasons. The Dodgers broke the color-bar in 1947 when they signed Jackie Robinson (above right). The city's basketball tradition (Patrick Ewing of the Knicks blocks a shot, top) was firmly established in Harlem's Renaissance Casino, where the Harlem Renaissance Big Five won 2,318 games in 22 seasons.

Mickey Mantle's
Restaurant and Sports Bar
42 Central Park South   New York, New York 10019   212 688 7777

THE FORTUNES OF THREE NEW YORK BASEBALL TEAMS 1903-1957

- The New York Giants (National League)
- The New York Yankees (American League)
- The Brooklyn Dodgers (National League)
- ○ won
- ◨ lost
- no World Series held

Broadway Nights

The first play to be produced in New York was Farquhar's *The Recruiting Officer* in 1732. In addition to taking over the British theatrical canon, New Yorkers also absorbed the English tradition of theatrical rioting (theaters in London had repeatedly been the sites of social disorder). The Continental Congress called for the suspension of "horse-racing, gambling, cockfighting, exhibitions of shows, plays and other expensive diversions and entertainments." One of the first acts of the occupying British army after the battle of Harlem Heights in 1776 was to reopen the John Street Theater.

Entertainment in New York during the early 19th century was closely tied to the area around the newly-built City Hall. The Park Theater was opened on Park Row, near Ann Street, in 1798.

It was a large structure, with a seating capacity of 2,400, with 42 boxes. (There was a gallery for "colored persons.")

With the opening of the Bowery Theater on the east side of the Bowery between Canal and Hester streets in 1826, the first great rival emerged to Broadway as the main focus for entertainment. Broadway theaters appealed to a more cultured and elegant audience; the Bowery was popular; where the Broadway stage was Anglophile, the Bowery was patriotic.

It was the opening of the IRT subway in 1904, which ran under Broadway from the Battery to 145th Street, which settled the theaters in the area around Longacre Square (at the intersection of Broadway and Seventh Avenue).

Renamed Times Square, the area was equidistant from Pennsylvania Station and Grand Central Terminal. With easy and rapid access from the rapidly-growing residential areas in the Bronx and Brooklyn, Broadway soon became synonymous with American theater as a whole.

More theaters were built in New York from 1900 to 1930 than in the preceding century, but innovation was expensive, and seldom welcome on Broadway. A parallel theater located "Off Broadway" (the Circle in the Square Theater opened in Greenwich Village in 1952) was by far the greatest source of cultural experiment.

New Yorkers had always been passionate in their enthusiasm for the theater. Visiting artists were awestruck by their reception. At the debut of the Viennese ballerina Fanny Elssler at the Park Theater in 1840, she wrote: *"The whole house rose, and such a shout ascended as stunned my senses, and made me involuntarily recoil. Men waved their hats, and women their handkerchiefs ... I stood confounded, with tears streaming down my face... Never before did I behold so vast an assembly so completely under the sway of one dominant feeling, and so entirely abandoned to its inspiration."*

The rivalry between the Bowery Theater (far left) opened in 1826, and Broadway was rooted in class and religion. In May 1849, rioting crowds of Bowery theater-goers, who favored the American actor Edwin Forrest, clashed with police outside the Astor Place Opera House where the English actor W.C. Macready was playing. Twenty-two people died. In the 1920s, Broadway theater, centered on Times Square (left), enjoyed its heyday.

Samuel Becket
Howard Clurman
Ticket Central
Playwrights Horizons
Judith Anderson
South St
Nat Horne
Actors Studio
INTAR
Douglas Fairbanks
John Houseman
Royale
Plymouth
Majestic
Broadhurst
St James
Nederlander
Victory
Minskoff
Criterion
Lambs
Lyceum
Writers
American Place
Palace
Cort
Shubert
Booth
Music Box
Edison
Lunt-Fontanne
Marquis
Helen Hayes
Richard Rodgers
Brooks Atkinson
Biltmore
Walter Kerr
Imperial
Longacre
Ethel Barrymore
Ambassador
Gershwin
Circle in the Square
Nell Simon
Virginia
Mark Hellinger
Winter Garden
Martin Beck
45th Street
John Golden
Irish Arts Center
St Clements
The Cubiculo
Ensemble Studio Theater
William Redfield
Tenth Ave
Ninth Ave
Eighth Ave
Seventh
Broadway
51st St
52nd St
53rd St
46th St
47th St
48th St
49th St
50th St
41st St
42nd St
43rd
44th St
45th St

Every bit as much as restaurants and shops, the theater obeyed the iron law of New York life by moving uptown. The burning of the Park Theater in 1848 broke the link which held the theater to the City Hall area, and by 1870 the theater district was moving steadily up Broadway until, by the 20th century, Times Square had become synonymous with the theater district (maps below, and left)

NEW YORK'S THEATRICAL HISTORY

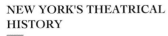

theater district pre-1850	
theaters 1850 1870	
1870-1900	still active
20th-century	still active

Broadway theater, even in its heyday, was generally escapist, "likeable" and positively inimical to artistic seriousness. The age of television dealt it a further blow. In the 1980s musicals brought in from England (right) became an increasingly important element on Broadway – a street with a more interesting past than promising future.

How the United Nations came to Turtle Bay

It was a commonplace among the exiled governments clustered in London during the Second World War that the new international organization, the League of Nations, must be located in the United States to ensure American involvement. But where in the United States? Delegations from San Francisco, Philadelphia, Boston, and other places arrived in London to pitch their cities to the new organization. New York City, in the midst of the worst housing crisis in its history, was slow to enter the competition. An Inspection Group sent from London favored North Stamford or Greenwich, Connecticut. Further discussions shifted attention to Westchester County, New York, and Fairfield County, Connecticut.

Temporary headquarters were set up in scattered hotels across Manhattan. Buildings on the Bronx campus of Hunter College were refitted and made available to the United Nations. In three weeks, the college gymnasium was transformed into a chamber for the first meeting of the Security Council in the United States on March 21, 1946.

Delegates clearly favored a midtown location, but real estate occupancy was high, and the city, as usual, had little money. By November 1946, the Headquarters Committee of the General Assembly revived the candidacies of San Francisco, Philadelphia, and Boston. New York was on the verge of dropping out of the picture. President Truman hinted at his preference when he offered use of the Presidio in San Francisco. The Russians saved the day by blocking any move to the west coast.

The United Nations Committee of New York City consisted of Mayor William O'Dwyer, the city's "Mr. Fixit", Robert Moses, one of the Rockefeller brothers, Arthur Hays Sulzberger (publisher of the *New York Times*), and Thomas J. Watson of IBM. Desperate not to lose the UN, they offered the whole of Flushing Meadows, rent-free. As the impasse deepened, UN Secretary-General Trygve Lie phoned Mayor O'Dwyer to explain that something more was needed to save the New York position. Moses mentioned Turtle Bay. He had long wanted to sweep away the slaughterhouses and factories which lined the East River in midtown. It was then that Willam Zeckendorf, a real estate developer, contacted O'Dwyer. He had secretly been buying land in Turtle Bay, and agreed to sell it to the the UN. But new organization had no money. Secretary-General Lie suggested that O'Dwyer and Moses contact Nelson Rockefeller. The

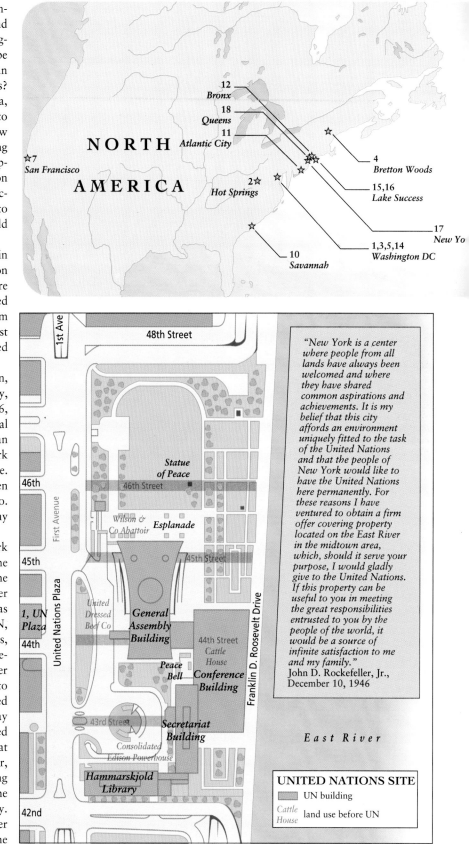

"New York is a center where people from all lands have always been welcomed and where they have shared common aspirations and achievements. It is my belief that this city affords an environment uniquely fitted to the task of the United Nations and that the people of New York would like to have the United Nations here permanently. For these reasons I have ventured to obtain a firm offer covering property located on the East River in the midtown area, which, should it serve your purpose, I would gladly give to the United Nations. If this property can be useful to you in meeting the great responsibilities entrusted to you by the people of the world, it would be a source of infinite satisfaction to me and my family."
John D. Rockefeller, Jr.,
December 10, 1946

UNITED NATIONS SITE
- UN building
- *Cattle House* land use before UN

ATLANTIC

OCEAN

EUROPE

8,9☆
London

☆13
The Hague

6
Yalta
☆

Siting the United Nations in the USA was a foreign policy aim of many countries – but where in the USA? (map above). The first Secretary-General, Trygve Lie, strongly favored a site on the east coast – New York, the financial center and leading metropolis of the new world order, combined the physical resources and communications needed for a truly international organization.

The building of the United Nations complex encouraged East Side development like the United Nations Plaza on East 44th St. (Kevin Roche, John Dinkeloo and Assocs., 1976, 1983, below). The design team for the Secretariat building (seen from across the East River in a 1950s postcard, below right) was led by Wallace K. Harrison.

Rockefeller family were famous for their tradition of incomparable public philanthropy and internationalisim.

During the tense weekend of December 7-8, 1946, while offers were coming in from the Mayor of Boston, secret meetings were taking place between the Rockefeller brothers, their father John D. Rockefeller, Jr., Mayor O'Dwyer, Robert Moses, Trygve Lie, and the US government. On Wednesday, December 11, the deal was announced: John D. Rockefeller, Jr., would give the UN $8,500,000 to buy Zeckendorf's land. "Why, Pa, that's most generous!" was Nelson Rockefeller's response to his father's offer. The city would spend serious money on improving the immediate neighborhood, and 1,612 apartments were secured for the UN staff at Parkway Village in Queens, Great Neck, and in Peter Cooper Village in Manhattan, at an average cost of $25 per room. Two days later a relieved General Assembly ratified the decision. On August 20, 1950, the first employees moved into the new Secretariat building.

Latest Arrivals 1

Until the 1960s, immigration to New York City was dominated by Europeans. Over 90 percent of the total national immigration in 1900 was from Europe. The National Origins Quota Act of 1921, and the Johnson-Reed Act of 1924, were designed to maintain the national racial and religious mix much as it was in 1890-1910, the latter act effectively restricting the numbers of Italians and Russian Jews.

These measures, notoriously discriminatory, had a more drastic impact upon New York City than elsewhere in the nation because the Russians, Jews, and Italians were immigrant groups who showed a strong preference for settlement in the five boroughs. The percentage of foreign-born residents declined steadily under the impact of "national origins" quotas, war, and depression, from 40.8 percent in 1910 to 23.6 percent in 1950. In the first half of this century, New York became a less "foreign" city; the withering ethnic enclaves in the city could be seen as a sign that the larger movement towards assimilation would prove irresistible.

In this period the percentage of foreign-born in the United States as a whole dropped by half. While New York followed the pattern, the city persistently had three or four times as high a proportion of immigrants as the nation. Legislative changes, beginning with the passage of the Hart-Celler Act in 1965, eradicated the discriminatory quota system, unwittingly opening the country to new immigration patterns. Family reunification has been the central principle of immigration legislation since the 1970s.

The post-1965 impact upon the ethnic composition in New York has been dramatic. In 1980, New York's 23.6 percent foreign-born population far exceeded Philadelphia's 5 percent, and Chicago's 11 percent. New York's immigrants were very diverse in national origin: three-quarters of all Dominicans, over half of all Jamaicans, Barbadians, Trinidadians, Guyanese and Haitians, nearly half of all Ecuadorians, and a third of the national total of Colombians have settled in New York.

Immigration changed the demographic profile of New York. In the 1980s, the total foreign-born population of the five boroughs rose by a quarter. The white non-hispanic population declined by 14 percent, while the total Hispanic population rose by nearly 27 percent. The Asian population doubled. In 1990, for the first time in the city's history, no single race or ethnic group formed a majority of the city's inhabitants.

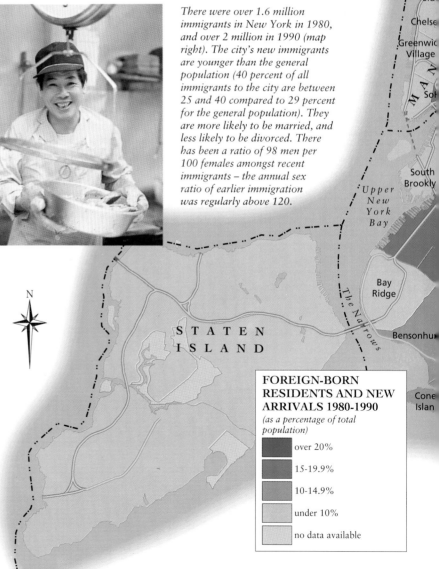

There were over 1.6 million immigrants in New York in 1980, and over 2 million in 1990 (map right). The city's new immigrants are younger than the general population (40 percent of all immigrants to the city are between 25 and 40 compared to 29 percent for the general population). They are more likely to be married, and less likely to be divorced. There has been a ratio of 98 men per 100 females amongst recent immigrants – the annual sex ratio of earlier immigration was regularly above 120.

FOREIGN-BORN RESIDENTS AND NEW ARRIVALS 1980-1990
(as a percentage of total population)

- over 20%
- 15-19.9%
- 10-14.9%
- under 10%
- no data available

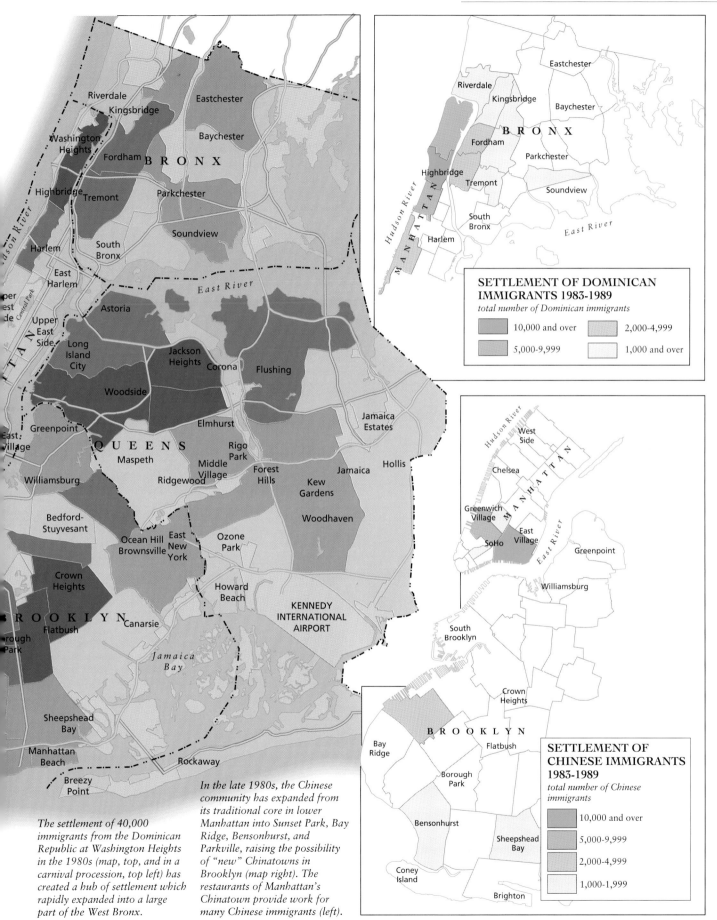

SETTLEMENT OF DOMINICAN
IMMIGRANTS 1983-1989

total number of Dominican immigrants

10,000 and over	2,000-4,999
5,000-9,999	1,000 and over

SETTLEMENT OF
CHINESE IMMIGRANTS
1983-1989

total number of Chinese immigrants

10,000 and over
5,000-9,999
2,000-4,999
1,000-1,999

The settlement of 40,000 immigrants from the Dominican Republic at Washington Heights in the 1980s (map, top, and in a carnival procession, top left) has created a hub of settlement which rapidly expanded into a large part of the West Bronx.

In the late 1980s, the Chinese community has expanded from its traditional core in lower Manhattan into Sunset Park, Bay Ridge, Bensonhurst, and Parkville, raising the possibility of "new" Chinatowns in Brooklyn (map right). The restaurants of Manhattan's Chinatown provide work for many Chinese immigrants (left).

Latest Arrivals 2

Immigrants made up just over 28 percent of the city's total population in 1990. They followed the pattern of earlier immigration in preferring to settle in areas already inhabited by immigrants from their home country. They seem also to be following the process observed when the Germans moved from Kleindeutschland to Yorkville in the 19th century. The immigrants are not evenly spread across the city. The highest proportion of immigrants is in Queens (over one-third), and the lowest (under 12 percent) in Staten Island. The Bronx and Staten Island received proportionately fewer immigrants than the three other boroughs, though the rate of growth of the immigrant population in both boroughs approached the growth rate of Queens between 1980 and 1990.

The percentage of foreign-born residents in Brooklyn grew substantially in the 1980s, from 23.8 percent to just over 29 percent. There was a substantial presence of non-hispanic Haitians, Jamaicans, and Guyanese concentrated in Community Districts 9 (Crown Heights), 14 (Flatbush/Midwood), and 17 (East Flatbush).

At the northern and southern extremities of Manhattan the growth of the immigrant population has redefined the shape of the borough's traditional ethnic enclaves. Just over half of the population of Manhattan Community District 12, which includes Washington Heights and Inwood, are foreign-born. The increase of the number of foreign-born residents in Bronx Community Districts 4, 5, and 7 revealed increases between 55 and 79 percent. (Half of the population of the Bronx speak a language other than English at home.) In 1980, Dominicans represented 9 percent of the city's Hispanic community. A decade later they represented 19 percent.

In the period 1983-9, 26,000 immigrants settled in Chinatown, causing an expansion of the community from its traditional core into the East Village, Stuyvesant Town, and the nearby lower East Side. There has also been a substantial growth of non-Chinese Asian immigration into Queens. After English and Spanish, Chinese is now on a par with Italian as the third most widely spoken language in the city. Koreans seem not to form residential enclaves where they have settled in Flushing, Jackson Heights, Corona, and Elmhurst in Queens. (In one Elmhurst elementary school, over half the students did not speak English as their native tongue; more than 30 languages were spoken by students.)

Half of all the city's Chinese-born immigrants, and half of all the Dominican-born, live in Manhattan (right). The immigrant areas have been traditional stepping-stones for entry into American society.

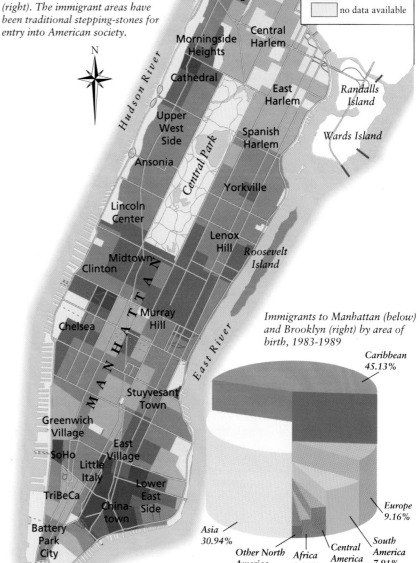

MANHATTAN: FOREIGN-BORN RESIDENTS
(as a percentage of total population)

- over 35%
- 25-34.9%
- 15-24.9%
- 5-14.9%
- less than 5%
- no data available

Immigrants to Manhattan (below) and Brooklyn (right) by area of birth, 1983-1989

Caribbean 45.13%
Europe 9.16%
South America 7.91%
Central America 3.23%
Africa 2.05%
Other North America 1.59%
Asia 30.94%

A Mexican child and a streetside flower-stall (far left), and a colorful West Indian carnival (below right) are just two examples of the changing impact of immigrant groups on the streetlife of New York City.

Since 1900, more than 33 million aliens have been admitted to the United States as immigrants. The immigrant population of New York has remained three or four times above the national level.

FOREIGN-BORN POPULATION, 1900-1980 (%)

	New York	United States
1900	37	13.7
1910	40.8	14.8
1920	36.1	13.2
1930	34	11.6
1940	28.7	8.8
1950	23.6	6.9
1960	20	5.4
1970	18.2	4.7
1980	23.6	6.2

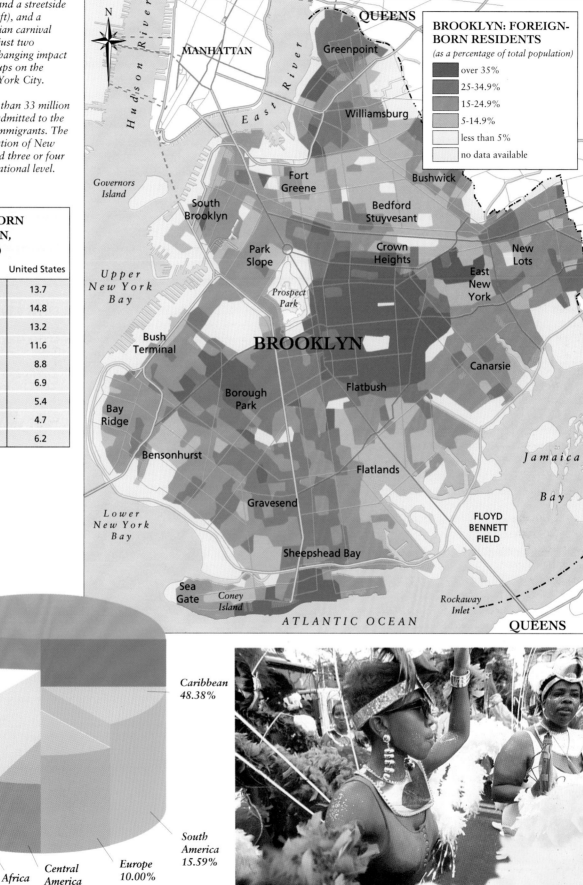

BROOKLYN: FOREIGN-BORN RESIDENTS
(as a percentage of total population)

- over 35%
- 25-34.9%
- 15-24.9%
- 5-14.9%
- less than 5%
- no data available

QUEENS

MANHATTAN

Greenpoint

Williamsburg

Bushwick

Fort Greene

Bedford Stuyvesant

South Brooklyn

Crown Heights

New Lots

Park Slope

East New York

Governors Island

Upper New York Bay

Prospect Park

Bush Terminal

BROOKLYN

Canarsie

Borough Park

Flatbush

Bay Ridge

Jamaica Bay

Bensonhurst

Flatlands

FLOYD BENNETT FIELD

Lower New York Bay

Gravesend

Sheepshead Bay

Sea Gate

Coney Island

Rockaway Inlet

ATLANTIC OCEAN

QUEENS

Hudson River

East River

Caribbean 48.38%

South America 15.59%

Europe 10.00%

Central America 5.73%

Africa 1.82%

Other North America 1.01%

Asia 17.46%

Public Housing

For over a century the city had struggled with the problems caused by tenements – from overcrowding and cockroaches to tuberculosis and emphysema – and mostly the losers in this unequal struggle were the poor. It was clear that the private provision of housing could never achieve either sufficient accommodation for a rapidly rising working-class population, or decent housing at an affordable price.

"Model tenements" were built to show landlords that improvements were possible; and mostly they soon fell into decay. The state legislature passed the Municipal Housing Act in 1934, which permitted the mayor, Fiorello La Guardia, for whom the goal of the city's housing policy was to "let in the sun", to create the Housing Authority of New York City, to develop housing projects to be financed by the sale of city bonds or by federal funds. In less than two years the first public housing project in the United States was opened, a project called the First Houses, based upon the rehabilitation and conversion of a group of eight tenements which lay between East 2nd and East 3rd Streets.

The policies of the New Deal overtly favored the building of single-family suburban homes as the engine to lift the nation's economy out of the Depression. There was little money available for low-cost housing in urban centers, and vast, unmet housing needs. But with the passing of the Wagner-Steagall Act in 1937, and the creation of the United States Housing Agency, the first "public housing" was built in the city. Over half a million low-rental apartments were built across the nation in the first two decades of the USHA; 30,000 of these apartments were built by the New York City Housing Authority. An additional 55,000 apartments were built under state and city programs.

In 1994 the City Housing Authority administered 179,715 apartments in 330 projects across the city. An estimated 600,000 residents currently live in public housing in New York City. With an operating budget of $1.2 billion, 105 Day Care Centers, 1.5 million windows, and 2,000 parks, the "projects" of the NYCHA represent a massive commitment to social welfare.

With a vigilant policy of non-discrimination on grounds of race, religion or ethnicity, the "projects" also represent an expression of national and local policies of racial integration. There was to be no replication of the city's ethnic neighborhoods and racial ghettoes in its public housing. Along with the contentious policies of rent control maintained after the Second World War, the social engineering implicit in the city's housing policies has certainly not solved the housing crisis, nor the problem of the homeless. But the city's experience of public housing forms an important tendon holding together the community. Housing is a social activity, and was recognized as such in New York.

In many parts of New York, rundown streets, overcrowded houses, and a general lack of amenities and open space (below) are endemic problems. Some housing projects, like the one pictured (below left), in the Kingsbridge district of the Bronx, attempt to provide more humane living conditions.

Frederick Ackerman, the first director of the Housing Authority of New York City, was intensely alive to the social responsibilities of housing. He favored open site plans, with garden apartments along the perimeter. But a debate was soon underway over the economic advantages of high-rise towers over low-rise for low income families. The critics' fears that public housing projects would create vertical sanitary slums were ignored when the Public Works Administration issued its Unit Plans in 1935, which specified acceptable design possibilities.

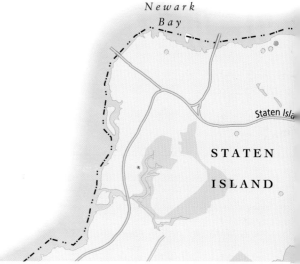

NEW YORK CITY PUBLIC HOUSING

public housing projects occupied:

- 1936-1949
- 1950-1965
- 1966-1980
- 1981-1991
- projects completed, but unoccupied
- projects under construction
- projects in planning

Administering New York City Housing Authority's 330 projects (right) is a major undertaking. Emergency service facilities are distributed throughout the city, and all aspects of routine maintenance, such as elevator safety and paintwork, are administered from a network of local offices.

Yonkers

Mount Vernon

New Rochelle

N

BRONX

Henry Hudson Parkway

Bronx River Parkway

Hutchinson River Parkway

Cross Bronx Expressway

Long Island Sound

125th St

Bronx-Whitestone Bridge

Throgg's Neck Bridge

East River

Astoria Boulevard

MANHATTAN

Hudson River

Long Island Expressway

QUEENS

Grand Central Parkway

Nassau

Brooklyn Queens Expressway

Van Wyck Expressway

Flatbush Ave.

Belt Parkway

Upper New York Bay

Prospect Expressway

BROOKLYN

Shore Parkway

The Narrows

ressway

Jamaica Bay

(Belt Parkway)

Lower New York Bay

ATLANTIC OCEAN

Broadway

For much of its history, Broadway *was* New York. To walk its length from the Bowling Green to Kingsbridge, starting with the former site of Mrs. Kocks' Dutch tavern at 1 Broadway is to understand how much of the city's story is to be found along its crowded length. As the center of fashion, commerce, and culture, Broadway in the 19th century set standards for style, consumption, and behavior which were emulated across the country.

In Dutch New Amsterdam, Broadway (De Heere Straet) was a broad dirt path whose west side was lined with pleasant rural cottages with gardens and orchards running down to the Hudson River. On the east side small artisans' huts and workshops straggled towards Wall Street and the limits of the city.

Under British rule, the distinction between the west and east side of the newly renamed Broad Way remained. The west side was the chosen location for St. Paul's Chapel and Trinity Church: it remained the more fashionable side. The British governor ordered the center of Broadway (as it came to be spelled) paved with pebbles, to form a gutter. Sidewalks were laid between Bowling Green and Trinity Church in 1709. Residents were allowed to plant trees. Broadway was lined with the homes of merchants, lawyers, and sea-captains.

The fire of 1776 destroyed much of colonial Broadway, and after the evacuation of the British army in 1783 the rebuilding of the city saw Broadway lined with three and four-story homes. It was still a street of private residences in the 1790s, but with the building of the City

Hotel above Trinity Church in 1794, and the opening of the Park Theater on Park Row four years later, the reconstructed city began to have a more northerly center-of-gravity. The street was graded as far as Canal Street in 1792, but the most fashionable retail businesses and shops were still located below Canal Street as late as the 1850s.

The streets below City Hall were increasingly given over to business while Broadway carried its bright lights northwards, decade by decade. The emergence of the "Ladies' Mile" of elegant shops between

The commercial, social, and theatrical hop-scotch along Broadway made the street a crowded, noisy spectacle, filled with energy (above, in 1875). It was "altogether the most showy, the most crowded, and the richest thoroughfare in America... collected into one promiscuous channel of activity and dissipation."
Putnam's Monthly, 1854

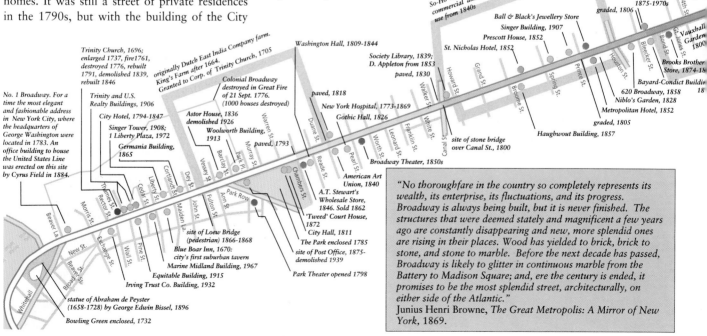

> "No thoroughfare in the country so completely represents its wealth, its enterprise, its fluctuations, and its progress. Broadway is always being built, but it is never finished. The structures that were deemed stately and magnificent a few years ago are constantly disappearing and new, more splendid ones are rising in their places. Wood has yielded to brick, brick to stone, and stone to marble. Before the next decade has passed, Broadway is likely to glitter in continuous marble from the Battery to Madison Square; and, ere the century is ended, it promises to be the most splendid street, architecturally, on either side of the Atlantic."
> Junius Henri Browne, The Great Metropolis: A Mirror of New York, 1869.

Union Square and Madison Square and the "Great White Way" of theaters above Times Square, both pointed to a street endlessly capable of self-renewal.

The decline of Broadway in the present century has been remorseless. Fashionable life and the luxury hotels fled to Fifth and Park Avenues. The theater district retained its importance, but the age of movies ushered in a deadly competitor. After 150 years as its glowing symbol, New York did not *need* Broadway. The reconstruction of Times Square, long overdue, suggests that it may be premature to write the street's obituary.

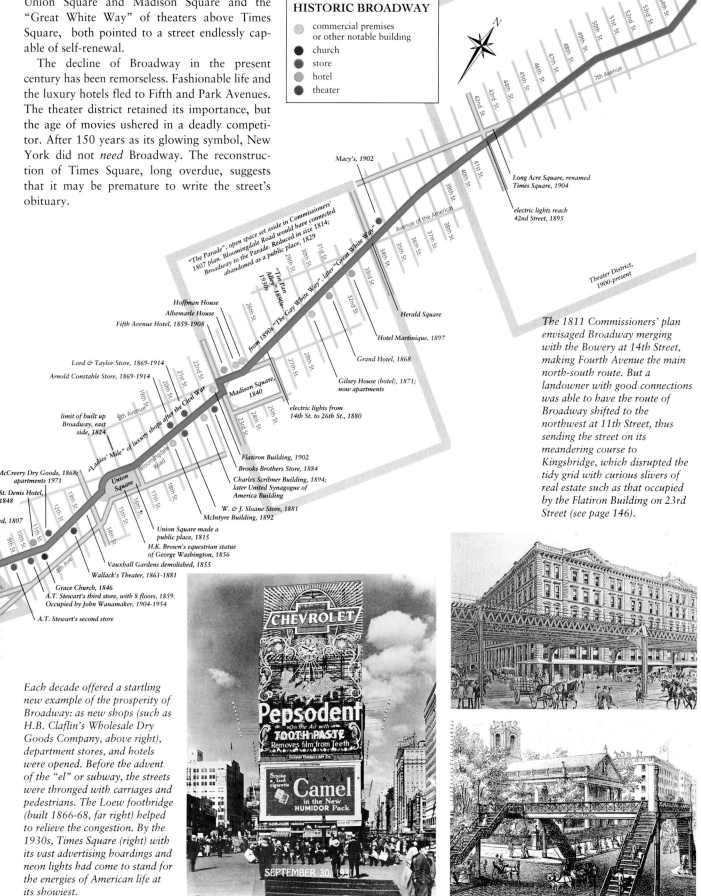

HISTORIC BROADWAY

- commercial premises or other notable building
- church
- store
- hotel
- theater

N

Macy's, 1902

Long Acre Square, renamed Times Square, 1904

electric lights reach 42nd Street, 1895

7th Avenue

Avenue of the Americas

Theater District, 1900-present

"The Parade", open space set aside in Commissioners' 1807 plan. Bloomingdale Road would have connected Broadway to the Parade. Reduced in size 1814; abandoned as a public place, 1829

"Tin Pan Alley", 1890s

from 1890s "The Gay White Way", later "Great White Way"

Hoffman House
Albemarle House
Fifth Avenue Hotel, 1859-1908

Herald Square

Hotel Martinique, 1897

Grand Hotel, 1868

Lord & Taylor Store, 1869-1914

Arnold Constable Store, 1869-1914

Gilsey House (hotel), 1871; now apartments

Madison Square, 1840

limit of built up Broadway, east side, 1824

electric lights from 14th St. to 26th St., 1880

"Ladies' Mile" of luxury shops after the Civil War

Bloomingdale Road

Flatiron Building, 1902

Brooks Brothers Store, 1884

Charles Scribner Building, 1894; later United Synagogue of America Building

W. & J. Sloane Store, 1881

McIntyre Building, 1892

McCreery Dry Goods, 1868; apartments 1971

St. Denis Hotel, 1848

Union Square

Union Square made a public place, 1815

H.K. Brown's equestrian statue of George Washington, 1856

Vauxhall Gardens demolished, 1855

Wallack's Theater, 1861-1881

...rd, 1807

Grace Church, 1846

A.T. Stewart's third store, with 8 floors, 1859. Occupied by John Wanamaker, 1904-1954

A.T. Stewart's second store

The 1811 Commissioners' plan envisaged Broadway merging with the Bowery at 14th Street, making Fourth Avenue the main north-south route. But a landowner with good connections was able to have the route of Broadway shifted to the northwest at 11th Street, thus sending the street on its meandering course to Kingsbridge, which disrupted the tidy grid with curious slivers of real estate such as that occupied by the Flatiron Building on 23rd Street (see page 146).

Each decade offered a startling new example of the prosperity of Broadway: as new shops (such as H.B. Claflin's Wholesale Dry Goods Company, above right), department stores, and hotels were opened. Before the advent of the "el" or subway, the streets were thronged with carriages and pedestrians. The Loew footbridge (built 1866-68, far right) helped to relieve the congestion. By the 1930s, Times Square (right) with its vast advertising hoardings and neon lights had come to stand for the energies of American life at its showiest.

Chronology 1609–1725

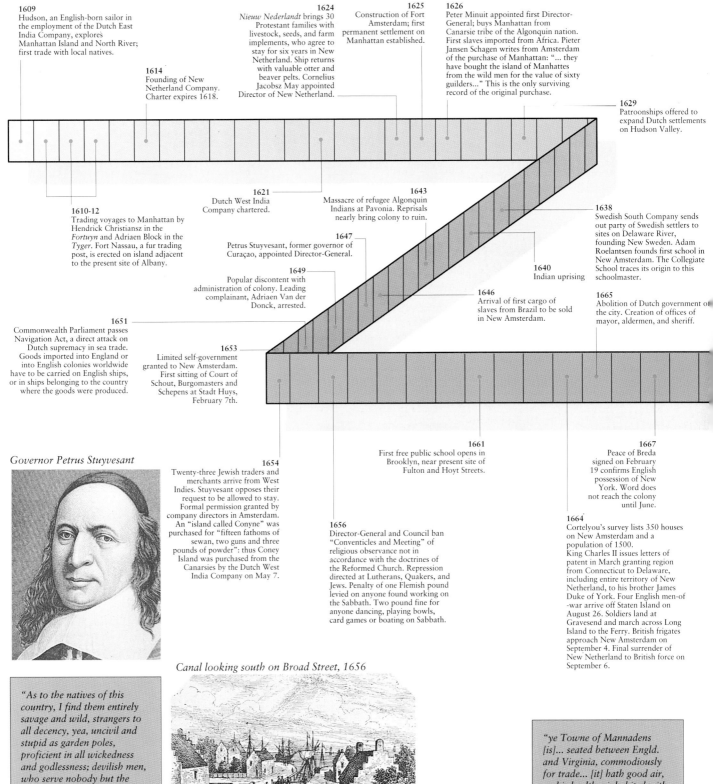

1609
Hudson, an English-born sailor in the employment of the Dutch East India Company, explores Manhattan Island and North River; first trade with local natives.

1614
Founding of New Netherland Company. Charter expires 1618.

1624
Nieuw Nederlandt brings 30 Protestant families with livestock, seeds, and farm implements, who agree to stay for six years in New Netherland. Ship returns with valuable otter and beaver pelts. Cornelius Jacobsz May appointed Director of New Netherland.

1625
Construction of Fort Amsterdam; first permanent settlement on Manhattan established.

1626
Peter Minuit appointed first Director-General; buys Manhattan from Canarsie tribe of the Algonquin nation. First slaves imported from Africa. Pieter Jansen Schagen writes from Amsterdam of the purchase of Manhattan: "... they have bought the island of Manhattes from the wild men for the value of sixty guilders..." This is the only surviving record of the original purchase.

1629
Patroonships offered to expand Dutch settlements on Hudson Valley.

1610-12
Trading voyages to Manhattan by Hendrick Christiansz in the *Fortuyn* and Adriaen Block in the *Tyger*. Fort Nassau, a fur trading post, is erected on island adjacent to the present site of Albany.

1621
Dutch West India Company chartered.

1643
Massacre of refugee Algonquin Indians at Pavonia. Reprisals nearly bring colony to ruin.

1647
Petrus Stuyvesant, former governor of Curaçao, appointed Director-General.

1638
Swedish South Company sends out party of Swedish settlers to sites on Delaware River, founding New Sweden. Adam Roelantsen founds first school in New Amsterdam. The Collegiate School traces its origin to this schoolmaster.

1640
Indian uprising

1649
Popular discontent with administration of colony. Leading complainant, Adriaen Van der Donck, arrested.

1646
Arrival of first cargo of slaves from Brazil to be sold in New Amsterdam.

1665
Abolition of Dutch government of the city. Creation of offices of mayor, aldermen, and sheriff.

1651
Commonwealth Parliament passes Navigation Act, a direct attack on Dutch supremacy in sea trade. Goods imported into England or into English colonies worldwide have to be carried on English ships, or in ships belonging to the country where the goods were produced.

1653
Limited self-government granted to New Amsterdam. First sitting of Court of Schout, Burgomasters and Schepens at Stadt Huys, February 7th.

Governor Petrus Stuyvesant

1654
Twenty-three Jewish traders and merchants arrive from West Indies. Stuyvesant opposes their request to be allowed to stay. Formal permission granted by company directors in Amsterdam. An "island called Conyne" was purchased for "fifteen fathoms of sewan, two guns and three pounds of powder": thus Coney Island was purchased from the Canarsies by the Dutch West India Company on May 7.

1661
First free public school opens in Brooklyn, near present site of Fulton and Hoyt Streets.

1667
Peace of Breda signed on February 19 confirms English possession of New York. Word does not reach the colony until June.

1656
Director-General and Council ban "Conventicles and Meeting" of religious observance not in accordance with the doctrines of the Reformed Church. Repression directed at Lutherans, Quakers, and Jews. Penalty of one Flemish pound levied on anyone found working on the Sabbath. Two pound fine for anyone dancing, playing bowls, card games or boating on Sabbath.

1664
Cortelyou's survey lists 350 houses on New Amsterdam and a population of 1500. King Charles II issues letters of patent in March granting region from Connecticut to Delaware, including entire territory of New Netherland, to his brother James Duke of York. Four English men-of-war arrive off Staten Island on August 26. Soldiers land at Gravesend and march across Long Island to the Ferry. British frigates approach New Amsterdam on September 4. Final surrender of New Netherland to British force on September 6.

Canal looking south on Broad Street, 1656

"As to the natives of this country, I find them entirely savage and wild, strangers to all decency, yea, uncivil and stupid as garden poles, proficient in all wickedness and godlessness; devilish men, who serve nobody but the Devil..."
The Rev. Jonas Michaëlius writing from New Amsterdam to his ecclesiastical superiors in Amsterdam, 1628

"ye Towne of Mannadens [is]... seated between Engld. and Virginia, commodiously for trade... [it] hath good air, and is healthy, inhabited with several sorts of Trades-men and marchants and mariners."
English description of Manhattan, 1661.

"On the 26th August [1664] there arrived in the Bay of the North River, near Staten Island, four great men-of-war, or frigates, well-manned with sailors and soldiers. They were provided with a patent or commission from the King of Great Britain to demand and take possession of this province, in the name of His Majesty... They intended, if any resistance was shown to them, to give a full broadside on this open place, then take it by assault, and make it a scene of pillage and bloodshed."
Reverend Samuel Drisus

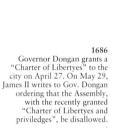

City Hall, 1700

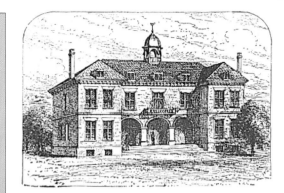

Governor Edmund Andros

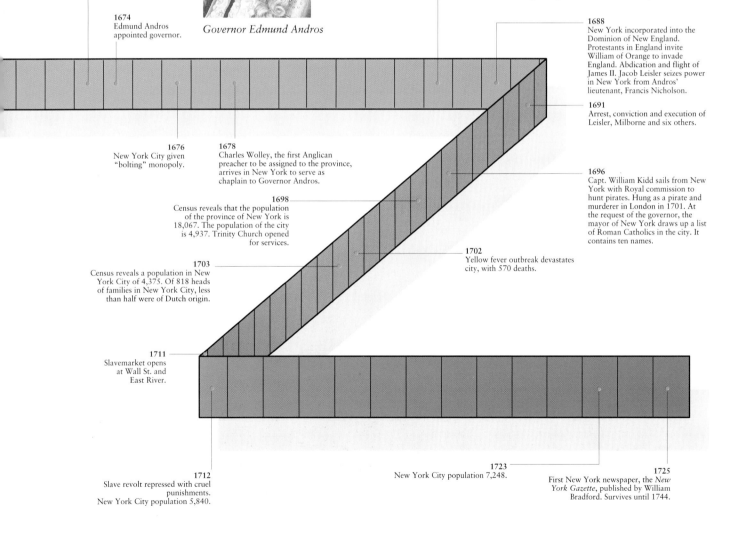

The residence of Jacob Leisler, who seized control of Fort James in the name of William of Orange in 1689. He was subsequently tried and executed for treason.

1673
Temporary restoration of Dutch rule (New York reverts to English rule in 1674).

1674
Edmund Andros appointed governor.

1686
Governor Dongan grants a "Charter of Libertyes" to the city on April 27. On May 29, James II writes to Gov. Dongan ordering that the Assembly, with the recently granted "Charter of Libertyes and priviledges", be disallowed.

1688
New York incorporated into the Dominion of New England. Protestants in England invite William of Orange to invade England. Abdication and flight of James II. Jacob Leisler seizes power in New York from Andros' lieutenant, Francis Nicholson.

1691
Arrest, conviction and execution of Leisler, Milborne and six others.

1676
New York City given "bolting" monopoly.

1678
Charles Wolley, the first Anglican preacher to be assigned to the province, arrives in New York to serve as chaplain to Governor Andros.

1696
Capt. William Kidd sails from New York with Royal commission to hunt pirates. Hung as a pirate and murderer in London in 1701. At the request of the governor, the mayor of New York draws up a list of Roman Catholics in the city. It contains ten names.

1698
Census reveals that the population of the province of New York is 18,067. The population of the city is 4,937. Trinity Church opened for services.

1702
Yellow fever outbreak devastates city, with 570 deaths.

1703
Census reveals a population in New York City of 4,375. Of 818 heads of families in New York City, less than half were of Dutch origin.

1711
Slavemarket opens at Wall St. and East River.

1712
Slave revolt repressed with cruel punishments.
New York City population 5,840.

1723
New York City population 7,248.

1725
First New York newspaper, the *New York Gazette*, published by William Bradford. Survives until 1744.

Chronology 1726–1800

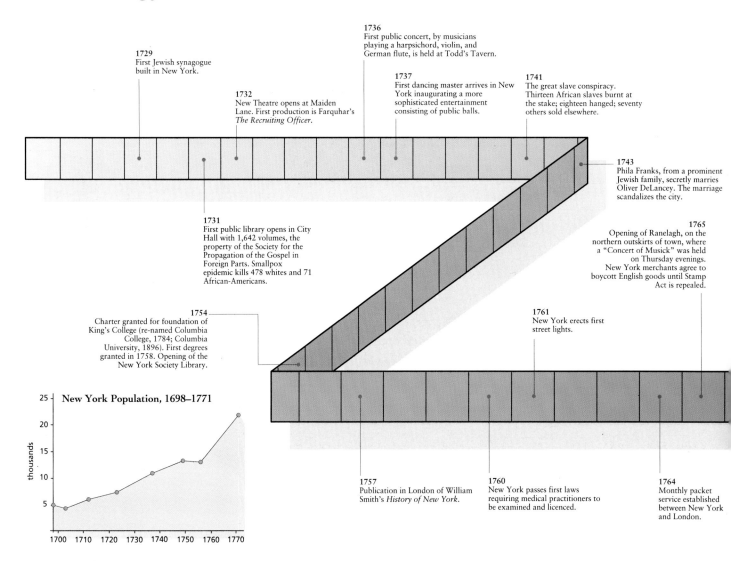

1729
First Jewish synagogue built in New York.

1736
First public concert, by musicians playing a harpsichord, violin, and German flute, is held at Todd's Tavern.

1732
New Theatre opens at Maiden Lane. First production is Farquhar's *The Recruiting Officer*.

1737
First dancing master arrives in New York inaugurating a more sophisticated entertainment consisting of public balls.

1741
The great slave conspiracy. Thirteen African slaves burnt at the stake; eighteen hanged; seventy others sold elsewhere.

1731
First public library opens in City Hall with 1,642 volumes, the property of the Society for the Propagation of the Gospel in Foreign Parts. Smallpox epidemic kills 478 whites and 71 African-Americans.

1743
Phila Franks, from a prominent Jewish family, secretly marries Oliver DeLancey. The marriage scandalizes the city.

1765
Opening of Ranelagh, on the northern outskirts of town, where a "Concert of Musick" was held on Thursday evenings. New York merchants agree to boycott English goods until Stamp Act is repealed.

1754
Charter granted for foundation of King's College (re-named Columbia College, 1784; Columbia University, 1896). First degrees granted in 1758. Opening of the New York Society Library.

1761
New York erects first street lights.

New York Population, 1698–1771

thousands
25
20
15
10
5

1700 1710 1720 1730 1740 1750 1760 1770

1757
Publication in London of William Smith's *History of New York*.

1760
New York passes first laws requiring medical practitioners to be examined and licenced.

1764
Monthly packet service established between New York and London.

Trinity Church, 1788

Burns' coffee house

"... about sun down, all the same negroes came to Hughson's [alehouse] again; some brought money and gave to Hughson for drink and dram; Ben played on the fiddle; Hughson's wife and daughter danced together in one part of the room, and the negroes in another; staid there until about seven that night:... they came there that night to frolic and merry make and did not talk about fires..."
Daniel Horsmanden, *Journal of the Proceedings Against the Conspirators, at New York in 1741.* The slave Ben, Hughson and his wife were among those executed for their part in the slave conspiracy.

"On the day preceded it [the "last day of Liberty" November1st], the Merchants of the City met at Barns' Tavern, the House of James DeLancey... and came to a Resolution to send for no goods from England, and sell none, should they be consigned to them, except the Stamp Act was repealed."
Robert R. Livingston to Robert Monckton, November 8, 1765

The north side of Wall Street in the 1780s.

Columbia College, chartered 1784

"A Cannonade from the Ships... seemed to infuse a panic thro' the whole of our troops who unfortunately were posted upon the left, where the enemy landed without the least opposition; for upon their approach to the Shore these dastardly sons of Cowardice deserted their lines & fled in the greatest Disorder & precipiture. I know not but I may venture to say Infected those upon the right, who speedily copied their vile conduct & then pursued them in their flight."
Major Nicolas Fish to John McKesson, Secretary of the New York Convention, September 19, 1776

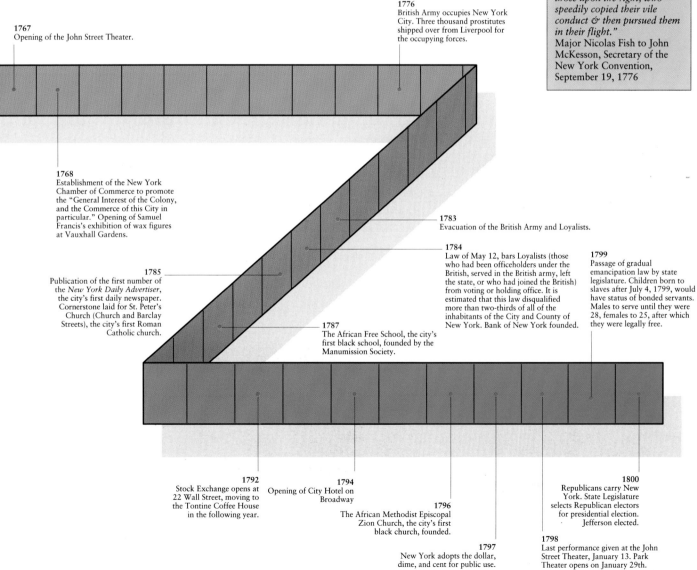

1767
Opening of the John Street Theater.

1776
British Army occupies New York City. Three thousand prostitutes shipped over from Liverpool for the occupying forces.

1768
Establishment of the New York Chamber of Commerce to promote the "General Interest of the Colony, and the Commerce of this City in particular." Opening of Samuel Francis's exhibition of wax figures at Vauxhall Gardens.

1783
Evacuation of the British Army and Loyalists.

1784
Law of May 12, bars Loyalists (those who had been officeholders under the British, served in the British army, left the state, or who had joined the British) from voting or holding office. It is estimated that this law disqualified more than two-thirds of all of the inhabitants of the City and County of New York. Bank of New York founded.

1799
Passage of gradual emancipation law by state legislature. Children born to slaves after July 4, 1799, would have status of bonded servants. Males to serve until they were 28, females to 25, after which they were legally free.

1785
Publication of the first number of the *New York Daily Advertiser*, the city's first daily newspaper. Cornerstone laid for St. Peter's Church (Church and Barclay Streets), the city's first Roman Catholic church.

1787
The African Free School, the city's first black school, founded by the Manumission Society.

1792
Stock Exchange opens at 22 Wall Street, moving to the Tontine Coffee House in the following year.

1794
Opening of City Hotel on Broadway

1796
The African Methodist Episcopal Zion Church, the city's first black church, founded.

1797
New York adopts the dollar, dime, and cent for public use.

1798
Last performance given at the John Street Theater, January 13. Park Theater opens on January 29th.

1800
Republicans carry New York. State Legislature selects Republican electors for presidential election. Jefferson elected.

Chronology 1801–1865

Chatham Square in 1812

1809
First Catholic receives the nomination of Tammany Hall for political office in New York. Steamship route opened to Philadelphia, by way of the Raritan River, an 18-mile stage to Trenton, and the Delaware River.

1812-5
War with Britain declared by Congress, June 18.

1817
Five New York shipowners announce the regular monthly sailing of packet service, called the Black Ball Line, between New York and Liverpool. Formation of New York Stock and Exchange Board.

1808
New York's first permanent circus, Pepe and Beschard's, opens on May 31 at Broadway and Worth Street.

1813
Burials below Canal Street prohibited.

The floor-plan for the Crystal Palace exhibition, which was held in 1853

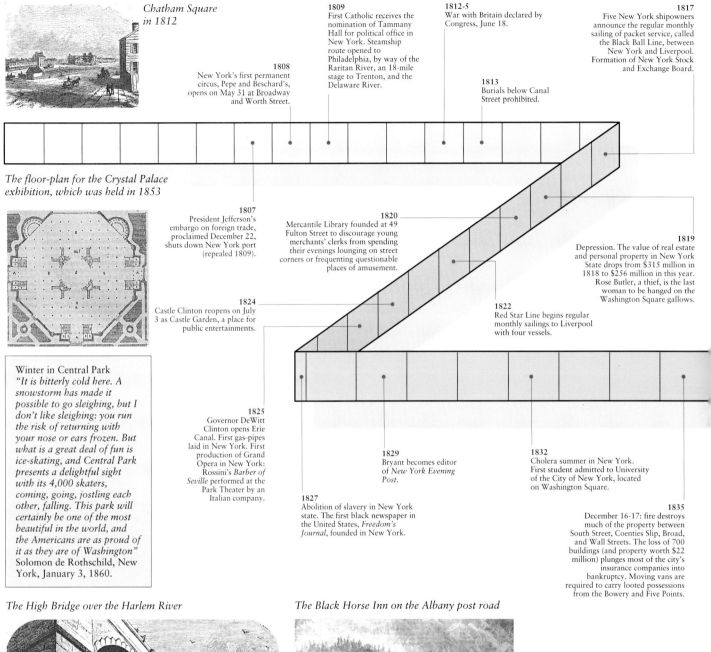

1807
President Jefferson's embargo on foreign trade, proclaimed December 22, shuts down New York port (repealed 1809).

1820
Mercantile Library founded at 49 Fulton Street to discourage young merchants' clerks from spending their evenings lounging on street corners or frequenting questionable places of amusement.

1819
Depression. The value of real estate and personal property in New York State drops from $315 million in 1818 to $256 million in this year. Rose Butler, a thief, is the last woman to be hanged on the Washington Square gallows.

1824
Castle Clinton reopens on July 3 as Castle Garden, a place for public entertainments.

1822
Red Star Line begins regular monthly sailings to Liverpool with four vessels.

Winter in Central Park
"It is bitterly cold here. A snowstorm has made it possible to go sleighing, but I don't like sleighing: you run the risk of returning with your nose or ears frozen. But what is a great deal of fun is ice-skating, and Central Park presents a delightful sight with its 4,000 skaters, coming, going, jostling each other, falling. This park will certainly be one of the most beautiful in the world, and the Americans are as proud of it as they are of Washington"
Solomon de Rothschild, New York, January 3, 1860.

1825
Governor DeWitt Clinton opens Erie Canal. First gas-pipes laid in New York. First production of Grand Opera in New York: Rossini's *Barber of Seville* performed at the Park Theater by an Italian company.

1829
Bryant becomes editor of *New York Evening Post.*

1832
Cholera summer in New York. First student admitted to University of the City of New York, located on Washington Square.

1827
Abolition of slavery in New York state. The first black newspaper in the United States, *Freedom's Journal*, founded in New York.

1835
December 16-17: fire destroys much of the property between South Street, Coenties Slip, Broad, and Wall Streets. The loss of 700 buildings (and property worth $22 million) plunges most of the city's insurance companies into bankruptcy. Moving vans are required to carry looted possessions from the Bowery and Five Points.

The High Bridge over the Harlem River

The Black Horse Inn on the Albany post road

Uptown in 1848:
"Walked about a little and contemplated the progress of uptown. The Fourth Avenue is so far built up as to have a city look as far as Thirty-first Street. All the cross streets have rows of houses starting up in them, and ten years more of this growth will carry the city beyond the Lower Reservoir [at 42nd Street]."
Diary of George Templeton Strong, November 20, 1848

An accommodation stage in the 1850s

Police charge on rioters during the Draft riots of 1863

An Englishman in New York, 1817
"'pon the whole, a walk through New York will disappoint an Englishman: there is, on the surface of society, a carelessness, a laziness, an unsocial indifference, which freezes the blood and disgusts the judgment. . . . I disapprove most decidedly of the obsequious servility of many London shopkeepers, but I am not prepared to go the length of those in New York, who stand with their hats on, or sit and lie along their counters, smoking segars, and spitting in every direction, to a degree offensive to any man of decent feelings . . ." Henry Fearon, *Sketches of America*, London, 1819

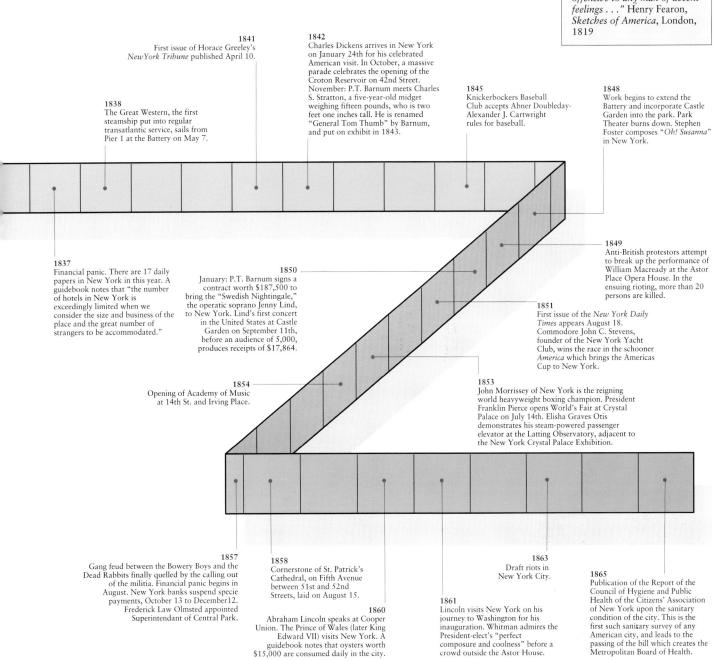

1841
First issue of Horace Greeley's *New York Tribune* published April 10.

1842
Charles Dickens arrives in New York on January 24th for his celebrated American visit. In October, a massive parade celebrates the opening of the Croton Reservoir on 42nd Street. November: P.T. Barnum meets Charles S. Stratton, a five-year-old midget weighing fifteen pounds, who is two feet one inches tall. He is renamed "General Tom Thumb" by Barnum, and put on exhibit in 1843.

1845
Knickerbockers Baseball Club accepts Abner Doubleday-Alexander J. Cartwright rules for baseball.

1848
Work begins to extend the Battery and incorporate Castle Garden into the park. Park Theater burns down. Stephen Foster composes *"Oh! Susanna"* in New York.

1838
The Great Western, the first steamship put into regular transatlantic service, sails from Pier 1 at the Battery on May 7.

1837
Financial panic. There are 17 daily papers in New York in this year. A guidebook notes that "the number of hotels in New York is exceedingly limited when we consider the size and business of the place and the great number of strangers to be accommodated."

1849
Anti-British protestors attempt to break up the performance of William Macready at the Astor Place Opera House. In the ensuing rioting, more than 20 persons are killed.

1850
January: P.T. Barnum signs a contract worth $187,500 to bring the "Swedish Nightingale," the operatic soprano Jenny Lind, to New York. Lind's first concert in the United States at Castle Garden on September 11th, before an audience of 5,000, produces receipts of $17,864.

1851
First issue of the *New York Daily Times* appears August 18. Commodore John C. Stevens, founder of the New York Yacht Club, wins the race in the schooner *America* which brings the Americas Cup to New York.

1854
Opening of Academy of Music at 14th St. and Irving Place.

1853
John Morrissey of New York is the reigning world heavyweight boxing champion. President Franklin Pierce opens World's Fair at Crystal Palace on July 14th. Elisha Graves Otis demonstrates his steam-powered passenger elevator at the Latting Observatory, adjacent to the New York Crystal Palace Exhibition.

1857
Gang feud between the Bowery Boys and the Dead Rabbits finally quelled by the calling out of the militia. Financial panic begins in August. New York banks suspend specie payments, October 13 to December 12. Frederick Law Olmsted appointed Superintendent of Central Park.

1858
Cornerstone of St. Patrick's Cathedral, on Fifth Avenue between 51st and 52nd Streets, laid on August 15.

1860
Abraham Lincoln speaks at Cooper Union. The Prince of Wales (later King Edward VII) visits New York. A guidebook notes that oysters worth $15,000 are consumed daily in the city.

1861
Lincoln visits New York on his journey to Washington for his inauguration. Whitman admires the President-elect's "perfect composure and coolness" before a crowd outside the Astor House.

1863
Draft riots in New York City.

1865
Publication of the Report of the Council of Hygiene and Public Health of the Citizens' Association of New York upon the sanitary condition of the city. This is the first such sanitary survey of any American city, and leads to the passing of the bill which creates the Metropolitan Board of Health.

Chronology 1866–1929

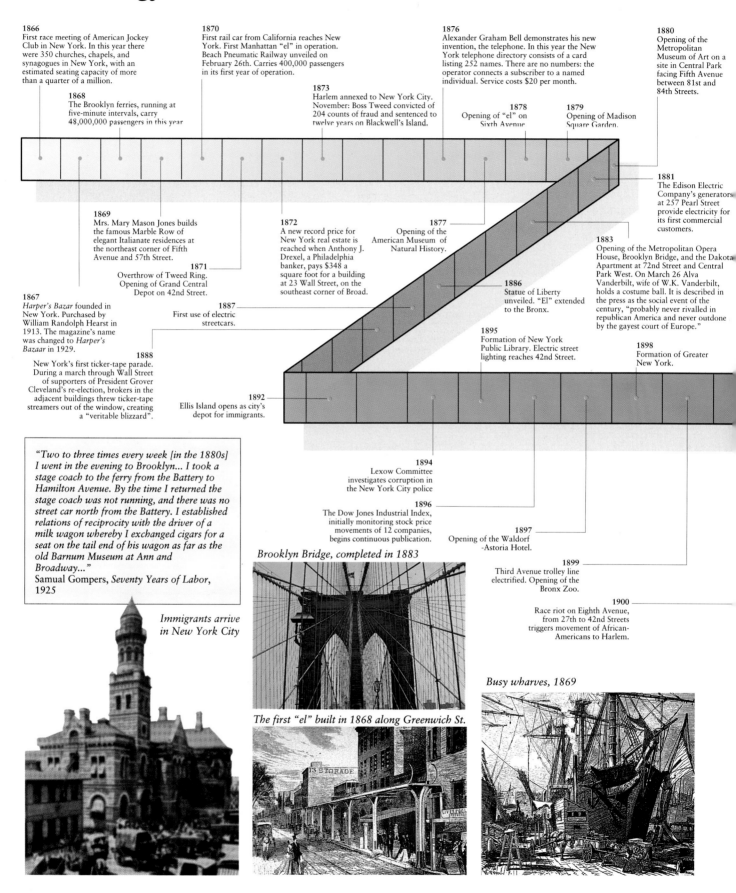

1866
First race meeting of American Jockey Club in New York. In this year there were 350 churches, chapels, and synagogues in New York, with an estimated seating capacity of more than a quarter of a million.

1870
First rail car from California reaches New York. First Manhattan "el" in operation. Beach Pneumatic Railway unveiled on February 26th. Carries 400,000 passengers in its first year of operation.

1876
Alexander Graham Bell demonstrates his new invention, the telephone. In this year the New York telephone directory consists of a card listing 252 names. There are no numbers: the operator connects a subscriber to a named individual. Service costs $20 per month.

1880
Opening of the Metropolitan Museum of Art on a site in Central Park facing Fifth Avenue between 81st and 84th Streets.

1868
The Brooklyn ferries, running at five-minute intervals, carry 48,000,000 passengers in this year

1873
Harlem annexed to New York City. November: Boss Tweed convicted of 204 counts of fraud and sentenced to twelve years on Blackwell's Island.

1878
Opening of "el" on Sixth Avenue

1879
Opening of Madison Square Garden.

1881
The Edison Electric Company's generators at 257 Pearl Street provide electricity for its first commercial customers.

1869
Mrs. Mary Mason Jones builds the famous Marble Row of elegant Italianate residences at the northeast corner of Fifth Avenue and 57th Street.

1872
A new record price for New York real estate is reached when Anthony J. Drexel, a Philadelphia banker, pays $348 a square foot for a building at 23 Wall Street, on the southeast corner of Broad.

1877
Opening of the American Museum of Natural History.

1883
Opening of the Metropolitan Opera House, Brooklyn Bridge, and the Dakota Apartment at 72nd Street and Central Park West. On March 26 Alva Vanderbilt, wife of W.K. Vanderbilt, holds a costume ball. It is described in the press as the social event of the century, "probably never rivalled in republican America and never outdone by the gayest court of Europe."

1871
Overthrow of Tweed Ring. Opening of Grand Central Depot on 42nd Street.

1867
Harper's Bazar founded in New York. Purchased by William Randolph Hearst in 1913. The magazine's name was changed to *Harper's Bazaar* in 1929.

1887
First use of electric streetcars.

1886
Statue of Liberty unveiled. "El" extended to the Bronx.

1895
Formation of New York Public Library. Electric street lighting reaches 42nd Street.

1898
Formation of Greater New York.

1888
New York's first ticker-tape parade. During a march through Wall Street of supporters of President Grover Cleveland's re-election, brokers in the adjacent buildings threw ticker-tape streamers out of the window, creating a "veritable blizzard".

1892
Ellis Island opens as city's depot for immigrants.

> "Two to three times every week [in the 1880s] I went in the evening to Brooklyn... I took a stage coach to the ferry from the Battery to Hamilton Avenue. By the time I returned the stage coach was not running, and there was no street car north from the Battery. I established relations of reciprocity with the driver of a milk wagon whereby I exchanged cigars for a seat on the tail end of his wagon as far as the old Barnum Museum at Ann and Broadway..."
> Samuel Gompers, *Seventy Years of Labor*, 1925

1894
Lexow Committee investigates corruption in the New York City police

1896
The Dow Jones Industrial Index, initially monitoring stock price movements of 12 companies, begins continuous publication.

1897
Opening of the Waldorf-Astoria Hotel.

1899
Third Avenue trolley line electrified. Opening of the Bronx Zoo.

1900
Race riot on Eighth Avenue, from 27th to 42nd Streets triggers movement of African-Americans to Harlem.

Immigrants arrive in New York City

Brooklyn Bridge, completed in 1883

The first "el" built in 1868 along Greenwich St.

Busy wharves, 1869

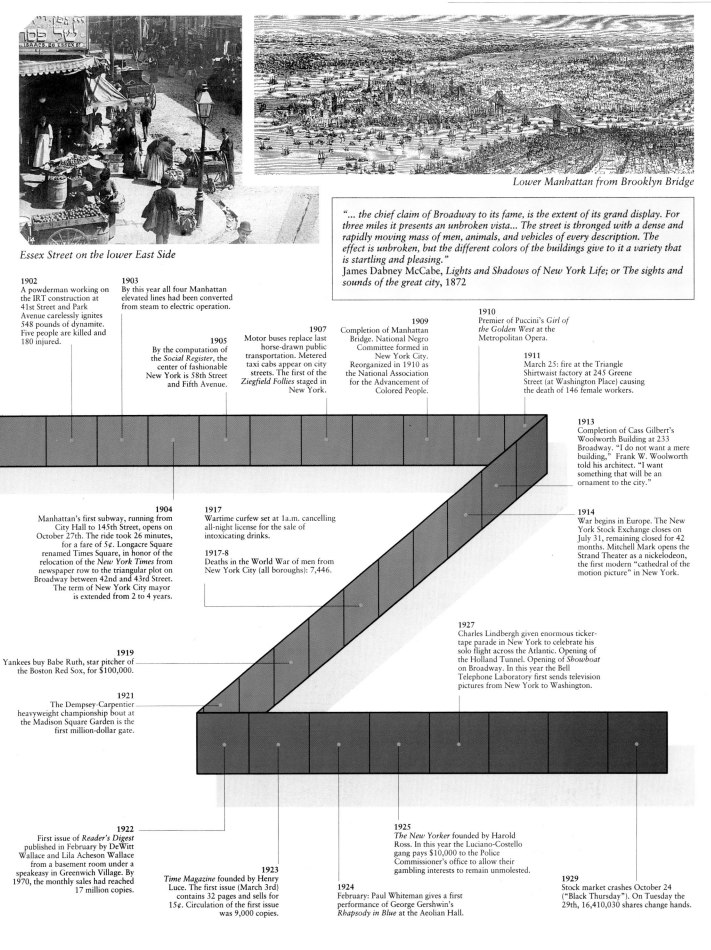

Lower Manhattan from Brooklyn Bridge

Essex Street on the lower East Side

"... the chief claim of Broadway to its fame, is the extent of its grand display. For three miles it presents an unbroken vista... The street is thronged with a dense and rapidly moving mass of men, animals, and vehicles of every description. The effect is unbroken, but the different colors of the buildings give to it a variety that is startling and pleasing."
James Dabney McCabe, *Lights and Shadows of New York Life; or The sights and sounds of the great city*, 1872

1902
A powderman working on the IRT construction at 41st Street and Park Avenue carelessly ignites 548 pounds of dynamite. Five people are killed and 180 injured.

1903
By this year all four Manhattan elevated lines had been converted from steam to electric operation.

1905
By the computation of the *Social Register*, the center of fashionable New York is 58th Street and Fifth Avenue.

1907
Motor buses replace last horse-drawn public transportation. Metered taxi cabs appear on city streets. The first of the *Ziegfield Follies* staged in New York.

1909
Completion of Manhattan Bridge. National Negro Committee formed in New York City. Reorganized in 1910 as the National Association for the Advancement of Colored People.

1910
Premier of Puccini's *Girl of the Golden West* at the Metropolitan Opera.

1911
March 25: fire at the Triangle Shirtwaist factory at 245 Greene Street (at Washington Place) causing the death of 146 female workers.

1913
Completion of Cass Gilbert's Woolworth Building at 233 Broadway. "I do not want a mere building," Frank W. Woolworth told his architect. "I want something that will be an ornament to the city."

1904
Manhattan's first subway, running from City Hall to 145th Street, opens on October 27th. The ride took 26 minutes, for a fare of 5¢. Longacre Square renamed Times Square, in honor of the relocation of the *New York Times* from newspaper row to the triangular plot on Broadway between 42nd and 43rd Street. The term of New York City mayor is extended from 2 to 4 years.

1917
Wartime curfew set at 1a.m. cancelling all-night license for the sale of intoxicating drinks.

1917-8
Deaths in the World War of men from New York City (all boroughs): 7,446.

1914
War begins in Europe. The New York Stock Exchange closes on July 31, remaining closed for 42 months. Mitchell Mark opens the Strand Theater as a nickelodeon, the first modern "cathedral of the motion picture" in New York.

1919
Yankees buy Babe Ruth, star pitcher of the Boston Red Sox, for $100,000.

1921
The Dempsey-Carpentier heavyweight championship bout at the Madison Square Garden is the first million-dollar gate.

1927
Charles Lindbergh given enormous ticker-tape parade in New York to celebrate his solo flight across the Atlantic. Opening of the Holland Tunnel. Opening of *Showboat* on Broadway. In this year the Bell Telephone Laboratory first sends television pictures from New York to Washington.

1922
First issue of *Reader's Digest* published in February by DeWitt Wallace and Lila Acheson Wallace from a basement room under a speakeasy in Greenwich Village. By 1970, the monthly sales had reached 17 million copies.

1923
Time Magazine founded by Henry Luce. The first issue (March 3rd) contains 32 pages and sells for 15¢. Circulation of the first issue was 9,000 copies.

1924
February: Paul Whiteman gives a first performance of George Gershwin's *Rhapsody in Blue* at the Aeolian Hall.

1925
The New Yorker founded by Harold Ross. In this year the Luciano-Costello gang pays $10,000 to the Police Commissioner's office to allow their gambling interests to remain unmolested.

1929
Stock market crashes October 24 ("Black Thursday"). On Tuesday the 29th, 16,410,030 shares change hands.

Chronology 1930–1994

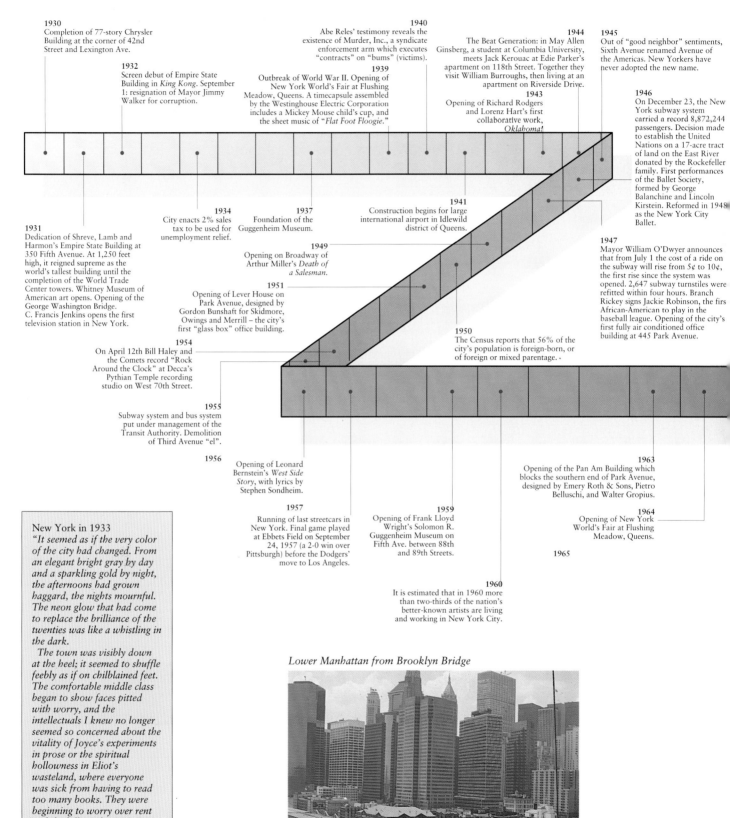

1930
Completion of 77-story Chrysler Building at the corner of 42nd Street and Lexington Ave.

1932
Screen debut of Empire State Building in *King Kong*. September 1: resignation of Mayor Jimmy Walker for corruption.

1940
Abe Reles' testimony reveals the existence of Murder, Inc., a syndicate enforcement arm which executes "contracts" on "bums" (victims).

1939
Outbreak of World War II. Opening of New York World's Fair at Flushing Meadow, Queens. A timecapsule assembled by the Westinghouse Electric Corporation includes a Mickey Mouse child's cup, and the sheet music of "*Flat Foot Floogie*."

1944
The Beat Generation: in May Allen Ginsberg, a student at Columbia University, meets Jack Kerouac at Edie Parker's apartment on 118th Street. Together they visit William Burroughs, then living at an apartment on Riverside Drive.

1943
Opening of Richard Rodgers and Lorenz Hart's first collaborative work, *Oklahoma!*

1945
Out of "good neighbor" sentiments, Sixth Avenue renamed Avenue of the Americas. New Yorkers have never adopted the new name.

1946
On December 23, the New York subway system carried a record 8,872,244 passengers. Decision made to establish the United Nations on a 17-acre tract of land on the East River donated by the Rockefeller family. First performances of the Ballet Society, formed by George Balanchine and Lincoln Kirstein. Reformed in 1948 as the New York City Ballet.

1931
Dedication of Shreve, Lamb and Harmon's Empire State Building at 350 Fifth Avenue. At 1,250 feet high, it reigned supreme as the world's tallest building until the completion of the World Trade Center towers. Whitney Museum of American art opens. Opening of the George Washington Bridge. C. Francis Jenkins opens the first television station in New York.

1934
City enacts 2% sales tax to be used for unemployment relief.

1937
Foundation of the Guggenheim Museum.

1941
Construction begins for large international airport in Idlewild district of Queens.

1949
Opening on Broadway of Arthur Miller's *Death of a Salesman*.

1951
Opening of Lever House on Park Avenue, designed by Gordon Bunshaft for Skidmore, Owings and Merrill – the city's first "glass box" office building.

1954
On April 12th Bill Haley and the Comets record "Rock Around the Clock" at Decca's Pythian Temple recording studio on West 70th Street.

1950
The Census reports that 56% of the city's population is foreign-born, or of foreign or mixed parentage.

1947
Mayor William O'Dwyer announces that from July 1 the cost of a ride on the subway will rise from 5¢ to 10¢, the first rise since the system was opened. 2,647 subway turnstiles were refitted within four hours. Branch Rickey signs Jackie Robinson, the first African-American to play in the baseball league. Opening of the city's first fully air conditioned office building at 445 Park Avenue.

1955
Subway system and bus system put under management of the Transit Authority. Demolition of Third Avenue "el".

1956
Opening of Leonard Bernstein's *West Side Story*, with lyrics by Stephen Sondheim.

1963
Opening of the Pan Am Building which blocks the southern end of Park Avenue, designed by Emery Roth & Sons, Pietro Belluschi, and Walter Gropius.

1957
Running of last streetcars in New York. Final game played at Ebbets Field on September 24, 1957 (a 2-0 win over Pittsburgh) before the Dodgers' move to Los Angeles.

1959
Opening of Frank Lloyd Wright's Solomon R. Guggenheim Museum on Fifth Ave. between 88th and 89th Streets.

1964
Opening of New York World's Fair at Flushing Meadow, Queens.

1965

1960
It is estimated that in 1960 more than two-thirds of the nation's better-known artists are living and working in New York City.

New York in 1933
"*It seemed as if the very color of the city had changed. From an elegant bright gray by day and a sparkling gold by night, the afternoons had grown haggard, the nights mournful. The neon glow that had come to replace the brilliance of the twenties was like a whistling in the dark.*
The town was visibly down at the heel; it seemed to shuffle feebly as if on chilblained feet. The comfortable middle class began to show faces pitted with worry, and the intellectuals I knew no longer seemed so concerned about the vitality of Joyce's experiments in prose or the spiritual hollowness in Eliot's wasteland, where everyone was sick from having to read too many books. They were beginning to worry over rent and the bills at the A. & P."
Harold Clurman, *The Fervent Years: The Story of the Group Theater and the Thirties* 1946

Lower Manhattan from Brooklyn Bridge

A rustic bridge in a secluded part of Central Park

A view of Broad Street in the city's financial district

In this year New York City has an industrial workforce of nearly one million, and a manufacturing payroll of close to three billion dollars.

1966
Subway fare rises to 20¢. Demolition of McKim, Mead & White's Pennsylvania Rail Road Station.

1968
Two hundred thousand students take part in giant antiwar rally in New York.

Daily News headline, October 30:
FORD TO CITY: DROP DEAD.

1982

Completion of tower 2 (1,350-feet-tall) of the World Trade Center complex, built by the Port Authority of New York & New Jersey.

1975

> "New York is an ugly city, a dirty city. Its climate is a scandal, its politics are used to frighten children, its traffic is madness, its competition is murderous. But there is one thing about it – once you have lived in New York and it has become your home, no place else is good enough."
> John Steinbeck, *New York Magazine*, Feb 1, 1953

1970
Subway fare raised to 30¢. August 10: women win the legal right to drink at McSorley's Old Ale House, at 15 East 7th Street, a bastion of male exclusivity since 1854.

NYSE registers its first 100 million share day.

1984

1973
NYSE registers its first 200 million share day. Publication of Jay McInerney's *Bright Lights, Big City*.

1990
Census reveals a median income in metropolitan New York of $38,445, a poverty rate of 11.7 percent, and a population made up of 18.2 percent blacks, 4.8 percent Asians, 15.4 percent Hispanics, and since 1980 a foreign immigration of 1,514,101.

1992
Reopening of restored Bryant Park. 68 of the city's 75 police precincts report decreases in total felonies compared with 1991.

The ornate entrance to the Empire State Building

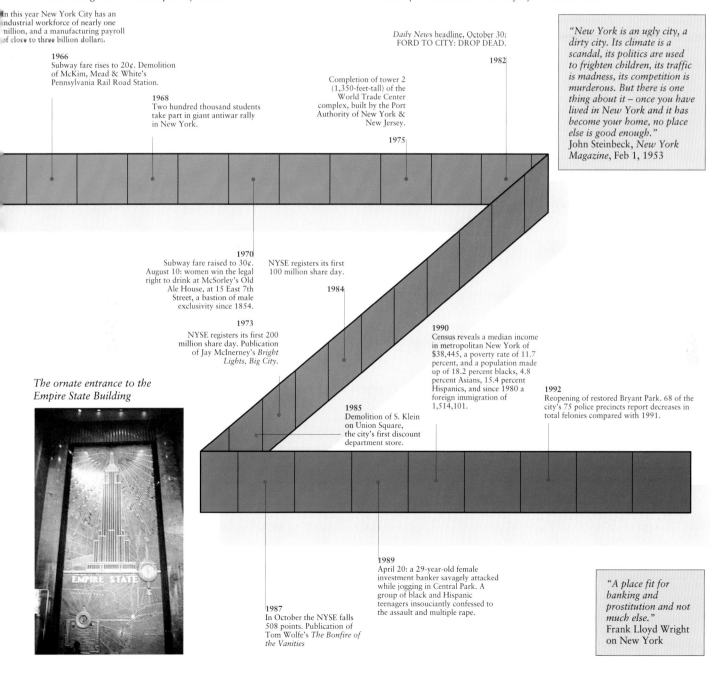

1985
Demolition of S. Klein on Union Square, the city's first discount department store.

1989
April 20: a 29-year-old female investment banker savagely attacked while jogging in Central Park. A group of black and Hispanic teenagers insouciantly confessed to the assault and multiple rape.

1987
In October the NYSE falls 508 points. Publication of Tom Wolfe's *The Bonfire of the Vanities*

> "A place fit for banking and prostitution and not much else."
> Frank Lloyd Wright on New York

Biographical Notes

Compiled by Stephanie Blackman, Perryn Callister, Helen Lewis, Laura Silverman, and Hwee Hwee Tan

Baker, Josephine (1906-1975) At the age of 13 Baker ran away from home to join a travelling vaudeville troupe. At 15, already showing mature talent as a dancer and comic, she appeared on Broadway. Her part African-American background confined Baker to "color" revues, such as *La Revue Négre* in Paris, 1925. The introduction of a black act in the *Folies Bergère* gave Baker her first solo appearance in Paris. Her combination of vaudeville routines with jazz, and a G-string decorated with bananas, made "Josephine" an overnight sensation. Her European successes were never matched in the United States, and Baker became a French citizen in 1937. During the war she was recruited by the French resistance, and received a military honor afterwards. Financial pressures brought Baker back to New York to perform where she was accused of being a communist who had consorted with fascists during the war. In the 1950s and 1960s Baker became so visible a campaigner for racial equality that she was at the side of the Rev. Martin Luther King, Jr., at the Lincoln Memorial during the March on Washington in 1963.

Balanchine, George (1904-1983) Born Georgy Balanchivadze, he left Russia in 1924 as part of a touring ballet company. In 1933 he formed his own company, *Les Ballets*. At this time he was approached by Lincoln Kirstein about forming the troupe of dancers that would eventually become the New York City Ballet in 1948. By 1964 they were permanently housed at the Lincoln Center's New York State Theater. Balanchine created over 150 works for the company, including *The Nutcracker* (1954) and *Don Quixote* (1965). He also enjoyed a long term collaboration with Igor Stravinsky, beginning in 1928 with *Apollo*. Success also came from choreographing a number of Broadway musicals and films. He continued as artistic director of the New York City Ballet until 1982 and died the following year. *(H.L.)*

Barnum, P.T. (1810-1891) Originally from Bethel, Connecticut, P.T. Barnum spent his early career fleecing customers in the store he ran with his uncle. After an acrimonious split with his uncle, Barnum entered popular journalism, starting a newspaper, *The Herald of Freedom*. Moving to New York in 1834, he embarked on a new career as an entrepreneur of popular entertainment, founding the American Museum on Broadway in 1841. Barnum marketed The American Museum as family entertainment, catering to all social classes, and even providing husbands and wives with an entertainment they could enjoy together. With a genius for publicity and able to tap public curiosity for (un)natural wonders, Barnum rode high on a wave of popularity until his death, assured legendary status as the first and perhaps the greatest of American showmen. *(P.C.)*

Berlin, Irving (1888–1989) Irving Berlin was born in Russia as Isadore Baline. His family emigrated to the United States and settled in New York City's lower East Side when he was five years old. Although he had no formal musical education, Berlin wrote approximately 800 songs, the most enduring of these coming from his scores for musicals. The most successful song of Berlin's early career was "*Alexander's Ragtime Band*" (1911), which popularized Ragtime throughout America. His later composition, "*There's No Business Like Show Business*" became the Battle Hymn of the theater in the United States. In 1919 he founded Irving Berlin Inc. to publish his music. From the 1920s to the 1960s Berlin wrote scores for many Broadway musicals, but his greatest success came in 1946 with *Annie Get Your Gun*. He also wrote scores for films, and a number of his Broadway shows were filmed. *(P.C.)*

Bernstein, Leonard (1918-1990) Born Louis Bernstein

Josephine Baker

in Lawrence, Massachusetts, he was called Leonard throughout his childhood, and eventually had his name legally changed. After attending Harvard College, he studied music at the Curtis Institute of Music in Philadelphia. In 1943 he joined the New York Philharmonic as assistant conductor. Bernstein established his reputation on November 14, 1943 when he unexpectedly had to substitute for a guest conductor. The following year, he presented his first symphony, *Jeremiah*, the ballet *Fancy Free*, and the musical *On the Town*. In 1945 he became the first American-born music director of the New York Philharmonic, remaining in this position for the next eleven years. Perhaps best known for his scores for musicals such as *Candide* (1956) and *West Side Story* (1957) and the film *On the Waterfront* (1954), he also wrote several books and toured extensively. He died in New York on October 4, 1990. *(L.S.)*

Blades, Ruben (1948-...) Singer, songwriter and political activist; studied law in New York City before returning to Panama where his musical success began. After a year as attorney for the Banco Nacional Panama (1973-74), he returned to New York, the major center of salsa music. From 1974 to 1983 he served as both a recording artist and legal adviser for Fania Records Inc. In 1978 he released *Siembra*, which became the highest selling salsa album ever. By 1984 he had moved to the bigger Elektra label. They issued his first English language album *Nothing But Trouble* which featured songs co-written with Lou Reed and Elvis Costello. He received Grammy nominations in 1983 and 1984. As

well as being involved with a number of political causes, particularly those relating to the Latino community, Blades has expanded his repetoire to include acting, appearing in such films as *The Milagro Beanfield War* and *The Color of Night*. *(H.L.)*

Bryant, William Cullen (1794-1878) Rising from a Massachusetts Calvinist background, Bryant was drawn to poetry as a child and was to become America's foremost poet and critic from the 1820s until the end of his long life. In 1825 he left his Massachusetts law practice for New York, and became the editor of the *New York Evening Post*, a position he held for half a century. He was a supporter of the conservative and respectable element within the Democratic Party, but broke with the pro-slavery elements over abolition. He was a passionate supporter of the Union cause in the Civil War. Never a prolific poet, his first book, *Poems*, appeared in 1821 and was followed by a volume in each decade of his life. He looked to the grand American West for inspiration while also being devoted to abolitionist principles and the Northern cause during the Civil War. "Personally, Bryant looks like one of the ancient patriarchs. His hair and beard, which he wears long, are of silvery white and of silken softness, and he might well sit for a model of Calchas. Though his face is deeply wrinkled, he is erect, lithe and vigorous as a man of thirty and, in his seventy-fourth year, is probably the best preserved New-Yorker in the neighborhood of Manhattan." *(S.B.)*

Cahan, Abraham (1860-1951) Russian-American

Jewish newspaper editor and novelist, Cahan emigrated to New York from Vilna in 1882. In 1897 he helped found the *Jewish Daily Forward*, which he edited for nearly fifty years. The *Forward*, which had a peak circulation of 250,000, was the voice of the Jewish socialist working class. Cahan was one of the first fiction writers to portray immigrants realistically, and also highlighted the problems of their Americanization. His fictional works include *Yekl: A Tale of the New York Ghetto* (1896), *The Imported Bridegroom and Other Stories of the New York Ghetto* (1898) and, most notably, *The Rise of David Levinsky* (1917). *(H.H.T.)*

Croker, Richard (1841-1922) Croker's family emigrated from Ireland to New York when he was a child. He entered politics in 1862 and then joined the "Young Democracy" faction of the Tammany Hall Democrats who opposed "Boss" Tweed in 1868. He served as an alderman from 1868 to 1870. After Tweed's downfall in 1871, he became a leading figure under "Honest John" Kelly, and became leader of Tammany Hall in 1885. "Boss" Croker dominated Democratic party politics for the next ten years, surviving a scandal involving police corruption in 1894. In 1897 he was responsible for engineering the election of Robert Van Wyck as the first mayor of Greater New York. At the turn of the century his political power began to fade and soon after he returned to an estate in his native Ireland, where he died in 1922. *(H.L.)*

Cuomo, Mario (1932-...) The son of Italian immigrants, Cuomo did not speak English until he entered school. He attended St. John's University and law school and even tried out for minor league baseball. He was running a successful law practice in Brooklyn when, in 1972, Mayor John Lindsay appointed him as mediator in a dispute over low income housing, which launched him on a career in local and state politics. In 1977 he ran for mayor of New York in the Democratic primary, but lost to Ed Koch. In the next year he was elected Lieutenant Governor. Elected Governor in 1982, he was re-elected in 1986 and 1990. There has been frequent speculation as to whether Cuomo would run for President, most notably in 1992. He has always declined, but gave a rousing nomination speech for Bill Clinton at the 1992 Democratic National Convention held at Madison Square Garden. In 1984 he published *Diaries of Mario Cuomo*, which gave an account of his winning campaign for Governor. Defeated by George Pataki in 1994. *(H.L.)*

Ellington, Duke (1899-1974) Ironically, the man who is considered to be the founder of modern jazz initially wanted to be a painter. Duke Ellington was born Edward Kennedy Ellington on April 29, 1899 in Washington, D.C. A deeply religious and superstitious man whose charisma with women was well documented, Ellington was playing by 1926 in Harlem's prestigious Cotton Club. From 1926 to 1945 he was composing on levels that no other jazz musician could achieve until years later. In addition to his composing skills, Ellington was a pianist and innovator, who transformed music recording by pioneering such devices as the now popular echo chamber. He was dubbed the Great Orchestrator of Jazz – almost everything concerning sound and instrumentation in jazz is traceable to him. Ellington died of pneumonia on May 25, 1974. The Duke once simply summed up his music as the transformation of memories into sounds. *(L.S.)*

Ellsworth, Elmer (1837-1861) Ellsworth resigned his regular army commission after the attack on Fort Sumter to recruit a regiment of New York firemen. He soon recruited more than 1,000 men, who elected him their colonel. New Yorkers raised $60,000 to equip the regiment with Sharp's rifles, and a gray, scarlet and blue uniform. Officially known as the 11th regiment New York State Volunteers, they departed from New York on April 29, 1861 for Annapolis. The 11th never quite lived down a reputation for disorderly conduct, but they were heroes of the day when they put out a fire at Willard's hotel on their arrival in Washington. Ellsworth was killed trying to cut down a southern flag flying from the Marshall House in Alexandria, Virginia. The dashing Ellsworth was the first commissioned officer in the Union Army to die in the Civil War, and New York's first military hero.

Gershwin, George (1898-1937) Born Jacob Gershwin to Russian-Jewish parents on Manhattan's lower East Side, Gershwin received minimal musical training and never became proficient at reading music. After early success on Broadway, his popularity continued to grow throughout the 1920s and 1930s with a series of musicals and film scores. Many of these contained lyrics by his brother Ira. In 1932 his *Of Thee I Sing* became the first musical to win a Pulitzer Prize for drama. His desire to be considered a serious composer resulted in his best known composition, *Rhapsody in Blue* (1924) and *An American in Paris* (1928) which combined jazz with classical orchestration. His opera *Porgy and Bess* (1935) also pushed the boundaries of that genre, albeit to a mixed critical response. Gershwin enjoyed his success, moving in fashionable circles and befriending film stars. He died of a brain tumor at the age of 38. *(H.L.)*

Goldman, Emma (1869-1940) Born into a Jewish family in Lithuania. Goldman emigrated to Rochester in 1886, and in New York City, in the aftermath of the Haymarket hangings of "Black Friday," she joined the German anarchist movement dominated by Johan Most. She encountered repression and squalor instead of the freedom and opportunity she had

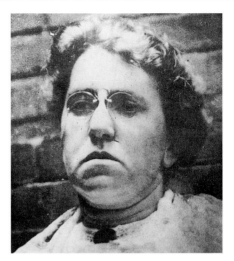

Emma Goldman

anticipated in the New World, and was soon known as a taunting, funny public speaker. Throughout the 1890s, "Red Emma" organized numerous demonstrations and achieved notoriety which was fed by every local sheriff and chief of police who tried to deny her a public platform. She boldly lectured on anarchism, the drama, the position of women in society, and wrote essays for whatever magazine was brave enough to publish someone so notorious. Arrested for opposing the draft in 1917, she was deported to Bolshevik Russia by the US government in 1920 along with 27 other "revolutionaries" under the 1918 Alien Exclusion Act. After Trotsky's bloody repression of the Kronstadt uprising in 1921, she became an even more persistent critic of Bolshevik totalitarianism than she had been of capitalist oppression in the United States. Her acclaimed autobiography, *Living My Life*, appeared in 1931. *(S.B.)*

Graham, Martha (1894-1991) The eldest of three girls, Martha Graham started life in Pittsburgh, Pennsylvania but by 1908 the family had relocated to Santa Barbara, California. It was the Oriental interpretations of dancer Ruth St. Denis, whom Graham first saw in 1910, that inspired her chosen path, and so on the death of her father in 1914, she enrolled at her idol's School of Dancing, "Denishawn." She soon progressed to both teach and choreograph extensively, spreading her own distinct style. Graham first performed in New York in April 1926 at the 48th Street Theater and would later collaborate with the New York City Ballet. Her long career effectively brought modern dance to New York and Graham is best known for her solo in the composition "Deep Song." *(S.B.)*

Greeley, Horace (1811-1872) Horace Greeley's life seems to have followed the tradition of the American Ideal – a poor boy rising by his own efforts to a position of great power. Entranced by literature from childhood, Greeley became an apprentice printer in 1826 and, after moving to New York in 1831, was employed in successive printing jobs. In 1841 Greeley borrowed a small amount of capital, launched the *Tribune*, and achieved an almost instant success. His frequent counsel "Go West, young man, and grow up with the country" became the cry of an era. From 1842 he was an active participant in New York politics, but was the most heavily beaten candidate who had ever sought the Presidency. He died shortly after this crushing defeat, aged 61. *(P.C.)*

Guinan, "Texas" (1884-1933) After a career with rodeos and theatrical companies and two failed marriages, Guinan arrived in New York in 1905. She won parts in musical comedies, and appeared in several hundred silent two-reel movies. She came into her own in Prohibition New York as hostess of the El Fay Club. "Hello, sucker!" was her greeting to customers. She and the New York police department played games: when the El Fay Club was closed down, she reappeared at the Del Fay, and then at the

George Gershwin

Texas Guinan Club, 300 Club, Club Intime and others. The police were unable to prove she owned any of these clubs, and each failed prosecution made her an ever-greater celebrity. Her wise-cracking, earthy style made Guinan one of the pathbreakers for the stage and cinema style of Mae West.

Hamilton, Alexander (1755-1804) A child of the West Indies, Hamilton sailed to New York in 1772. He enrolled at King's College (now Columbia University) from which he emerged as a passionate defender of American rights against Crown prerogatives. After spending six years in the Continental Army and serving on General Washington's staff, he developed a burning nationalistic faith, which manifested itself in support for the proposed Constitution. Hamilton was among the fifty-five delegates sent to the Great Convention of 1787 and was one of the authors of *The Federalist*, a collection of newspaper essays which was to powerfully affect the American philosphy of government. Hamilton was appointed Secretary of the Treasury in 1789, where he showed his great talent for administration as well as being a trusted personal advisor to George Washington. Hamilton was killed in a duel with Aaron Burr in Weehawkin over a slight. *(S.B.)*

Hellman, Lillian (1905-1984) She was born in New Orleans, and came to New York at the age of six. Hellman attended New York University for two years, and then got a job with the publishing company of Horace Liveright. She married Arthur Kober, lost her job at Liveright, reviewed books and worked as a play reader. After a stay in Hollywood working for MGM, Hellman's first play, *The Children's Hour*, opened on Broadway in 1934 and ran for 691 performances. She had a longterm relationship with Dashiell Hammett, to whom she dedicated her first play. It was her period as a fellow-traveller which was the source of many recriminations in later decades. Her second great Broadway success came with Tallulah Bankhead's performance as Regina Giddens in *The Little Foxes* in 1939. Hellman believed that the theater could be a force for social change, and remained loyal to an Ibsenite commitment to social realism on the stage. Her last great theatrical triumph was *Toys in the Attic* (1960). Hellman's sharp-tongued autobiographical writings (*An Unfinished Woman*, 1969; *Pentimento*, 1974; *Scoundrel Time*, 1976), gave her many chances to even scores. *(H.L.)*

Holiday, Billie (1915-1959) Known as Lady Day and the Angel of Harlem, Holliday had a hard childhood and after moving to New York she became a prostitute. Her singing career began in Harlem bars in 1931, where she was an instant success. A collaboration with Benny Goodman in 1933 was followed by work with Count Basie and Artie Shaw. She also toured Canada and played Chicago and New York City clubs. Her first solo concert, held at New York's Town Hall in 1946, was followed by several film appearances. Periods in hospital and prison on drugs charges marked Holliday's unhappy private life. After nearly a year in prison she returned in

Lillian Hellman

Alexander Hamilton

March 1948 for a sellout concert at Carnegie Hall. Ten years of touring the United States and a 1954 tour of Europe followed, but her addiction to heroin worsened. As she was admitted to the Metropolitan Hospital in New York for the last time, the police tried to arrest her for possession of illegal drugs. *Lady Sings the Blues*, a bitter autobiography, was published in 1956. *(H.L.)*

Hopper, Edward (1882-1967) Hopper trained at the New York School of Art under Robert Henri (1900-1906) before embarking on the first of several trips to Europe. On his return in 1910 he set up a studio on E. 59th St. He made his living as a commercial artist and illustrator, painting in his spare time. In 1913 he moved his studio to 3 Washington Square, where he lived until his death. That same year he sold his first painting at the New York Armory Show for $250. In 1920 he had the first one man exhibition at the Whitney Studio Club (147 W. 4th St.). In 1924 he married Jo Nivison, who was his inspiration for all subsequent portrayals of women in his work. Hopper continued to fund his painting with work as an illustrator but received official recognition with a retrospective exhibition at the New York Museum of Modern Art in 1933. Other major exhibitions followed in 1950, 1964, and 1980. *(H.L.)*

Hosack, David (1769-1835) Earned his BA at Princeton University in 1789, and studied medicine at the University of Pennsylvania. Became Professor of Botany, Columbia University, 1795-1807 (during this period he founded the Elgin Botanical Garden on the land where Rockefeller Center is now sited). He was physician and consultant physician at the New York Hospital, 1797-1835. He was the attending physician at the duel between Burr and Hamilton at Weehawkin in 1804. Hosack introduced vaccination into the United States, and was the most prominent physician in New York City in his time, with extensive acquaintances in the city's artistic and intellectual life.

Hughes, Archbishop John Joseph (1797-1864) He did not leave Ireland until he was 21, when he emigrated to the United States with the idea of becoming a priest. He had an assortment of jobs before being admitted into the seminary in 1820. On October 15, 1826, he was ordained by the Philadelphia diocese. In 1838 he was consecrated as coadjutor bishop of New York. After the death of Bishop DuBois in 1824 Hughes was installed as bishop of New York. In this role he reduced debt, diminished the power of trustees and advocated the development of parochial Catholic schooling. In July 1850 New York was made an archdiocese and Hughes was appointed archbishop. He courted controversy by opposing abolitionism and arguing that Irish imigrants should not "Go West" but should remain in the cities where they would stay under the guidance of the Church.

(H.L.)

Hughes, Langston (1902-1976) Born in Joplin, Missouri. When he was thirteen, he received his first accolade for his poetic talents when elected class poet by his grammar school. Although influenced by Carl Sandburg, he strove to develop his own unique style of verse while consistently maintaining the theme of America's racial inequality. Hughes was an avid traveller throughout his life, but felt most at home in Harlem which he viewed as a microcosm of Black America. A prolific writer, by 1965 he had published nine volumes of poetry, two novels, eight volumes of short stories and sketches, a two volume autobiography, and numerous plays, essays, and translations. Even after his death on May 22, 1967, several more works were published posthumously. Although Hughes is perhaps best known for his poetic contributions to the Harlem Renaissance of the 1920s, his productivity in numerous genres, and advocacy of an optimistic vision of a racially harmonious America, established him as a humanitarian as well as a creative genius. *(L.S.)*

Irving, Washington (1783-1859) Born in New York City, the youngest of a large merchant family. At 18 he was apprenticed to a lawyer, which only lasted for three years. After two years in Europe, he returned to pass the bar examination in 1806 but remained financially dependent upon his family until the publication of *The Sketch Book* (1820) which established his reputation as a writer. It contained two of his most popular short stories, "*The Legend of Sleepy Hollow*" and "*Rip Van Winkle*." In the late 1820s Irving wrote a succession of profitable romantic biographies and histories. From 1815 to 1832 he lived in Europe and served as Secretary of the American Legation in London in 1829 and as the American Minister to Spain from 1842 to 1846. He never married, and retired to Tarrytown, New York, where he died. Irving was the city's first great man of letters. *(L.S.)*

Jacobs, Jane (1916-...) A sociologist and architectural writer, she was born in Scranton, PA. After a year at the *Scranton Tribune*, she moved to New York. She married the architect, Robert H. Jacobs, who, she says, taught her enough to enable her to become associate editor of *Architectural Forum*. In 1962 she published *The Death and Life of Great American Cities*, an exciting polemic on urban planning that attacked the teachings of Ebenezer Howard, the Garden City movement and the fashionable "decentrists." A former resident of Greenwich Village, she now lives in Toronto, Canada. *(H.H.T.)*

La Guardia, Fiorello (1882-1947) The son of Italian-Jewish parents, LaGuardia's first political position was as deputy attorney-general of New York (1915-17). During the First World War he served with the American Air Force in Italy. On his return he entered Congress (1917-21 and 1923-33) as a Republican. In 1933 he became mayor of New York and held the position until 1945. His popularity stemmed from his

Washington Irving

advocacy of housing programs and labor safety laws. He was an early opponent of Hitler's anti-Semitism and was appointed civil administrator of Allied Occupied Italy. In 1946 he became the director-general of the UNRRA but died the following year. One of New York's airports is named after him. (H.L.)

Fiorello La Guardia

Lazarus, Emma (1849-1887) A precocious product of the German-Jewish community in New York, Lazarus's poems were praised by Emerson. She translated the works of Heine, and wrote a novel about Goethe. Her poem "The New Colossus," written in 1883, was inscribed on the base of the Statue of Liberty as a powerful statement of American ideals:
*"Your huddled masses yearning to breathe free,
The wretched refuse of your teeming shore.
Send these, the homeless, the tempest-tost to me,
I lift my lamp beside the golden door."*

Lee, Spike (1957-...) Born Shelton Lee, this son of a jazz musician graduated from Morehouse College and New York University's Film School. His first feature film *She's Gotta Have It*, released in 1986, made an auspicious debut, winning the Prix de Jeunesse at the Cannes Film Festival. His other films include *Do The Right Thing* (1989), *Jungle Fever* (1991) and *Malcolm X* (1992). All three were shot on location in New York. As well as directing, Lee also writes, edits, and acts in his films. (H.L.)

Letterman, David (1947-...) The apparent victor in the ongoing talk show wars, Letterman got his start as a performer at *The Comedy Store* in Los Angeles in 1975. This resulted in his becoming a guest host of Johnny Carson's *The Tonight Show*. Next came a daytime chat show that lasted only four months. Although shortlived, it won two Emmy awards. *Late Night with David Letterman* began in 1982, broadcast from the NBC studios in Rockefeller Center, New York City. This highly successful program, which ran until 1993, was a break from traditional talk show fare, featuring instead such

popular gimmicks as "Stupid Pet Tricks" and the "Top Ten Lists." These were interspersed with the more usual celebrity guests. In 1993, after wrangles as to who should succeed Johnny Carson, CBS managed to steal Letterman away from NBC with a three year contract worth $42 million. From a specially refurbished Ed Sullivan Theater "Dave" continues his reign as the number one late night host. (H.L.)

Melville, Herman (1819-91) Born in Pearl Street, New York, Melville joined a whaling ship that led him to adventures in the Marquesas and Tahiti. Many of his early novels – *Typee* (1846), *Omoo* (1847), *Redburn* (1849) and *White-Jacket* (1850) were based on his experiences in the South Seas. He returned in 1844 and, after a few years in New York, took a farm near Pittsfield, MA. There he wrote his masterpiece, *Moby Dick* (1851), which he dedicated to his neighbor, Nathaniel Hawthorne. His later novels – the symbolic *Pierre* (1852), and the satirical *Confidence Man* (1857) were unappreciated. In 1863 he returned to New York where he became a customs inspector. Now regarded as one of America's greatest novelists, recognition only came thirty years after his death. (H.H.T.)

Miller, Arthur (1915-...) The son of an Austrian Jewish manufacturer, Miller was born in New York City. His university education was disrupted in the 1930s because of the economic depression, but by working in a warehouse for two years he was able to earn enough money to support himself at the University of Michigan, studying journalism. Miller has been married three times, the second marriage being to Marilyn Monroe, for whom he wrote the script for the film *The Misfits* (1961). His first Broadway play, *The Man Who Had All the Luck* (1944) ran for only one week, but his next plays, *All My Sons* (1947), *Death of a Salesman* (1949), and *The Crucible* (1953) established him as a major playwright and are now renowned as modern theatrical classics. (S.B.)

Olmsted, Frederick Law (1822-1903) After a failed attempt to support himself as a farmer, he secured a commission in the early 1850s from the *New York Times* to travel in the South and write a series of articles on the effect of slavery on the Southern economy. Published in three volumes, they are among the most detailed visitor-accounts of Southern attitudes and values. He was appointed superintendant of Central Park in 1858 and soon after architect-in-chief. His design of Central Park was the most influential piece of landscape design in the 19th century, and his management of the park construction was universally praised for its honesty. After the Civil War, he planned parks in Brooklyn, Chicago, Buffalo, and Boston, was the designer of the World's Columbian Exposition at Chicago, and the grounds of the national capital at Washington, D.C. He secured Yosemite as a national reservation. (H.H.T.)

Powell, Adam Clayton, Jr. (1908-1972) Educated at Colgate and Columbia Universities, Powell entered the ministry and eventually succeeded his father at the Abyssinian Baptist Church in Harlem. He continued to serve there until 1971. He founded the *People's Voice*, a newspaper through which he demanded better conditions for blacks. In 1941 he became the first African-American elected to the New York City Council. Four years later he entered the U.S. House of Representatives. His political success centered around the 13,000 members of his church in Harlem. Powell was excluded from the House in 1967 for allegedly using government funds for private purposes. In a special election to find a replacement he was overwhelmingly reelected. On his return he was stripped of twenty two years of seniority and fined $25,000. Powell's case went to the Supreme Court, where in June 1969, the Court ruled that the House had unconstitutionally excluded him from Congress. In 1970 he failed to be renominated.(H.L.)

Robinson, Jackie (1919-1972) Born Jack Roosevelt Robinson near Cairo, Georgia. He attended UCLA for three years after winning an athletic scholarship. During the Second World War Robinson joined the army and became a second lieutenant in 1943. After

receiving a medical discharge in 1943, he played professional football in Hawaii and baseball for the Kansas City Monarchs – a member of the Negro National League. In April 1947, Robinson became the first African-American to play in the major leagues after signing with the Brooklyn Dodgers. During his ten-year career with the team, during which time he had a career batting average of 311, he was voted Rookie of the Year (1947), Most Valuable Player (1949), and led the team in winning six pennants and one World Series. Robinson retired from the sport in 1956 and became involved in business, politics, and civil rights activities. In 1962 he was elected to the Baseball Hall of Fame. (L.S.)

Robinson, Luther ("Bill," "Bojangles") (1878-1949) The grandson of a slave, Robinson was orphaned as a baby and was raised in Richmond, VA, by his grandparents. He ran away to Washington, D.C., where he worked as a stable boy, and it was in Washington where he first saw travelling minstrel shows. He joined one such group as a young dancer, and appeared in a New York production of the minstrel show *The South Before the Civil War* in 1892. He formed an act with George Cooper and pursued a career in vaudeville. From 1908 he was billed as "The Dark Cloud of Joy." For most of his early career Robinson appeared in the black vaudeville circuit, but after his successful "downtown" appearance along with Adelaide Hall in Lew Leslie's *Blackbirds* in 1928, Robinson worked for better-paying white audiences. In the 1930s he appeared in fourteen films, four featuring Shirley Temple (including *The Little Colonel*, (1935), and *Rebecca of Sunny Brook Farm*, (1938), in which he appeared as an antebellum butler. His fluid, masterful softshoe and tap performances endeared Robinson to the movie-going public, and won him many admirers in white society. Robinson celebrated his 65th birthday by dancing down Broadway from Columbus Circle to 44th Street.

Rockefeller, David (1915-...) The son of John D. Rockefeller Jr., David Rockefeller was educated at Harvard, graduating in 1936. He published *Unused*

Bill "Bojangles" Robinson

Resources and Economic Waste in 1940, and served as secretary to Mayor LaGuardia, 1940-41. His long career at Chase Bank began in 1946 when he was appointed assistant manager of the foreign department. He became chairman and CEO of Chase in 1969, a post he held until 1980-81. The Chase Manhattan Bank Tower and Plaza (an 800 feet tower between Pine and Liberty Streets designed by Skidmore, Owings and Merrill, 1960), and Rockefeller's long service as chairman of the Downtown Lower Manhattan Association, 1958-75, was an indication of his commitment to the survival of the downtown business and financial interests.

Roosevelt, Theodore (1859-1919) Of an old New York family of Dutch, Scottish and Irish descent, Roosevelt was educated at Harvard before joining the New York legislature at the age of 23. He was defeated in the famous mayoral election of 1886. Roosevelt served first as a state Assemblyman, then as New York City's Police Commissioner, the U.S. Civil Service Commissioner, and assistant secretary of the Navy. In 1898 he left government to form and lead the Roughriders in the Cuban war. It was a titanic public relations triumph. On his return he was elected governor of New York state. In 1901 he was nominated Vice President. The assassination of William McKinley that year made Theodore Roosevelt President, where he was to remain for seven and a half years. At the age of 42 he was a young president but had plentiful political experience and transformed the White House into a volcano of political activism. He was re-elected in 1904 and oversaw the implementation of the Square Deal, the development of the Great White Fleet (U.S. Navy) and the regulation of trusts and monopolies, which earned him the nickname "trustbuster." In 1905 he was awarded the Nobel Peace Prize for mediating the end of the Russo-Japanese war. By 1912 he was standing for President as the Progressive candidate, a party he had helped form in 1910. He lost the election to Woodrow Wilson. He continued his role as explorer, hunter and zoologist and campaigned heavily for United States intervention in World War I. Teddy Roosevelt, the man of action, died in his sleep at home on Long Island. *(S.B.)*

Rosenberg , Ethel Greenglass (1915-1953) The daughter of Jewish immigrants, Ethel Greenglass grew up on Sheriff Street in the lower East Side, where her father had a little shop repairing sewing machines. A graduate of Seward Park High School in 1931, she studied stenography and worked as a secretary. Her political activity began in 1935. She was an active trades unionist, and while singing in a choir at a rally for the International Seamen's Union met Julius Rosenberg, who had joined the Communist Party in the mid-1930s. They married in 1939, and lived for the ten years of their lives together at Knickerbocker Village, a low-cost housing project in New York. From 1941 to 1945 Rosenberg worked as a junior engineer in the United States Signal Corps. In 1950 he was accused of having recruited his brother-in-law, David Greenglass, for espionage. Ethel was arrested on conspiracy charges. Despite the weakness of the evidence against her, in what many people feel to have been a miscarriage of justice, Ethel was convicted with her husband and given a death sentenced by the trial judge, Irving Kaufman. Legal appeals kept the Rosenbergs alive, but when President Eisenhower refused her last clemency appeal she was electrocuted immediately after her husband on June 19, 1953. *(H.L.)*

Roth, Henry (1906-...) Roth's first novel, *Call it Sleep* (1934), is an intense, impressionistic account of a Jewish boy's first years among the immigrants in New York City's lower East Side. It had a modest success when first published, but was forgotten until 1964, when several critics praised it in the *New York Times* Book Review as a neglected American classic. It went on to sell more than a million copies. Roth held a variety of jobs – hospital attendant, maple syrup vendor, and water-fowl farmer. Sixty years passed before he published another novel, *Mercy of the Rude Stream* (1994), the first of six new novels he has completed. *(H.H.T.)*

Rothstein, Arnold (1882-1928) The son of wealthy and respected upper West Side Jews, Rothstein was a

President Theodore Roosevelt

most unlikely candidate for entrance into the New York criminal fraternity. Whilst a teenager, he became acquainted with Big Tim Sullivan, leader of Tammany Hall, who encouraged his career as a runner for local gambling houses. Rothstein opened his own casino in 1909, and became widely known as a gambler and bankroller of gambling operations. He was rumored to be involved in the fixing of the 1919 World Series. During the Prohibition era Rothstein was involved in rum-running, narcotics, and labor racketeering. Rothstein's biographer states, "He led crime into the business era," and so New York's well known Broadway playboy and gambler laid the groundwork for what would become the organized crime syndicates formed in the 1930s. *(S.B.)*

Sanger, Margaret (1883-1966) Sanger started her career in public health in 1912 as a nurse on the lower East Side. After watching a woman die from a self-induced abortion, she began her life-long campaign for birth control. After a short but informative spell in Paris in 1914, she began distributing pamphlets on "Family Limitation." Consequently she was forced to flee to Great Britain to avoid prosecution for sending "obscene" material by post. On her return in 1916, in defiance of New York law, Sanger opened a birth control clinic in the Brownsville section of Brooklyn. This was closed down and she was briefly imprisoned. More clinics followed as did the American Birth Control League, which Sanger founded in 1921. Her work reached an international stage with the first World Population Conference in Geneva in 1927. She also created a national lobby group that sought changes in legislation throughout the 1930s. The culmination of her work was the Planned Parenthood Federation of America, which began in 1952. *(H.L.)*

Schultz, Dutch (1902-1935) Born Arthur Flegenheimer, Schultz took his name from an old Bronx gangster. His "career" started with burglary but soon progressed to bootlegging, ownership of speakeasies and police rackets in the Bronx and parts of Manhattan. Several gang wars were the result of his rise to the top. In 1933 he was acquitted of a charge of income tax evasion but was forced into hiding months before the trial. As a result he lost control of his businesses to his rivals. New York Special Prosecutor, Thomas E. Dewey, targeted Schultz and in October 1935 the gangster broached the idea of assassinating his nemesis. The other crime

bosses were opposed to the idea because of adverse publicity. Schultz's fall from grace was complete and on October 23 1935, he and three body guards were gunned down in a New Jersey restaurant. *(H.L.)*

Schuyler, Louisa Lee (1837-1926) The great-granddaughter of Alexander Hamilton, she was privately educated, and entered the world of female charitable work with the formation of the Woman's Central Association of Relief in 1861. Her effective organizational skills helped make this body the leading auxiliary of the U.S. Sanitary Commission. She formed the State Charities Aid Association in 1872, to encourage volunteer visitors to poorhouses, public hospitals, and schools. Schuyler was an effective lobbyist on behaf of the mentally ill, and procured state support for their transfer from county almshouses to state-supported institutions.

Scorsese, Martin (1942-...) Scorsese was educated at New York University's Film School and taught there from 1968-70. His first feature film, *Who's That Knocking at My Door*, appeared in 1968. He made commercials and edited before returning to direction with *Boxcar Bertha* in 1972. His admittedly personal films reflect Scorsese's Italian-American background and are concerned with the twin influences of the Catholic church and life "on the streets." He gained critical acclaim with *Mean Streets* (1973), *Taxi Driver* (1976) and *Raging Bull* (1980). Recent successes include *Cape Fear* (1992) and *The Age of Innocence* (1993). Highly regarded as an actor's director, he launched the careers of Robert De Niro and Harvey Keitel. He has also directed pop videos, documentaries, and a Broadway show. *(H.L.)*

Stieglitz, Alfred (1864-1946) At the age of six, the young Alfred Stieglitz moved with his family from Hoboken, New Jersey, to Manhattan. His education began at the City College, but by 1879 he was studying at the University of Bonn, where he soon abandoned his chosen field of mechanical engineering to concentrate on photography. He returned to America after the death of his sister Flora in1890, but not before he had travelled and photographed extensively in Europe. Stieglitz remained in New York City for the remainder of his life, taking pictures, encouraging the development of art photography, editing photographic publications, the most successful being *Camera Work* (1902), and organizing exhibitions of his own and other contemporary work. He was an early American advocate of modern art. Moreover, Alfred Stieglitz inspired many Amerian galleries to regard photography as serious art, worthy of collection and preservation. *(S.B.)*

Strasberg, Lee (1901-1982) Strasberg's family emigrated to the United States from Poland when he was seven years old. They lived on the lower East side. He began acting as a teenager but his professional career got its start in 1920 with the Theater Guild where he worked as an actor and stage manager. He was also a founder member of the Group Theater. Between 1941-48 he worked in Hollywood but returned to New York to join the Actors' Studio which had been founded the previous year by members of the Group Theater. There he was responsible for the rise of method acting and the teaching of the doctrines of Stanislavsky. Marlon Brando, Paul Newman, and James Dean were amongst his pupils. He continued as artistic director of the Actors' Studio until his death. In 1969 he established the Lee Strasberg Institute of Theater. His acting debut in the movies did not come until 1974 in *The Godfather Part II.* *(H.L.)*

Stuyvesant, Petrus (1592-1672) The son of a Dutch Reformed Church *dominie*, Stuyvesant pursued a military career as a young man. Appointed governor of the Dutch possession of Curaçao in the Leeward Islands, in 1644 he led an attack on the island of St. Martins during the course of which he sustained a leg wound which led to amputation of his right leg. In 1646 he was commissioned by the States-General as Director-General of New Netherlands. He was the last and most powerful of the Dutch rulers of New Netherlands, surrendering to the *force majeur* of the British in 1664. Stuyvesant purchased the "Great Bouwerie" for 6,400 guilders, an estate which ran from 5th Street to 17th, between the East River and Fourth Avenue. No liberal in matters of piety and religion, he sought to ban Lutheran, Quaker, and Jewish observance in New York. In his eyes government should be based upon the submissiveness and obedience of the people.

Taylor, Lawrence (1959-...) Born in Williamsburg, this 6'3" linebacker known as "L.T." was a star player at the University of North Carolina. In 1981 Taylor was the New York Giants' first round draft pick. He spent his entire career at the club, retiring in 1994 after the Giants failed to win the conference championship. Generally considered to be the quickest linebacker ever, Taylor enjoyed huge success on the field, helping the Giants win the Superbowl in 1986 and 1990. He was voted the N.F.L.'s Most Valuable Player in 1986 and appeared in the N.F.L. Pro-Bowl every season from 1981 to 1990. Away from football, Taylor's personal life has been less stellar, including periods in rehabilitation clinics for treatment of drug and alcohol addiction. *(H.L.)*

Tharp, Twyla (1941- ...) Tharp studied music and dance as a child but graduated with a degree in pyschology. Her breakthrough in dance came when she joined the Paul Taylor Dance Co. (1963-65) and then founded her own troupe in 1965. She has made her name as a freelance choreographer working with the Joffrey Ballet and the American Ballet Theater. Her skill is in combining popular music with traditional ballet techniques. This is shown in works that use the music of the Beach Boys, Frank Sinatra, David Byrne, and Jelly Roll Morton. National prominence came in 1976 when the American Ballet Theater danced the premiere of *Push Comes to Shove* which she choreographed for Mikhail Baryshnikov. She has also choreographed two Broadway shows and the films *Hair* (1979) and *White Nights* (1985) which starred Baryshnikov. *(H.L.)*

Tilden, Samuel (1814-1886) A farmer's son, Tilden studied law at Yale before starting a practice that specialized in serving railway companies. He was elected to the New York Assembly and became a member of the Free Soil faction of the Democratic Party. Between 1866 and 1874 he was chairman of the New York State Democratic Committee. During this time he re-organized the party, destroyed "Boss" Tweed and broke the hold of Tweed's Ring on the government of the city. By 1874 he was Governor of New York and was responsible for exposing the "Canal Ring," a bipartisan group that stole funds designated for enlargement and repair of the State's canal system. In 1876 he ran in the bitter and contentious presidential race against Rutherford Hayes. An Electoral Commission was created by Congress to settle the dispute over electoral votes but their decision favored his opponent. Tilden subsequently faded from politics, but on his death bequeathed a considerable fortune to found a free library in New York. *(H.L.)*

Trump, Donald J. (1946-...) The multi-millionaire real-estate developer and entrepreneur was born the middle child of a close-knit, traditional family in Queens, New York. An assertive and aggressive child, he was considered a leader in his neighborhood and at 13 was enrolled in the New York Military Academy. He graduated in 1964 and entered Fordham University in the Bronx. Two years later he left and entered the Wharton School of Finance at the University of Pennsylvania, graduating in 1968. Trump worked full-time for his father, a real estate developer, until 1971 when he moved to Manhattan and set up a series of major development projects which made him his fortune. His most famous development is probably Trump Tower, adjacent to Tiffany's, on 57th Street and Fifth Avenue. Trump is a master of self-serving publicity, manipulating his own visibility like a virtuoso violinist. *(P.C.)*

Tweed, William "Boss" (1823-1878) Tweed trained as a chairmaker and bookkeeper before being elected in 1852 as a Democratic party Alderman in New York. A year later he entered Congress and then became chairman of the New York Board of Supervisors (1856), School Comissioner (1856-57), and a State Senator (1867-71). In 1870 he was made Commissioner of Public Works for the city and had

almost complete control of Tammany Hall, Democratic politics in the city and great influence in the state legislature. As head of the Tweed Ring, he and his associates stole liberally from the public coffers. In one such case the New York County Courthouse, planned at $500,000, eventually cost $8 million. In 1871 the *New York Times* exposed the fraud. Samuel Tilden destroyed the ring and saw Tweed sentenced to twelve years imprisonment. Released on bail in 1875, he fled to Spain in order to avoid a civil suit to recover the stolen money. He was identified by a series of cartoons that had appeared in *Harpers Weekly* and was arrested. Extradited to New York in 1876, he died in the Ludlow St. Jail, still under prosecution for the return of $6 million. *(H.L.)*

Vanderbilt, Cornelius (1794-1877) He was born in Port Richmond, Staten Island, to parents of Dutch ancestry. Despite the fact that he did not receive any schooling past the age of eleven, he became the leading figure in the New York shipping business and railroad transportation and became a millionaire many times over. Vanderbilt started his career at 16 by transporting freight and passengers between Staten Island and New York City in a boat he bought for $100. This led in 1818 to becoming an associate of Thomas Gibbons and in 1829 starting his own program of steamship ownership, which resulted in him controlling the majority of the shipping business in New York harbor and along the Hudson River to Albany. In his later year he constructed the New York Central Railroad system. Never one to take no for an answer (he once had his wife committed to an insane asylum because she refused to move to the exclusive Washington Square), he epitomized the hard-driving robber barons of American industry. In his will he left a vast fortune and his name to found a university in Tennessee. *(L.S.)*

Warhol, Andy (1930?-1987) The only certain fact about Andy Warhol's earliest beginnings is that he was named Andrew Warhola by his Czechoslovakian immigrant parents. Dates of his birth range from

Walt Whitman

1928-1931. A sensitive child, he had three nervous breakdowns between the ages of eight and ten. After graduating from the Carnegie Institute of Technology in 1949 with the aspiration of becoming a public school art teacher, Warhol entered the field of commerical art initially for the financial security. The illustrations he made for book covers, record jackets, and magazines perfected his signature print-like style that emerged in the 1960s when he purposefully established himself as a serious artist. Perhaps best known for his Marilyn pictures and Campbell Soup Cans, Warhol was also a playwright and movie director, as well as one of the great luminaries in the city's party scene. Even up to his death he was continually changing the traditional concept of "original artwork" in favor of art determined by content. *(L.S.)*

Wharton, Edith (1862-1937) Born to the aristocracy of Knickerbocker New York, Edith Newbold Jones was educated by private tutors in New York and Europe. Marriage to a Boston banker, Edward Wharton, in 1885 was not a great success, and Wharton turned to writing as a career. Her great subject as a novelist was the New York aristocracy (*The House of Mirth*, 1905, *The Age of Innocence*, 1920), which she observed with a notably cool and unsentimental eye. She lived in France from 1907.

Whitman, Walt (1819-1902) Born one of nine to a barely literate Long Island family, Whitman published his first volume, *Leaves of Grass*, in 1855 after only five years of formal education and a career in journalism. This collection of poems, warmly praised by Emerson, was to be the source of three decades of revision and expansion, and contains many of his greatest works, including the famous "*Song of Myself*." During the Civil War, Whitman spent time comforting the wounded of both sides and this experience inspired him to write a cycle of war poems entitled *Drum-Taps* (1865). After a stroke, Whitman retired to Camden, New Jersey, in 1873, already a legend and hero, the dominating figure in American poetry in the 19th century. *(S.B.)*

Bibliography

Chapter 1

Colden, Cadwalader, *History of the Five Indian Nations of Canada* (London, 1747)

Crosby, A.W., *The Columbian Exchange: Biological and Cultural Consequences of 1492* (Greenwood Press: Westport, CT, 1972)

De Vorsey, Louis, "The New Land: The Discovery and Exploration of Eastern North America," in *North America: The Historical Geography of a Changing Continent*, ed. Robert D. Mitchell and Paul A. Groves (Hutchinson: London, 1987)

Driver, H.E., *Indians of North America* (University of Chicago Press: Chicago, 1961)

Grumet, Robert Steven, *Native American Place Names in New York City* (Museum of the City of New York: New York, 1981)

Miller, William J., *The Geological History of New York* (Kennikat Press: Port Washington, N.Y, 1970) First published 1914

Morison, S.E., *The European Discovery of America: The Northern Voyages AD 500-1600* (Oxford University Press: New York, 1971)

Nilsson, Tage, *The Pleistocene: Geology and Life in the Quaternary Ice Age* (Ferdinand Enke Verlag, and Dordrecht: D. Reidel Publishing Co.: Stuttgart, 1983)

Weslager, C.A. *The Delaware Indians: A History* (Rutgers University Press: New Brunswick, 1972)

Chapter 2

Documents Relating to the Colonial History of the State of New York. Compiled by John Romeyn Brodhead from manuscripts transcribed from archives in Netherlands, France and England. Commissioned by the state of New York (Albany, 1856-58)

Beauchamp, Dr William M., *Aboriginal Place Names of New York* in Bulletin No.108, New York State Museum (Albany, 1907)

Boxer, C.R., *The Dutch Seaborne Empire 1600-1800* (Alfred A. Knopf: New York, 1965)

Butler, Jon, *The Huguenots in America: A Refugee People in New World Society* (Harvard University Press: Cambridge, MA, 1983)

Debo, Angie, *A History of the Indians of the United States* (University of Oklahoma Press: Norman, 1970)

Fox, Dixon Ryan, *Yankees and Yorkers* (New York University Press: New York, 1940)

Jameson, J. Franklin, ed., *Narratives of New Netherland 1609-1664* (Charles Scribner's Sons: New York, 1909; reprinted Barnes & Noble: New York, 1967) Translations from 17th-century Dutch sources relating to the settlement, growth and administration of the colony.

Kenney, Alice P., *Stubborn for Liberty: The Dutch in New York* (Syracuse University Press: Syracuse, New York, 1975)

Kessler, Henry H. and Eugene Rachlin, *Peter Stuyvesant and His New York* (Random House: New York, 1959)

Merrell, James H., "'The Customes of our Country': Indians and Colonists in Early America," in Philip D. Morgan, ed., *Diversity and Unity in Early North America* (Routledge: London and New York, 1993)

Raesly, Ellis Lawrence, *Portrait of New Netherland* (Columbia University Press: New York, 1945)

Rensselaer, Mrs Schuyler van, *History of the City of New York in the Seventeenth Century*, 2 vols. (Macmillan: New York, 1909)

Reynolds, Donald Martin, *The Architecture of New York City: Histories and Views of Important Structures, Sites, and Symbols* (Macmillan: New York, 1984)

Rink, Oliver A., "The People of New Netherland: Notes on Non-English Immigration to New York in the Seventeenth Century," *New York History*, LXII (January 1981), 5-42

Rink, Oliver A., *Holland on the Hudson: An Economic and Social History of Dutch New York* (Cornell University Press: Ithaca, New York and London: and New York Historical Association: Cooperstown, 1986)

Swieringa, Robert P., *The Dutch in America: Immigration, Settlement, and Cultural Change* (Rutgers University Press: New Brunswick, N.J., 1985)

Trelease, Allen W., *Indian Affairs in Colonial New York* (Cornell University Press: Ithaca, 1960)

Van der Donck, Adriaen, *Description of the New Netherland*, ed. Thomas F. O'Donnell (Syracuse University Press: Syracuse, 1968)

van der Zee, Henri and Barbara, *A Sweet and Alien Land: The Early History of New York* (Macmillan: London, 1978)

White, Norval, *New York: A Physical History* (Atheneum: New York, 1987)

Wilson, Charles, *The Dutch Republic* (McGraw-Hill: New York, 1968)

Chapter 3

Abbott, Carl, "The Neighborhoods of New York, 1760-1775", *New York History*, 45 (1974), 35-54

Abbott, Wilbur C., *New York in the American Revolution* (1929; reprinted Haskell House: New York, 1975).

Andrews, Charles M., *The Colonial Period of American History*, 4 vols. (Yale University Press: New Haven, 1934-40)

Andrews, Charles M., *The Colonial Background of the American Revolution: Four Essays in American Colonial History* (Yale University Press: New Haven, 1924)

Archdeacon, Thomas, *New York City, 1664-1710: Conquest and Change* (Cornell University Press: Ithaca, 1975)

Barck, Oscar T., Jr., "The Occupation of New York City by the British," in *History of the State of New York*, ed. A.C. Flick, vol. 4, The New State (Columbia University Press: New York, 1933), 33-71

Bonomi, Patricia U., *A Factious People: Politics and Society in Colonial New York* (Columbia University Press: New York, 1971)

Bridenbaugh, Carl, *Cities in the Wilderness: The First Century of Urban Life in America, 1625-1742* (Alfred A. Knopf: New York, 1938)

Bridenbaugh, Carl, *Cities in Revolt; Urban Life in America, 1743-76* (Alfred A. Knopf: New York, 1955)

New York (Colony). Council. *Calendar of Council Minutes 1668-1783*, New York State Library *Bulletin*, 58 (April 1901; reprinted Harrison: Harbor Hill Books, New York, 1987)

Cappon, Lester J., et al, eds., *Atlas of Early American History: The Revolutionary Era, 1760-1790* (Princeton University Press: Princeton, 1976)

Countryman, Edward, *A People in Revolution: The American Revolution and Political Society in New York, 1760-1790* (Johns Hopkins University Press: Baltimore, 1981)

Countryman, Edward, *The American Revolution* (Hill & Wang: New York, 1985)

Cray, Robert E., Jr., *Paupers and Poor Relief in New York City and Its Rural Environs, 1700-1830* (Temple University Press: Philadelphia, 1988)

Davis, Thomas J., "New York's Long Black Line: A Note on the Growing Slave Population, 1676-1790," reprinted in Wendell Tripp, *Coming and Becoming: Pluralism in New York State History* (New York State Historical Association: Cooperstown, N.Y., 1991)

Davis, Thomas J., *A Rumor of Revolt: The "Great Negro Plot" in Colonial New York* (The Free Press: New York, 1985)

East, Robert A. and Jacob Judd, eds., *The Loyalist Americans: A Focus on Greater New York* (Sleepy Hollow Restorations: Tarrytown, 1975)

Friedman, Bernard, "The Shaping of the Radical Consciousness in Provincial New York," *Journal of American History*, 56 (March 1970), 781-801.

Gerlach, Larry R., ed., *The American Revolution: New York as a Case Study* (Wadsworth Publishing Co.: Belmont, CA, 1972)

Gipson, Lawrence Henry, *The Coming of the Revolution, 1763-1775* (Harper & Row: New York, 1962)

Goodfriend, Joyce D., *Before the Melting Pot: Society and Culture in Colonial New York City, 1664-1730* (Princeton University Press: Princeton, 1992)

Greenberg, Douglas, *Crime and Law Enforcement in the Colony of New York 1691-1776* (Cornell Universitry Press: Ithaca and London, 1974)

Greene, Evarts B. and V.D. Harrington, *American Population before the Federal Census of 1790* (Columbia University Press: New York, 1932)

Hartog, Hendrik, *Public Property and Private Power: The Corporation of the City of New York in American Law, 1730-1870*, (University of North Carolina Press: Chapel Hill, 1983)

Johnston, Henry P., *The Battle of Harlem Heights September 16, 1776, with a Review of the Events of the Campaign* (Macmillan: New York, 1897).

Jones, Thomas (1731-1792), *History of New York During the Revolutionary War ...*, 2 v. (New York Historical Society: New York, 1879)

Jordan, Winthrop D., *White Over Black: American Attitudes Toward the Negro, 1550-1812* (University of North Carolina Press: Chapel Hill, N.C.,

1968)

Kammen, Michael, *Colonial New York: A History* (Charles Scribner's Sons: New York, 1975)

Klein, Milton M., *New York in the American Revolution: A Bibliography* (New York State American Revolution Bicentennial Commission: Albany, 1974)

Klein, Milton M., *The Politics of Diversity: Essays in the History of Colonial New York* (Kennikat Press: Port Washington, New York, 1974)

Klein, Milton M., ed., *New York: The Centennial Years, 1676-1976* (Kennikat Press: Port Washington, N.Y., 1976

Launitz-Schürer, Jr., Leopold S., *Loyal Whigs and Revolutionaries: The Making of the Revolution in New York 1765-1776* (New York University Press: New York, 1980)

Leder, Lawrence, "...Like Madmen through the Streets": The New York City Riot of June, 1690, *New York Historical Society Quarterly*, 39 (October 1955), 405-15

Leder, Lawrence, "The Politics of Upheaval in New York, 1689-1709," *New York Historical Socety Quarterly*, 44 (October 1960), 413-27

McCormick, Charles Howard, *Leisler's Rebellion* (Garland Publishing, Inc.: New York and London, 1989)

McKee, Samuel, *Labor in Colonial New York, 1664-1776* (Columbia University Press: New York, 1935)

McManus, Edgar J., *A History of Negro Slavery in New York* (Syracuse University Press: Syracuse, 1966)

McParland, Eugene P., "Colonial Taverns and Tavernkeepers of British New York," *The New York Genealogical and Biographical Record*, 103 (Octover 1972), 193-202 et seq.

Mohl, Raymond, "Poverty in Early America, A Reappraisal: The Case of Eighteenth-Century New York City," *New York History*, 50 (1969), 5-27

Morris, R.B., ed., *Select Cases of the Mayor's Court of New York City, 1674-1784* (Washington, 1935)

Murrin, John M., "English Rights as Ethnic Aggression: The English Conquest, the Charter of Liberties of 1683, and Leisler's Rebellion in New York" in *Authority and Resistence in Early New York*, ed. William Pencak and Conrad Edick Wright (The New-York Historical Society: New York, 1988), 56-94

Nash, Gary B., *The Urban Crucible: Social Change, Political Consciousness, and the Origins of the American Revolution* (Harvard University Press: Cambridge, MA, 1979)

Norton, Thomas Elliot, *The Fur Trade in Colonial New York* (University of Wisconsin Press: Madison, 1947)

"Old New York Coffee Houses," *Harper's New Monthly Magazine*, 64 (March 1992), 481-99.

Olson, Edwin, "The Slave Code in Colonial New York," *Journal of Negro History*, 29 (1944), 147-65

Pierson, William H. Jr., *American Buildings and Their Architects*, vol. 1, *The Colonial and Neoclassical Styles* (Anchor Press/Doubleday: Garden City, N.Y., 1976)

Reich, Jerome R. *Leisler's Rebellion: A Study of Democracy in New York,*

1664-1720 (University of Chicago Press: Chicago, 1953)

Ritchie, Robert C., *The Duke's Province: A Study of New York Politics and Society* (University of North Carolina Press: Chapel Hill, 1977)

Rothschild, Nan A., *New York City Neighborhoods: The 18th century* (Academic Press: New York, 1990)

Scott, Kenneth, "The Slave Insurrection in New York in 1712," *New York Historical Society Quarterly*, 45 (1961), 43-74

Scott, Kenneth, "Jacob Leisler's Fifty Militiamen," *New York Genealogical and Biographical Record*, 94 (April 1963), 65-72

Still, Bayrd, *Mirror for Gotham: New York as Seen by Contemporaries from Dutch Days to the Present* (New York University Press: New York, 1956)

Szasz, Ferenc M., "The New York Slave Revolt of 1741: A Re-Examination," *New York History*, 48 (1967), 215-30

Wertenbaker, Thomas J., *The Golden Age of Colonial Culture* (New York University Press: New York, 1949)

Wertenbaker, Thomas J., *Father Knickerbocker Rebels: New York City during the Revolution* (Charles Scribner's Sons: New York, 1948)

Wilkenfeld, Bruce M., "New York City Neighborhoods, 1730," *New York History*, 57 (April 1976), 165-182

Wilson, James Grant (1832-1914), ed., *Memorial History of the City of New York*, 4 vols. (New York History Co.: New York, 1892-93) Stevens, J.A., "Life in New York at the Close of the Colonial Period," Vol. 2, Ch.12

Wood, Gordon S., *The Creation of the American Republic, 1776-1787* (University of North Carolina Press: Chapel Hill, 1969)

Yoshpe, Harry B., "A Record of Manumissions in New York during the Colonial and Early National Periods," *Journal of Negro History*, 27 (1941), 78-107

Yoshpe, Harry B., *The Disposition of Loyalist Estates in the Southern District of the State of New York* (Columbia University Press, New York, 1939)

Chapter 4

Albion, Robert Greenhalgh, "New York Port in the New Republic, 1783-1793," *New York History*, 21 (October 1940), 388-403

Blackmar, Elizabeth, *Manhattan for Rent, 1785-1850* (Cornell University Press: Ithaca, 1989)

DePeyster, Frederic, *History of the Tontine Building. Founded 1792. Demolished in May, 1855* (George F. Nesbitt: New York, 1855)

Dodge, William E., *Old New York* (Dodd, Mead: New York, 1880)

Evans, Meryle, "Knickerbocker Hotels ... 1800-1850," *New York Historical Society Quarterly*, 36 (1952), 377

Fay, Theodore, *Views in New York ...* (Peabody: New York, 1831)

"From Boston to New York Thirty Years Ago," *The Knickerbocker*, XLII, i (July 1853), 62-5

Harlow, Alvin F., *Old Bowery Days: The Chronicle of a Famous Street* (D. Appleton & Co.: New York, 1931)

Kostof, Spiro, *The City Shaped: Urban Patterns and Meanings Through History* (Little, Brown: Boston, 1991)

Launitz-Schürer, Jr., Leopold S., "Whig-Loyalists: The DeLanceys of New York," *New-York Historical*

Society Quarterly, 56 (July 1972), 179-198.

Lossing, Benjamin J., "Historic Houses of America: The DeLancey Mansion," *Appleton's Journal*, XI (6 June 1874), 705-8. Engraving of Fraunces' tavern as it was in 1874

Luke, Myron H., *The Port of New York 1800-1810: The Foreign Trade and Business Community* (New York, 1950)

Mates, Julian, *The American Musical Stage before 1800* (Rutgers University Press: New Brunswick, 1962)

Miller, John C., *The Federalist Era 1789-1801* (Harper & Row: New York, 1960)

Mohl, Raymond A., *Poverty in New York, 1783-1825* (New York, 1971)

Myer, John Walden, "The Gothic Revival in New York," *Bulletin of the Museum of the City of New York*, April 1940.

Pomerantz, Sidney, *New York: An American City 1783-1803* (Columbia University Press: New York, 1938)

Porter, Kenneth Wiggins, *John Jacob Astor: Business Man*, 2 vols. (Harvard University Press: Cambridge, MA, 1931; Russell & Russell: New York, 1966)

Reps, John W., *Town Planning in Frontier America* (Princeton University Press: Princeton, 1969)

Reps, John W., *The Making of Urban America: A History of City Planning in the United States* (Princeton University Press: Princeton, 1965)

Rock, Howard B., *Artisans of the New Republic: The Tradesman of New York City in the Age of Jefferson* (New York University Press: New York, 1984)

Scott, Kenneth, "A Scot Visits New York, 1810-1811," *New York Genealogical and Biographical Record*, 105 (January 1964), 2-10

Shea, John Gilmary, ed., *The Catholic Churches of New York City* (L.G. Goulding & Co.: New York, 1878)

Stevens, John Austin, *Progress of New York in a Century: 1776-1876: an Address delivered before the New York Historical Society, December 7, 1875* (Printed for the Society: New York, 1876)

White, Shane, *Somewhat More Independent: The End of Slavery in New York City, 1770-1810* (University of Georgia Press: Athens, 1991)

Zeichner, Oscar, "The Loyalist Problem in New York after the Revolution," *New York History*, 31 (July 1940), 284-302

Chapter 5

Blake, Nelson M., *Water for the Cities* (Syracuse University Press: Syracuse, 1956)

Browne, Junius Henry, "The Problem of Living in New York," *Harper's New Monthly*, 65 (November 1882), 918-24

Burnham, A., "The New York Architecture of Richard Morris Hunt," *Journal of the Society of Architectural Historians*, 11 (May 1952), 9-14

Carman, Harry James, *The Street Surface Railway Franchises of New York City*, Studies in History, Economics and Public Law, No. 88 (Columbia University Press: New York, 1919)

"Commerce in the City of New York," *Hunt's Merchant Magazine*, 13 (July 1845)

[Cook, Clarence,] "New York Daguerreotyped. Group First: Business-Streets, Mercantile Blocks, Stores and

Banks" *Putnam's Monthly Magazine*, 1 (February 1853), 121-136; (April 1853), 353-368. "The Benevolent Institutions of New York" (June 1853), 673-686; "Public Buildings of New York," *Putnam's Monthly Magazine*, 3 (January 1854), 10-15; "Places of Public Amusement: theaters and Concert Rooms," (February 1854), 141-152; "New York Daguerreotyped. Private Residences," (March 1854), 233-248.

Ernst, Robert, *Immigrant Life in New York 1825-1863*. 1949 (Ira J. Friedman, Port Washington, N.Y., 1965)

Foster, George G., *New York by Gas-Light and Other Urban Sketches*, ed. Stuart M. Blumin (University of California Press, Berkeley, 1990)

Gilder, Rodman, *The Battery* (Houghton Mifflin, Boston, 1936)

Gilfoyle, Timothy J., "The Urban Geography of Commercial Sex: Prostitution in New York City, 1790-1860," *Journal of Urban History*, 13 (August 1987)

Gilfoyle, Timothy J., "Strumpets and Misogynists: Brothel 'Riots' and the Transformation of Prostitution in Antebellum New York City," *New York History*, 68 (January 1987), 45-65.

Greene, Joseph Warren Jr., "New York City's First Railroad: The New York and Harlem, 1832 to 1867," *New York Historical Society Quarterly*, 9 (January 1926), 107-123

Hawes, Elizabeth, *New York, New York: How the Apartment House Transformed the Life of the City (1869-1930)* (Knopf: New York, 1993)

Hone, Philip, "Commerce and Commercial Character," *Hunt's Merchants Magazine*, 4 (February 1841), 129-146

The Diary of Philip Hone, ed. Allan Nevins, 2 vols. (Dodd, Mead & Co.: New York, 1927)

Huxtable, Ada Louise, *Classic New York* (Anchor: New York, 1964)

Knobel, Dale T., *Paddy and the Republic: Ethnicity and Nationality in Antebellum America* (Wesleyan University Press: Middletown, CT, 1986)

Krout, John A. and Clifford L. Lord, "Sports and Recreation" in Alexander C. Flick, ed., *History of the State of New York*, 10, Ch.7

"Lafayette Place," *The Knickerbocker*, II (July 1833), 71

Leach, Richard H., "The Impact of Immigration on New York, 1840-1860," *New York History*, 31 (1950), 15-30

Lockwood, Charles, *Manhattan Moves Uptown: An Illustrated History* (Houghton Mifflin: Boston, 1976)

Miller, Douglas T., "Immigration and Social Stratification in Pre-Civil War New York," in *Coming and Becoming: Pluralism in New York State History* (New York State Historical Association: Cooperstown, NY, 1991), 173-184

Mushkat, Jerome, *Fernando Wood: A Political Biography* (Kent State University Press: Kent, OH, 1990)

Richard Moody, *The Astor Place Riot* (Indiana University Press: Bloomington, 1958)

The Papers of Frederick Law Olmsted. Vol. 3, *Creating Central Park 1857-1861* ed. Charles E. Beveridge and David Schuyler and Jane Turner Censer (Johns Hopkins University Press: Baltimore and London, 1983)

Rubin, Julius, "An Innovating Public Improvement: The Erie Canal," in *Canals and American Economic Development*, ed. Carter Goodrich (Columbia University Press: New York, 1961), 15-66

Shaw, Ronald E., *Erie Water West: A History of the Erie Canal 1792-1854* (University of Kentucky Press: Lexington, 1966)

Spann, Edward K., *The New Metropolis: New York City 1840-1857* (Columbia University Press: New York, 1981)

Vaux, Calvert, "Parisian Buildings for City Residents," *Harper's Weekly*, 2 (19 December 1857), 809-810

Weisman, W., "Commercial Palaces of New York: 1845-1875," *Art Bulletin*, 36 (December 1954), 285-302

Chapter 6

Alpern, Andrew, *Apartments for the Affluent* (McGraw Hill: New York, 1975)

Baker, Paul R., *Richard Morris Hunt* (The MIT Press: Cambridge, MA and London, 1980)

Baldwin, Charles C., *Stanford White* (Dodd Mead: New York, 1931)

Bernstein, Iver, *The New York City Draft Riots: Their Significance for American Society and Politics in the Age of the Civil War* (Oxford University Press: New York, 1990)

Boyer, M. Christine, *Manhattan Manners: Architecture and Style 1850-1900* (Rizzoli: New York, 1985)

Bremner, Robert H., "The Impact of the Civil War on Philanthropy and Social Welfare," *Civil War History*, 12 (December 1966), 293-303

Burchard, John and Albert Bush-Brown, *The Architecture of America: A Social and Cultural History* (An Atlantic Monthly Press Book: Little Brown, Boston, 1961)

Buttenweiser, Anne L., "Shelter for What and For Whom? On the Route Toward Vladeck Houses, 1920 to 1940," *Journal of Urban History*, 12 (August 1986), 391-413

Cantor, Jay E., "A Monument of Trade: A.T. Stewart and the Rise of the Millionaire's Mansion in New York," *Winterthur Portfolio 10* (University Press of Virginia: Charlottesville, 1975)

Comer, John P., *New York City Building Control: 1800-1941* (Columbia University Press: New York, 1942)

Condit, Carl W., *The Port of New York: A History of the Rail and Terminal System from the Beginnings to Pennsylvania Station* (University of Chicago Press: Chicago, 1980)

Cook, Adrian, *The Armies of the Streets: The New York City Draft Riots of 1863* (University Press of Kentucky, Lexington, KY, 1974)

Crapsey, Edward, "A Monument to Trade," *The Galaxy*, 9 (1870), 94-101. [On A.T. Stewart]

Cudahy, Brian J., *Under the Sidewalks of New York*, rev. ed., (The Stephen Greene Press: Pelham Books, New York, 1989)

Ford, James, et al, *Slums and Housing with Special Reference to New York City: History, Conditions, Policy*, 2 v. (Harvard University Press: Cambridge, 1936)

French, Lillie Hamilton, "Shopping in New York," *The Century Magazine*, 61 (March 1901), 644-658

Gardner, Deborah S., "'A Fashion of Paradise': A.T. Stewart's Department Store, 1862-1875," in *A Needle, a*

Bobbin, a Strike: Women Needle Workers in America (Temple University Press: Philadelphia, 1984)

Hower, Ralph M., *History of Macy's of New York, 1858-1919* (Harvard University Press: Cambridge, MA, 1943)

Lee, Basil Leo, *Discontent in New York City, 1861-1865* (Washington, D.C., 1943)

Leach, William R., "Transformations in a Culture of Consumption: Women and Department Stores, 1890-1935," *Journal of American History*, 71 (September 1984), 319-342

Leonard, Ellen, *Three Days' Reign of Terror, or the July Riots in 1863 in New York* (New York, 1867) Pamphlet reprinted from *Harper's Magazine*, January 1867

McKay, Donald A., *The Building of Manhattan*. Illustrated by the author (Harper & Row: New York, 1987)

McKay, Ernest A., *The Civil War and New York City* (Syracuse University Press: Syracuse, 1990)

Maurice, Arthur Bartlett, *Fifth Avenue* (Dodd, Mead: New York, 1918)

Nadel, Stanley, *Little Germany: Ethnicity, Religion, and Class in New York City, 1845-80* (University of Illinois Press: Urbana and Chicago, 1990)

Percy, Townsend, *Appleton's Dictionary of New York* (Appleton: New York, 1879)

Resseque, Harry E., "A.T. Stewart's Marble Palace – The Cradle of the Department Store," *New York Historical Society Quarterly*, 48 (April 1964), 131-162

Scheiner, Seth M., *Negro Mecca: A History of the Negro in New York City, 1865-1920* (New York University Press: New York, 1965)

Syrett, Harold C., *The City of Brooklyn, 1865-1898* (Columbia University Press: New York, 1944)

Trachtenberg, Alan, *Brooklyn Bridge: Fact and Symbol* (Oxford University Press: New York, 1965)

Van Rensselaer, Mariana Griswold, "Fifth Avenue," *Century Magazine*, November 1893, 5-18

Van Rensselaer, "The Madison Square Garden," *Century Magazine*, March 1894, 732-747

Van Rensselaer, "Recent Architecture in America, II. Public Buildings Continued," *Century Magazine*, July 1884, 323-334

Van Rensselaer, "People in New York," *Century Magazine*, February 1895, 534-548

Van Rensselaer, "Recent Architecture in America. V. City Dwellings," *Century Magazine*, February 1886, 548-558

Van Rensselaer, "The Mother City of Greater New York," *Century Magazine*, May 1898, 138-140

Chapter 7

Richard Plunz, *A History of Housing in New York City: Dwelling Type and Social Change in the American Metropolis* (Columbia University Press: New York, 1990)

Anderson, Jervis, *This Was Harlem: A Cultural Portrayal* (Farrar, Straus and Giroux: New York, 1982)

Balfour, Allan, *Rockefeller Center: Architecture as Theater* (McGraw-Hill: New York, 1978)

Bard, Erwin Milkie, *The Port of New York Authority* (Columbia University Press: New York, 1939)

Erenberg, Lewis A., *Steppin' Out: New York Nightlife and the Transformation of American Culture, 1890-1930* (University of Chicago Press: Chicago and London, 1981)

Gillman, Lucy P., "Coney Island," *New York History*, 36 (July 1955), 255-290

Glickman, Toby and Gene, *The New York Red Pages: A Radical Tourist Guide* (Praeger: New York, 1984)

Green, Martin, *New York 1913: The Armory Show and the Paterson Strike Pageant* (Charles Scribner's Sons: New York, 1988)

Gurock, Jeffrey, *When Harlem Was Jewish 1870-1930* (Columbia University Press: New York, 1979)

Henderson, Mary C., *The City and the Theater: New York Playhouses from Bowling Green to Times Square* (James T. White: Clifton, N.J., 1973)

Hood, Clifton, *722 Miles The Building of the Subways and How They Transformed New York* (Simon & Schuster: New York, 1993)

Kenneth T. Jackson, "The Capital of Capitalism: the New York Metropolitan Region, 1890-1940," in *Metropolis 1890-1940*, ed. Anthony Sutcliffe (Mansell: London, 1984), 319-354

Johnson, James Weldon, *Black Manhattan*, with a new preface by Allan H. Spear (Atheneum: New York, 1975). First published 1930

Jones, Pamela, *Under the City Streets* (Holt, Rinehart and Winston: New York, 1978)

Jordy, William H., *American Buildings and Their Architects:, Vol. 4: The Impact of European Modernism in the Mid-Twentieth Century* (Doubleday: Garden City, N.Y., 1972)

Kasson, John F., *Amusing the Million: Coney Island at the Turn of the Century* (Hill & Wang: New York, 1978)

Krinsky, Carole Herselle, *Rockefeller Center* (Oxford University Press: New York, 1978)

Latimer, Margaret, *Two Cities: New York and Brooklyn the Year the Great Bridge Opened* (Brooklyn Educational and Cultural Alliance: Brooklyn, 1983)

Mayer, Grace, *Once Upon a City: New York from 1890 to 1910 as photographed by Byron* (Macmillan: New York, 1957)

McKay, Claude, *Harlem Shadows* (Harcourt, Brace: New York, 1922)

Marcuse, Peter, "The Beginning of Public Housing in New York," *Journal of Urban History*, 12 (August 1986), 353-390

Miller, John Anderson, *Fares, Please! A Popular History of Trolleys, Horse-Cars, Street-Cars, Buses, Elevateds, and Subways* (D. Appleton-Century: New York, 1941; reissued Dover: New York, 1960)

Miller, Rita Seiden, ed., *Brooklyn USA: The Fourth Largest City in America* (Brooklyn College Press: New York, 1979)

Mollenkopf, John Hull, ed., *Power, Culture, and Place: Essays on New York City* (Russell Sage Foundation: New York, 1988)

Nevins, Allan and John A. Krout, eds., *The Greater City: New York 1898-1948* (Columbia University Press: New York, 1948)

Noffsinger, James Phillip, *The Influence of the Ecole des Beaux-Arts on the Architects of the United States* (Catholic University of America Press: Washington, D.C., 1955)

Osofsky, Gilbert, *Harlem: The Making of a Ghetto* (Harper & Row: New York, 1963)

Ottley, Roi, *New World A-Coming* (Houghton Mifflin: Boston, 1943)

Paine, Albert Bigelow, "The New Coney Island," *Century Magazine*, August 1904, 528-538

Parry, Albert, *Garrets and Pretenders: A History of Bohemianism in America* (Covici-Friede: New York, 1933)

Pilat, Oliver and Jo Ranson, *Sodom by the Sea: An Affectionate History of Coney Island* (Doubleday, Doran: Garden City, N.Y., 1941)

Ralph, Julian, "Coney Island," *Scribner's Magazine*, July 1896, 3-20

Roth, Leland M., *McKim, Mead & White: Architects* (Harper & Row: New York, 1983)

Sante, Luc, *Low Life: Lures and Snares of Old New York* (Farrar, Straus & Giroux: New York, 1991)

Shanly, Charles Dawson, "Coney Island," *Atlantic Monthly*, 34 (1874), 306-312

Silver, Nathan, *Lost New York* (Houghton Mifflin: Boston, 1967)

Stern, Robert A.M., Gregory Gilmartin and John Montague Massengale, *New York 1900: Metropolitan Architecture and Urbanism 1890-1915* (Rizzoli: New York, 1983)

——, Gregory Gilmartin and Thomas Mellins, *New York 1930: Architecture and Urbanism Between the Two World Wars* (Rizzoli: New York, 1987)

Tauranac, John, *Elegant New York: The Builders and the Buildings 1885-1915* (Abbeville Press: New York, 1985)

Taylor, William R., ed., *Inventing Times Square: Commerce and Culture at the Crossroads of the World* (Russell Sage Foundation: New York, 1991)

Taylor, William R., *In Pursuit of Gotham: Culture and Commerce in New York* (Oxford University Press, New York and Oxford, 1992)

Ware, Caroline F., *Greenwich Village 1920-1930: A Comment on American Civilization in the Post-War Years* (Houghton Mifflin: Boston, 1935)

Works Progress Administration, *New York City Guide* (Guilds' Committee for Federal Writers' Publications: New York, 1939)

Chapter 8

Ashton, Dore, *The New York School: A Cultural Reckoning* (Viking Press: New York, 1973)

Caro, Robert A., *The Power Broker: Robert Moses and the Fall of New York* (Alfred A. Knopf: New York, 1974)

Collier, Peter, and David Horowitz, *The Rockefellers: An American Dynasty* (Jonathan Cape: London, 1976)

Dudley, George A., *A Workshop for Peace: Designing the United Nations Headquarters* (The Architectural History Foudation/The MIT Press: Cambridge, MA, 1994)

Foner, Nancy, ed., *New Immigrants in New York* (Columbia University Press: New York, 1987)

Guilbaut, Serge, *How New York Stole the Idea of Modern Art: Abstract Impressionism, Freedom, and the Cold War*, trans. Arthur Goldhammer (University of Chicago Press: Chicago, 1983)

Harrison, Helen A., guest curator, *Dawn of a New Day: The New York World's Fair, 1939/40* (The Queens Museum/New York University Press: New York, 1980)

Kim, Illsoo, *New Urban Immigrants: The Korean Community in New York* (Princeton University Press: Princeton, 1981)

Laguerre, Michael S., *American Odyssey: Haitians in New York City* (Cornell University Press: Ithaca, 1984)

LeBlanc, Sydney, *Whitney Guide: 20th Century American Architecture 200 Key Buildings* (Whitney Library of Design: New York, 1993)

Lie, Trygve, *In the Cause of Peace: Seven Years with the United Nations* (Macmillan: New York, 1954)

Makielski, S.J., Jr., *The Politics of Zoning: The New York Experience* (Columbia University Press: New York, 1966)

Moore, William, Jr., *The Vertical Ghetto: Everyday Life in an Urban Project* (Random House: New York, 1969)

Moscow, Alvin, *The Rockefeller Inheritance* (Doubleday & Co.: Garden City, N.J., 1977)

Naifeh, Steven W., *Culture Making: Money, Success, and the New York Art World*. Princeton University Undergraduate Studies in History, 2 (The History Department of Princeton University: Princeton, 1976)

Paris, Arthur E., "New York as a Third World City" in *New York: City as Text*, ed. Christopher Mulvey and John Simons (Macmillan: London, 1990), 166-176

Plunz, Richard, ed., *Housing Form and Public Policy in the United States* (Praeger: New York, 1980)

Plunz, Richard, *A History of Housing in New York City: Dwelling Type and Social Change in the American Metropolis* (Columbia University Press: New York, 1990)

Rosenberg, Harold, "Tenth Street: A Geography of Modern Art," *Art News Annual*, no. 28, 1959, 120-143

Salins, Peter D., ed., *New York Unbound: The City and the Politics of the Future* (Basil Blackwell: New York and Oxford, 1988)

Sandler, Irving, *The New York School: The Painters and Sculptors of the Fifties* (Harper & Row: New York, 1978)

Simpson, Charles R., *SoHo: The Artist in the City* (University of Chicago Press: Chicago, 1981)

Sternlieb, George, "New York's Housing: A Study in Immobilisme," *The Public Interest*, no. 16 (Summer 1969), 123-141

Tobier, Emanuel, "Gentrification: The Manhattan Story," *New York Affairs*, 5 (1979), 13-25

Warner, Sam Bass, Jr., *The Urban Wilderness: A History of the American City* (Harper & Row: New York, 1972)

Wallock, Leonard, ed., *New York: Culture Capital of the World 1940-1965* (Rizzoli: New York, 1988)

Wright, Gwendolyn, *Building the Dream: A Social History of Housing in America* (MIT Press: Cambridge, MA, 1981)

Discovering New York

NEW YORK IN AMERICAN LITERATURE

Washington Irving, *Knickerbocker's History of New York*, 1809

James Fenimore Cooper, *Home as Found*, 1838

Herman Melville, *Pierre; or, The Ambiguities*, 1852, *Bartleby, the Scrivener*, 1853

Walt Whitman, *Leaves of Grass*, 1856

William Allen Butler, *Nothing to Wear*, 1857

Horatio Alger, Jr., *Ragged Dick; or, Street Life in New York* 1868

Rebecca Harding Davis, *John Andross*, 1874

Henry James, *Washington Square*, 1881

H.C. Bunner, *The Story of a New York House*, 1887

William Dean Howells, *A Hazard of New Fortunes*, 1890

Richard Harding Davis, *Van Bibber and Others*, 1892

Stephen Crane, *Maggie*, 1893

Paul Leicester Ford, *The Honorable Peter Sterling*, 1894

Abraham Cahan, *Yekl: A Tale of the New York Ghetto*, 1896

Montagu Glass, *Potash and Perlmutter*, 1910

Ernest Poole, *The Harbor*, 1915

Lillian D. Wald, *The House on Henry Street*, 1915

Anzia Yezierska, *Hungry Hearts*, 1920

Edith Wharton, *The Age of Innocence*, 1920

Anne Nichols, *Abie's Irish Rose*, 1924

John Dos Passos, *Manhattan Transfer*, 1925

Alfred Kreymborg, *Manhattan Men*, 1929

Horace Gregory, *Chelsea Rooming House*, 1930

Michael Gold, *Jews Without Money*, 1930

Charles Reznikoff, *By the Waters of Manhattan*, 1930

Hart Crane, *The Bridge*, 1930

Countee Cullen, *One Way to Heaven*, 1931

Manuel Komroff, *A New York Tempest*, 1932

Albert Halper, *Union Square*, 1933

Daniel Fuchs, *Summer in Williamsburg*, 1934

Henry Roth, *Call It Sleep*, 1934

Waldo Frank, *The Death and Birth of David Markand*, 1934

John O'Hara, *BUtterfield 8*, 1935

Jerome Weidman, *I Can Get It For You Wholesale*, 1937

A.J. Liebling, *Back Where I Came From*, 1938

Kenneth Fearing, *The Big Clock*, 1946

Sholem Asch, *East River*, 1946

William Blake, *The Copperheads*, 1949

Langston Hughes, *Simple Speaks His Mind*, 1950

Ralph Ellison, *Invisible Man*, 1952

William P. McGivern, *The Big Heat*, 1953

Elizabeth Janeway, *Leaving Home*, 1953

Arthur Miller, *A View From the Bridge*, 1955

Truman Capote, *Breakfast at Tiffany's*, 1958

Paddy Chayefsky, *Marty*, 1953

Grace Paley, *The Little Disturbances of Man*, 1960

Edward Lewis Wallant, *The Pawnbroker*, 1961

Herbert Gold, *Salt*, 1963

Chester Himes, *Cotton Comes to Harlem*, 1965

Hortense Calisher, *The New Yorkers*, 1969

Wallace Markfield, *Teitlebaum's Window*, 1970

Irvin Faust, *The File on Stanley Patton Buchta*, 1970

Jerome Charyn, *Marilyn the Wild*, 1976

Gore Vidal, *1876*, 1976

William Styron, *Sophie's Choice*, 1980

James T. Farrell, *Sam Holman*, 1983

Meyer Liben, *New York Street Games*, 1984

Jay McInerny, *Bright Lights, Big City*, 1984

Tom Wolfe, *The Bonfire of the Vanities*, 1987

Larry Beinhart, *You Get What You Pay For*, 1988

E.L. Doctorow, *Billy Bathgate*, 1989

Bret Easton Ellis, *American Psycho*, 1991

Caleb Carr, *The Alienist*, 1994

NEW YORK HISTORY: WHERE TO GO

Black Fashion Museum, *(By appointment)*
155 West 126th Street   Tel: 212 666 1320
Highlights the importance of African-Americans to the development of fashion in the USA. Costumes from the theater and cinema.

Brooklyn Historical Society,
128 Pierrepont Street, Brooklyn   Tel: 718 624 0890
Includes exhibitions on the Dodgers, the Brooklyn Bridge and Coney Island.
Admission Fee

Ellis Island Museum of Immigration,
Ellis Island   Tel: 212 363 7620
Museum includes oral history listening room. Recreates experiences of immigrant families.
Free admission

Fraunces Tavern Museum,
54 Pearl Street, at Broad Street   Tel: 212 425 1778
Restored and reconstructed early American house. Built in 1719 as a residence, became a warehouse in 1730. Acted as a theater 1737–39, later became a tavern.
Free admission

Harbor Defense Museum of New York City,
230 Fort Hamilton, Brooklyn   Tel: 718 630 4349
Located at an active military base, museum features small arms, uniforms, artillery equipment dating to the 18th century, and an array of military miniatures.
Free admission

Lower East Side Tenement Museum,
97 Orchard Street   Tel: 212 431 0233
History of European immigrants in lower East Side. Preserves and interprets the life of immigrants, Walking tours and dramatic performances available.
Admission Fee

Morris-Jumel Mansion,
Edgecombe Ave. at 161st St.   Tel:212 923 8008
Admission free

Museum of Bronx History,
3266 Bainbridge Avenue and East 208th Street   Tel: 212 881 8900
History of the Bronx from 1758.
Admission Fee

Museum of the City of New York,
1220 Fifth Avenue at 103rd Street   Tel: 212 534 1672
More than three million objects held. Costumes, works of art, and household objects create a picture of New York's past. Includes multi-media and audio visual presentations.
Admission Fee

Museum of American Financial History
24 Broadway   Tel: 212 908 4519/908 4110

National Museum of the American Indian
1 Bowling Green   Tel: 212 668 6624

New York City Fire Museum,
278 Spring Street   Tel: 212 691 1303
Comprehensive collection of fire-fighting tools from the 18th, 19th and 20th centuries.

New York City Transit Museum,
Boerum Pl. at Schermerhorn St., Brooklyn Heights   Tel: 718 330 3060
A 1930s subway station displays restored classic subway cars and restored ticket office.
Admission Fee

New York Historical Society,
170 Central Park West, at West 77th Street   Tel: 212 873 3400
Comprehensive collection of portraits and landscapes, archive of prints and photographs.
Admission Fee

Old Merchant's House,
29 East 4th Street   Tel: 212 777 1089
Greek Revival House, almost untouched since the 1860s. Walking tours and lectures regularly held.
Admission Fee

Police Academy Museum, *(By appointment)*
235 East 20th Street   Tel: 212 477 9753
Law enforcement memorabilia dating back to the time of the Dutch.
Free admission

Queens County Farm Museum,
73-50 Little Neck Parkway, Floral Park, Queens   Tel: 718 347 3276
New York agricultural history on a 200-year-old farm.
Admission Fee

Queens Museum,
Flushing Meadow, Corona Park   Tel: 718 592 2405
Housed in what was the New York City Pavillion for the 1939 Fair. Includes a restored Panorama, a 9355-square-foot architectural model of New York City's five boroughs.
Admission Fee

Schomburg Center for Research in Black Culture of the New York Public Library,
515 Lenox Avenue at 135th Street   Tel: 212 491 2200

South Street Seaport Museum,
207 Front Street   Tel: 212 669 9424
Changing exhibition on maritime New York. Adjacent to a working print shop.
Admission Fee

Studio Museum in Harlem,
144 West 125th Street   Tel: 212 864 4500
Shows work by African-American, African and Caribbean artists.
Admission Fee

The Jewish Museum,
170 Central Park   Tel: 212 399 3430
Admission Fee

Index

In this index, references to illustrations are set in *italic*. References to double page spreads are set in **bold**

Acknowledgments

Page 8/9 New Amsterdam (Manhattan) c.1660: Peter Newark's Pictures, Bath, England
Page 10 Fort of the Iroquois, Champlain fights with Hurons; neg. no. 15103, Courtesy Department Library Services, American Museum of Natural History
Page 12 Eric Homberger
Page 13 New York City, the First Settlement on Manhattan, 1623: Peter Newark's Pictures, Bath, England
Page 16 Defeat of the Iroquois at Lake Champlain; neg. no. 15100, Courtesy Department Library Services, American Museum of Natural History
Page 17 Corn Planting and Maple Sugar Making by the American Indians; neg. no. 38575, Courtesy Department Library Services, American Museum of Natural History
Page 19 and 20 Eric Homberger
Page 21 Österreichische Nationalbibliothik Bild-Archiv und Porträt-Sammlung, A-1015 Wien1, Yosefsplatz 1; photo-Atelier, E 17.066
Page 22 The "Duke" map of New York in 1664: Peter Newark's Pictures, Bath, England
Page 25 Eric Homberger
Page 26/27 Hartgers View, engraving by Kryn Frederycks: I.N. Phelps Stokes Collection, Miriam & Ira D. Wallach Division of Art, Prints & Photographs, The New York Public Library, Astor, Lenox and Tilden Foundations
Page 29 Visscher Map of Novum Belgium, 1651–55: Peter Newark's Pictures, Bath, England
Page 30/31 Eric Homberger
Page 33 The Castello Plan 1665 from the Manuscript Atlas of Johannes U̇ngboons, plate 76: Royal Geographical Society: no: M.R. United States 5.191, neg no. T673, portfolio 5.I.D.
Page 35 Eric Homberger
Page 36 Map of New York in 1766–67 Surveyed by lieutenant Bernard Rutzer: Peter Newark's Pictures, Bath, England
Page 38–41 Eric Homberger
Page 43 Top: The Massacre of St. Bartholomew, Paris. German, 16th-century woodcut. Bibbliotheque de Protestantisme, Paris: Lauros-Giraudon/The Bridgeman Art Library, London. Center: Eric Homberger
Page 44 and 47 Eric Homberger
Page 48 Stuart Gilbert (American 1755–1828) George Washington, 1795: National Gallery of Art, Washington. Andrew W. Mellon Collection
Page 49 A View of the Attack Against Fort Washington, watercolor, Nov. 16 1776 by Thomas Davies, 1776-B-93. I.N. Phelps Stokes Collection, Miriam & Ira D. Wallach Division of Art, Prints & Photographs, The New York Public Library, Astor, Lenox and Tilden Foundations
Page 51 Top: B.F. Stevens's facsimile of British Headquarters Colored Manuscript of New York and Environs, 1782: Royal Geographical Society. Bottom: View of Narrows between Long Island and Staten Island by Captain Archibald Robertson; The New York Public Library, Astor, Lenox and Tilden Foundations
Page 52/53 New York from Governor's Island, 1820; Museum of the City of New York, The J. Clarence Davies Collection
Page 54 View of the City and Harbor of New York, 1796 by Charles Balthazar Julien, Fevret de Saint-Memin. 1794-B-121. I.N. Phelps Stokes Collection. Miriam & Ira D. Wallach Division of Art, Prints & Photographs, The New York Public Library, Astor, Lenox and Tilden Foundations
Page 55 and 56 Eric Homberger
Page 58 In Harlem Lane: Emmet Collection, Miriam & Ira D. Wallach Division of Art, Prints & Photographs, The New York Public Library, Astor, Lenox and Tilden Foundations
Page 59/60 Eric Homberger
Page 61 Center Eric Homberger: Bottom right: A View of Broad Street, Wall Street, and the City Hall, watercolor, 1797 by John Joseph Holland: 1797-B-120, I.N. Phelps Stokes Collection, Miriam & Ira D. Wallach Division of Art, Prints & Photographs, The New York Public Library, Astor, Lenox and Tilden Foundations
Page 62 Eric Homberger
Page 63 Center: Eric Homberger: Top: Broadway, New York, colored etching with aquatint, issued 1836, by Thomas Hornor, engraver, John Hill. 1835-E-103. I.N. Phelps Stokes Collection, Miriam & Ira D. Wallach Division of Art, Prints & Photographs, The New York Public Library, Astor, Lenox and Tilden Foundations. Bottom right: Launch of the Steam Frigate Fulton the First, engraving, 1815: artists, William H. Morgan (possibly) and John James Barralet, engraver, Benjamin Tanner. 1814-E-87; I.N. Phelps Stokes Collection. Miriam & Ira D. Wallach Division of Art, Prints & Photographs, The New York Public Library, Astor, Lenox and Tilden Foundations
Page 64, 65 and 66 Eric Homberger
Page 67 Astor Papers, Maps of Real Estate transactions 1830s. Page 118, 1834. The New-York Historical Society
Page 68 Eric Homberger
Page 69 Eno Collection, Miriam & Ira D. Wallach Division of Art, Prints & Photographs, The New York Public Library, Astor, Lenox and Tilden Foundations
Page 70 Croton Aqueduct at Harlem River, 1825: Museum of the City of New York, 38.299.5
Page 71 and 72 Eric Homberger
Page 73 Samuel B. Waugh, The Bay Harbor of New York, 1855. Museum of the City of New York. 33.169.1
Page 75 Eric Homberger

Page 76 Erie Canal Celebrations, Anthony Imbert. Museum of the City of New York. 49.415.1
Page 77 Top left: Eric Homberger. Top right: Hudson River RR Station, 1851. Museum of the City of New York. 52.100.12
Page 78 Nicolino Calyo, View of the Great Fire in New York, December 16 & 17, 1835. Museum of the City of New York
Page 79 and 80 Eric Homberger
Page 81 Top: Five Points, 1827, from Valentine's Manual, 1855. McSpedon & Baker, Lithographers. Museum of the City of New York. Center right: Eric Homberger
Page 82 G.P. Hall, Manhattan Company Reservoir, 1825. Museum of the City of New York. 29.100.1579
Page 83 Eric Homberger
Page 84 Top: Eric Homberger. Bottom: The Times, 1837 by Edward W. Clay. Museum of the City of New York. 29.100.2355
Page 85 Top: Eric Homberger. Center: Irish Immigrants, 1855. From the painting by Samuel B. Waugh. Peter Newark's Pictures, Bath, England
Page 86 Right: Eric Homberger. Bottom left: Astor Place House 1850. Museum of the City of New York. 52.100.23D
Page 87 and 88 Eric Homberger
Page 89 Eric Homberger. Center right: Fashionable Turn-outs in Central Park, artwork by T. Worth, published by Currier & Ives in 1869. Bottom: Facsimile of a survey showing land incorporated into Central Park. Harvard College Library
Page 90 New York City in 1860. Peter Newark's Pictures, Bath, England
Page 91, 92, 93 and 94 Eric Homberger
Page 96 The Life of a Fireman. Currier & Ives print of 1861. Peter Newark's Pictures, Bath, England
Page 97 Eric Homberger
Page 98 Eric Homberger. Center bottom: New York City in 1877, A German Beer Hall in the Bowery, illustration from The Graphic, February 10, 1877. Peter Newark's Pictures, Bath, England
Page 99 Eric Homberger
Page 100 Top: Madison Square, New York City, in the 1880s, Peter Newark's Pictures, Bath, England. Center: House of Alexander T. Stewart, c.1890. Museum of the City of New York
Page 101 Eric Homberger
Page 102 Bottom left: Macy's First Store, 6th Avenue and 14th Street, 1858–1901. Museum of the City of New York
Page 103 Eric Homberger
Page 105 Flatiron Building, 1905. Broadway and Fifth Avenue. Museum of the City of New York
Page 106 Eric Homberger
Page 107 Eric Homberger. Top center: New York City, elevated railroad c.1875. Peter Newark's Pictures, Bath, England
Page 108 The Harlem River, 1895, photo by William Henry Jackson, gift of Miss Barblett Cowdrey, Museum of the City of New York
Page 109 Brooklyn Bridge, drawing by Schell and Hogan for Harper's Weekly. Museum of the City of New York
Page 110 Minding the Baby, the Baby Yells – a whirlwind scene, Grotham Court. The Jacob A. Riis Collection, no.189. Museum of the City of New York
Page 111 Top left: Bandit's Roost, 39½ Mulberry Street. The Jacob A. Riis Collection, no.101. Museum of the City of New York. Top right: Rear Tenement in Roosevelt Street. The Jacob A. Riis Collection, no.97. Museum of the City of New York. Center left: Scene on the Roof of the Barracks, Mott Street. The Jacob A. Riis Collection, no.117. Museum of the City of New York
Page 114 W. Louis Sontag, Jr., The Bowery at Night c.1895, watercolor, gift of Mrs W.B. Miles. Museum of the City of New York
Page 115 Grand Central Terminal, 1906. Museum of the City of New York
Page 116 New York Central System poster of 1926. Peter Newark's Pictures, Bath, England
Page 118 Chrysler, Daily News, Chanin, Lincoln & Lefcourt Buildings, New York City, from postcard of late 1930s. Peter Newark's Pictures, Bath, England
Page 119 Empire State Building, New York City; from a postcard of the late 1930s Peter Newark's Pictures, Bath, England
Page 120 Workman on the Empire State Building, 1931, photo by Lewis W. Hine. Peter Newark's Pictures, Bath, England
Page 122 Francis Guy, Winter Scene in Brooklyn. The Brooklyn Museum, Brooklyn, 97.13
Page 123 and 124 Eric Homberger
Page 125 Jasper Francis Cropsey, Grimes Hill, Staten Island, 1866. The Brooklyn Museum, 39.409
Page 126 Entrance Kiosk, City Hall Station, Interborough Rapid Transit Subway, New York City, c.1904. New York Transit Museum Archives, Brooklyn
Page 127 Ticket Hall, City Hall Station. New York Transit Museum Archives, Brooklyn
Page 128 Coney Island, Luna Park, photo: Adolph Witteman, The Leonard Hassam Bogart Collection. Museum of the City of New York
Page 129 Ah There! Coney Island, 1897. Museum of the City of New York
Page 130 Abe Reles; Municipal Archives Collection, Department of Records & Information Services, City of New York

Page 131 Right: Murder Inc. victim. Bottom, top left: Meyer Lansky; Bottom, top right: Benjamin Siegal; bottom left, Charles Luciano; bottom right: Albert Anastasia; Municipal Archives Collection, Department of Records & Information Services, City of New York
Page 133 Top: George Benjamin Luks, Mister Street 1905, oil on canvas; The Brooklyn Museum, 40.339 Bottom left: Immigration into the U.S.A., Hester Street in the Jewish Quarter on New York City's lower East Side, c.1900; Peter Newark's Pictures, Bath, England
Page 135 Top: Backyards, Greenwich Village, oil on canvas, by John Sloan 1871–1951. Collection of Whitney Museum of American Art, New York. Center right: Eugene O'Neil, 1933, gift of Mrs, Eugene O'Neil. Museum of the City of New York, 34.74.18. Bottom right: Bleecker Street, March 27, 1920. The Hopkins Collection; Museum of the City of New York
Page 136 Left: European Immigrants into New York Pass the Statue of Liberty in the 1890s. Peter Newark's Pictures, Bath, England. Bottom: Immigrants on Ellis Island, New York, c.1910. Peter Newark's Pictures, Bath, England
Page 137 Immigrants into U.S.A., Ellis Island, 1910. Peter Newark's Pictures, Bath, England
Page 139 Center left: Billie Holliday. Peter Newark's Pictures, Bath, England. Center right: King Oliver's Creole Jazz Band in 1920. Peter Newark's Pictures, Bath, England. Bottom left: Harlem Street Scene, 135th Street and Lennox Avenue. Schomburg Center for Research in Black Culture, The New York Public Library. Bottom right: Harlem; The Cotton Club. Peter Newark's Pictures, Bath, England
Page 140 Woolworth Building, 1913. The Underhill Collection, Museum of the City of New York. Bottom right: Grand Central Station, New York: Robert Harding Picture Library, London
Page 142 Right: Skyviews Survey, Inc.: Pic.no. 150489M. Bottom: Rockefeller Center Mangement Corporation
Page 143 Radio City Buildings, Rockefeller Center, New York City from postcard of the late 1930s. Peter Newark's Pictures, Bath, England
Page 144 Top: Hudson River Bridge: The Port Authority of New York & New Jersey. Botton left: The Port Authority of New York & New Jersey. Bottom right: Opening day, Holland Tunnel, November 13, 1927. The Port Authority of New York & New Jersey
Page 145 Bottom left: LaGuardia Airport: The Port Authority of New York & New Jersey. Bottom right: Container Terminal complex at Port Newark, Elizabeth in New Jersey: The Port Authority of New York & New Jersey
Page 146 Malcolm Swanston
Page 147 Top: Eric Homberger. Bottom: Malcolm Swanston
Page 148 Top: Eric Homberger. Bottom: Malcolm Swanston
Page 149 Eric Homberger
Page 150 Left: Eric Homberger. Right: Malcolm Swanston
Page 151 Malcolm Swanston
Page 152 Brooklyn Bridge, Georgia O'Keefe, 77.11. The Brooklyn Museum, Brooklyn
Page 153 Left: Arcaid, Surrey, England. © Richard Bryant/1992. Right: The Andy Warhol Foundation for the Visual Arts, Inc., New York
Page 154 Sheepshead Bay Racetrack, 1893, Coney Island; Museum of the City of New York, The Byron Collection
Page 155 Left: Peter Newark's Pictures, Bath, England. Center: Eric Homberger. Right: Popperfoto, Northampton, England.
Page 156 Eric Homberger
Page 157 Peter Newark's Pictures, Bath, England
Page 159 Left: UN Plaza, photo Geofrey Taunton, Sylvia Cordaiy Picture Library, Littlehampton, West Sussex, England. Right: Eric Homberger
Page 160 Top: Fred Chase, The Link Picture Library, London. Bottom: Orde Eliason, The Link Picture Library, London
Page 162 Donna Decesare, The Link Picture Library, London
Page 163 Brian Palmer, The Link Picture Library, London
Page 164 Top: Queens, 6029-22B; Charles Harbull Archive. Bottom: 6831-2-22; Charles Harbull Archive
Page 166 Broadway in 1875, New York City. Peter Newark's Pictures, Bath, England
Page 167 Bottom left: Eric Homberger. Bottom right: Times Square, September 30, 1931; Museum of the City of New York
Page 168 to Page 177 Eric Homberger
Page 178 Josephine Baker, The Theater Collection, Museum of the City of New York
Page 179 Top: Emma Goldman, gift of Harry Bland, Museum of the City of New York. Bottom: George Gershwin, Peter Newark's Pictures, Bath, England
Page 180 Top: Eric Homberger. Bottom left: Lillian Hellman, The Theater Collection, Museum of the City of New York. Bottom right: Eric Homberger
Page 181 Left: Fiorello H. LaGuardia: Peter Newark's Pictures, Bath, England. Right: Bill "Bojangles" Robinson, The Theater Collection, Museum of the City of New York
Page 182 President Theodore Roosevelt, photo by Rockwood, New York, 1902. Peter Newark's Pictures, Bath, England
Page 183 Watt Whitman, September 1887, photo by George Cox, gift of Mrs Clarence Clough Buel, 40.146. Museum of the City of New York